LIFE AMONG THE SCIENTISTS

LIFE AMONG THE SCIENTISTS

An Anthropological Study of an Australian Scientific Community

MAX CHARLESWORTH
LYNDSAY FARRALL
TERRY STOKES
DAVID TURNBULL

OXFORD
UNIVERSITY PRESS

Melbourne
Oxford   Auckland   New York

OXFORD UNIVERSITY PRESS AUSTRALIA

Oxford New York Toronto Delhi Bombay
Calcutta Madras Karachi Petaling Jaya Singapore
Hong Kong Tokyo Nairobi Dar es Salaam Cape Town
Melbourne Auckland
and associated companies in Berlin Ibadan

OXFORD is a trade mark of Oxford University Press

National Library of Australia
Cataloguing-in-Publication data:

Life among the scientists.
    Bibliography.
    Includes index.
    ISBN 0 19 554999 6.

    1. Walter and Eliza Hall Institute of Medical Research.
    2. Scientists—Australia. 3. Scientists—Australia—
    Professional ethics. 4. Scientists—Australia—Conduct
    of life. 5. Science—Australia—Moral and ethical
    aspects. I. Charlesworth, Max, 1925–

509'.2'2

Edited by Christine Connor
Designed by Steven Randles
Cover designed by Roy Walshe
Typeset by Typeset Gallery Sdn. Bhd.
Printed by Impact Printing, Melbourne
Published by Oxford University Press,
253 Normanby Road, South Melbourne, Australia

CONTENTS

ACKNOWLEDGEMENTS

The authors wish to express their gratitude to Sir Gustav Nossal, Director of the Walter and Eliza Hall Institute of Medical Research, for his unfailing and invaluable support of this project. Without that support our work simply would not have been possible. Grateful thanks are also due to the former Manager of the Institute, Dr Margaret Holmes, the present General Manager, Dr Margaret Brumby, the Assistant Director, Professor Donald Metcalf, and to all those members of the Institute who cheerfully tolerated our often very obtrusive presence and who were willing to spend considerable amounts of time talking to us. No 'natives' could have been friendlier! We would especially like to thank Dr Roland Scollay and Dr Graham Mitchell. Our thanks also to Dr John Schrader, Dr Graham Brown, Dr Ross Coppell, Dr Suzanne Cory, Dr Jerry Adams, Dr Robin Anders, Dr Ken Shortman, Dr Emanuela Handman, Dr Tom Mandel, Dr Ian Mackay, Dr Jacques Miller, Dr Elsmaree Baxter, Dr David Kemp, Dr Richard Simpson, Dr Allan Sturgess, Warren Alexander, Anthea Baxter, Michael Graham, Wilford Tiu, Anne Wilson, and Yvette Wilson. Outside the Institute we were helped by a number of people to whom we express our gratitude: Dr Michael Alpers of the Papua New Guinea Institute of Medical Research and his co-workers, as well as Dr Gael Jennings, Dr John Mathews, and a number of immunologists in other institutes in Australia, the United States and Europe. Dr Faith Thompson and Associate Professor Janice Reid were members of our research team early in the project and we thank them warmly for their valuable work and their helpful criticism. Gratitude is also due to those who read and commented on the first draft of this book. Professor Donald Denoon, Mrs S. Harris, Dr Hilary Charlesworth, Dr Charles Guest, and John Hutnyk. The word-processing of our material was expertly done by Mrs Judy Barber and her staff in the School of Humanities at Deakin University. The project was supported by a seeding grant from the Deakin University Foundation, grants from the School of Humanities, Deakin University, and the University of Wollongong and most substantially by funding from the Australian Research Grants Scheme. The University of Melbourne also provided a home for us for some two years. To all those bodies, many thanks.

We are also grateful to the following for permission to reproduce copyright material: Nigel Barley and British Museum Publications for an extract from *The Innocent Anthropologist*, 1986; Bertolt Brecht, John Willett and Ralph Mannheim (translators) and Methuen, London, for an extract from *Plays, Poetry and Prose*: *Poems, 1913–1956*; James Clifford and Harvard University Press for an extract from *The Predicament of Culture*, 1988; Louis Dumont and The University of Chicago Press for an extract from *Essays on Individualism*: *Modern Ideology in Anthropological Perspectives*, 1986; Ian Langham and Kluwer Academic Publishers for an extract from *The Building of British Social Anthropology*, 1981; Bruno Latour for an extract from *Laboratory Life:The Social Construction of Scientific Facts*, Sage, Beverly Hills, 1979; Christine Larmer and Basil Blackwell for an extract from *Witchcraft and Religion*, 1984; Claude Lévi-Strauss and Harper and Row for an extract from *The Raw and the Cooked*, 1975; Ian Mitroff and Elsevier Publishing for the 'Ideal Scientist Profile' from *The Subjective Side of Science*, 1974; Paul Rabinow and University of California Press for an extract from *Reflections on Fieldwork in Morocco*, 1977; Paul Rabinow and Kluwer Academic Publishers for an extract from 'Discourse and Power' in *Dialectical Anthropology*, vol. 10, 1985; Mrs W.E.H. Stanner for an extract from W.E.H. Stanner, 'On the study of Aboriginal religion', 1961.

PREFACE

Four people, with very different scholarly backgrounds in the history of science and the philosophy of science, contributed to this study and to the writing of the book. However, for a number of good stylistic reasons it was decided not to use the royal 'we' but the more modest 'I' instead. Henceforth then, 'we' will speak with one voice.

INTRODUCTION

Since the turn of the century, scores of men and women have penetrated deep forests, lived in hostile climates, and weathered hostility, boredom and disease in order to gather the remnants of so-called primitive societies. By contrast to the frequency of these anthropological excursions, relatively few attempts have been made to penetrate the intimacy of life among tribes which are much nearer at hand. This is perhaps surprising in view of the reception and importance attached to their product in modern civilized societies: we refer of course to tribes of scientists and to their production of science. Whereas we now have fairly detailed knowledge of the myths and circumcision rituals of exotic tribes, we remain relatively ignorant of the details of equivalent activity among tribes of scientists whose work is commonly heralded as having startling or at least extremely significant effects on our civilization.

Bruno Latour and Steve Woolgar, *Laboratory Life: The Social Construction of Scientific Facts*[1]

This is an attempt to understand how a small group of scientists at a particular research institute, and in a specific scientific field, do science, as distinct from what the received scientific mythology *says* they do and what philosophers of science and other science watchers *suppose* they do. Through this account, I hope to throw some light on that mysterious and fascinating realm of human activity we call 'science' and on those special people we call 'scientists'. I hope also that it may enable scientists themselves to stand off from, reflect upon, and become more self-conscious about, what they are doing. Again, my picture of the 'life-world' of a group of scientists may help to demystify (but not necessarily to debunk) the scientific process. In our civilization science (and its Siamese twin, technology) has a centrally important place and it is all too easy to fall into an attitude of uncritical awe before it. It is also easy to treat science as though it were separate from the culture of which it is a part and were an autonomous realm of its own. This apparent autonomy of science lands us in difficulties when we attempt to engage in any kind of critical appraisal of it, since the critic of science seems to be anti-science. On the other hand, seeing science embedded in, rather than separate from, the social context which makes it possible, enables us to think of it as similar to art, or music, or architecture, or cooking, all of which we have no difficulty in critically appraising. To write film criticism is not to be anti-film, and to critically analyse science from a sociological/anthropological standpoint is not to be anti-science.

In my view, scientific knowledge is, in a sense, 'constructed', and social and personal factors play a large part in that construction. In other words, scientific knowledge does not come about by the scientist directly confronting nature and reading off how it works; neither is it an asocial enterprise in which the individual scientist goes it alone. Again, scientific knowledge is not a purely 'objective' and impersonal business in which personal or 'subjective' factors play no part. Not only does science necessarily take place within a specific social context, but that context forms and shapes the very style and content of science. By studying one group of scientists, then, I may be able to show, in one small area, how, and to what extent, scientific knowledge is shaped or 'constructed'. And from that particular example it may be possible to derive some general ideas about science at large.

The scientific sub-culture

The group or community of the scientists, technicians and associated staff in question belong to the prestigious Walter and Eliza Hall Institute of Medical Research in Melbourne, Australia. The Institute is concerned with a range of biomedical issues, but it is mainly interested in the investigation of the human immune system, the complex set of intricate and ingenious mechanisms that enable our bodies to repel invading organisms that would otherwise cause disease and disablement. The human immune system is under constant attack from a bewildering variety of enemies—bacteria, viruses, parasites, poisonous substances—and what someone has called 'a barrage of stray biological junk'. Usually, the immune system is able to detect and neutralize these invaders. But as the new and terrible disease of AIDS (Acquired Immune Deficiency Syndrome) has shown, when the immune system collapses or is subverted, our bodies soon succumb to the diseases that infiltrate once our defences are down. Immunology, the study of the immune system, is part of the biological or life sciences and, like these latter, has been deeply affected by the astonishing revolution—the 'eighth day of creation' as it has been called—that followed the discovery of the structure of DNA (deoxyribonucleic acid), the very stuff of life, in 1953. My group of scientists is caught up in this new scientific revolution which appears to promise, ultimately, an explanation of the mystery of life.

The group of research scientists at the Walter and Eliza Hall Institute, like any other group of people with a common focus of interests and purposes, has its own distinctive set of shared beliefs and attitudes and practices and assumptions and expectations; it has its own way of going about things; it has its own language, its special in-words and shop-talk and gossip. You could even say that it has its own distinctive rituals (including 'rites of passage') and its own heroic stories or sustaining myths. It certainly has its own way of forming and educating (socializing) its members and its own strict rules for deciding who are 'good' scientists and who are 'bad', who are 'in' and who are 'out', who are worthy of being funded and who are not. In other words, it is a small sub-culture all of its own. Or, one can say that it is a distinctive 'life-world'—a complex set of beliefs, attitudes, practices, relationships, and networks which make science possible. It is also, of course, a part of the larger culture or world of Science with a capital S, and beyond that, of the complex set of beliefs and attitudes and material factors that make science possible and that we call 'Western culture'. But the little world of our 310 life scientists also has its own distinctive identity and autonomy as a sub-culture and it can be studied as such.

My involvement with this group came about almost by chance. I am not a scientist but I am interested in the philosophy and sociology of science, trying to understand the curious set of activities we call 'science'. Some five years ago I was invited to give a talk at the Wednesday staff seminar at the Institute and I decided to speak on recent developments in the sociology of science. In particular I focused on attempts to approach science, and scientists, in an 'anthropological' way—viewing scientists as though they belonged to a 'tribe' with a distinctive 'culture' of its own.

The Director and several of the younger scientists at the Institute were interested in what I had to say and, after some negotiation, the Director very courageously offered, so to speak, the Institute as a subject for research. And that is how I began.

Studying up

Anthropologists investigate the micro-cultures of small groups of native peoples like the Nuer and the Dinka in Africa, or the Warlpiri and the Aranda in Central Australia; sociologists study the small but rich life-words of American white-collar workers, or French bakers, or Polish peasants, or poor Mexican families. Anthropologists and sociologists try to work out how these groups fabricate a world for themselves and how they live within those worlds. In much the same way, the sub-culture or life-world constructed by our group of life-scientists at the Institute can also be a legitimate object of anthropological and sociological investigation.

Laura Nader, an American anthropologist, has complained that in the past anthropologists have tended to 'study down', that is they have been mainly concerned with groups and communities and peoples who were thought to be 'inferior', more 'primitive', less developed, or less modern, or lower in class or status, than they themselves (white Western—most often male—anthropologists).[2] The same is true of a good deal of sociology which has been for the most part focused upon marginal, and 'deviant', and lower class groups, and to a great extent has neglected the various groups that make up the social 'establishment'. So we have a multitude of sociological accounts of petty criminals and drug addicts and prostitutes and religious eccentrics, but relatively few accounts of judges and lawyers and medicos and academics (including anthropologists and sociologists themselves). Nader urges anthropologists to 'study up', that is, to turn their enquiry upon so-called upper class, high social status, professional groups. The life-world or sub-culture of the judiciary deserves just as much anthropological and sociological attention as that of the various deviant groups who face the judges in the courts; and the exotic culture of the anthropological and sociological 'tribe' demands just as much attention and investigation as that of the native peoples and lower status groups they study so earnestly, and write books and theses about, and make a living out of. Margaret Mead and the rich and strange academic culture she represented ought to be as interesting to the anthropologists, and as much grist to their scholarly mill, as the Samoans she made her reputation from.[3]

We ought, then, to be able to 'study up' and investigate communities of scientists in more or less the same way as we investigate other communities—Samoans, the Nuer, street corner youths, white collar workers, Voodoo devotees, Rastafarians, migrant women—

trying to see how they make their life-worlds and how they live in those worlds; how those worlds cohere and function; how they are structured; how the implicit rules and conventions they embody determine what is valuable and important and what is not (and even what is *true* and what is not) and enable the group to decide who is 'in' and who is 'out' and so to preserve its purity and exclusiveness; how various rituals mark and symbolize the stages of a member's progress within a group (analogues of birth, puberty, initiation to adult life, marriage and death); how mythical rationales or justifications sustain the life of the group ('The land of the Dinka was given by the Gods and is the centre of the universe'; 'A university is a community of scholars dedicated to seeking the truth'; 'Science is the objective and dispassionate study of the observable facts'); how the stories of culture heroes help to provide legitimacy and induce solidarity among the members of the group (the Ancestor Spirit Gunabibi of the Australian Aborigines who emphasizes the death-and-resurrection rhythm of human life; the Roman Horatius who epitomizes soldierly courage; Abraham Lincoln who showed that every American boy can make it from log cabin to White House; Crick and Watson who, by sheer brash genius, discovered the structure and function of DNA and 'solved' the mystery of life). Societies and cultures are in a sense constructed (very much as languages are) or invented by human beings, so that what social scientists have to study are man-made constructs, and their primary concern is how the latter are constructed and the rules and conventions that govern all that happens within them. Understanding a society or culture is like understanding the grammar of a language; in other words, understanding the rules and conventions which enable people to find meaning in their social relationships, institutions, rituals and symbols.[4]

To achieve that understanding, the social sciences require an interpretive approach which focuses upon what things mean or signify: what do the Papua New Guineans mean by their custom of cassowary sacrifice; what is the point of the secrecy which pervades Australian Aboriginal culture; how are we to interpret the importance given to psychoanalysis by middle-class Americans; how are we to understand the significance of the introduction of the 'ideology' of physics into biology in the 1950s? Learning how to 'read' the social phenomena, grasping the point of such and such a custom, getting the hang of a certain style of behaviour, is all-important in anthropology. As Geertz puts it: 'Understanding the form and pressure of ... natives' inner lives is ... like grasping a proverb, catching an allusion, seeing a joke—or ... reading a poem'.[5]

Observers and observed

This view of the social sciences sees them then as being primarily concerned with interpreting the meanings of social and cultural phenomena—customs, institutions, symbols, rituals etc.—all of them, as we have seen, man-made or invented very much as languages are made or invented. But this leads to a further point, namely that the anthropologist and sociologist cannot observe the social and cultural facts in a wholly neutral and objective way, that is, in the way in which a scientific device—a thermometer or a voltmeter—might register the heat of a pot of water or the electrical charge in a car battery. Social scientists are always to some extent part of the situation they are observing. One has always to remember that in the last resort anthropology and sociology come down to 'people studying people', and the people who are studying (social scientists) are as much a part of, and as much affected by, the exchange as the people studied. As Studs Terkel once remarked: 'I realised quite early in this adventure that interviews, conventionally conducted, were meaningless. Conditioned clichés were certain to come. The question and answer technique may be of some value in determining favoured detergent, toothpaste, deodorant, but not in the discovery of men and women'.[6]

A social science investigation is then always a personal trans-action between the so-called 'observer' and the so-called 'subjects'. Thus an attempt to understand and interpret the life of a group—the African Azande or the Salk Institute endocrinologists at La Jolla in California—is always to some extent a resultant of interaction and (often implicit) negotiation between the anthropologists/sociologists and their informants and subjects in the culture they are investigating. As it has been put: 'Despite their desire to view their subjects solely as sources of information and their attempts to avoid personal involvement in their subjects' affairs, they (anthropologists) discover that they cannot remain completely detached'.[7] Again, inevitably, the entrance of an observer from 'outside' into a community changes the situation. When Evans-Pritchard goes among the Azande, what he is studying henceforth is not the Azande in their natural state, so to speak, but the Azande-as-reacting-to-the-presence-among-them-of-a-non-Azande(Evans-Pritchard)-who-is-observing-them. And what Latour is investigating is not the Salk Institute community of scientists in a pristine state, but a sub-culture in a 'contaminated', as-observed-by-the-anthropologist-Bruno-Latour, state. (There is a nice story about Trikoli Nath Pandey, an anthropologist who did extensive fieldwork among the Zuni people previously studied by the great Kroeber. When Pandey observed to one of her Zuni informants that the Zuni people seemed to have changed a good deal over the years, the informant replied: 'So have the anthropologists. You are not asking me what Mr Kroeber used to ask'.)[8]

I must make it clear that I am not myself a professional anthropologist who has gone though the initiation test of field-work among a pre-literate tribe. I ought also say that my conception of the anthropological method is a very broad one in that I do not make any hard and fast distinction between anthropology and sociology, nor do I hesitate to use historical and other perspectives in seeking to understand the scientific life-world. In my view, what is essential to anthropology is its interpretive aim and anything that contributes to that aim is grist to anthropology's mill.

It is this interpretive mode of enquiry which I have employed here—looking at a group of life-scientists in a research institute in a way which (within the limitations just spelled out) will, if I am successful, bring out the point of what they are doing and also enable me to make larger and more general points about science and scientists in general. Observation and the gathering of data are of course important: I have in fact spent a good deal of time observing my group of scientists and collecting data of all kinds about them and the context in which they live and move and have their being. But what is of primary concern to me is *reading* and *interpreting* the data so as to understand how scientists organize their world. At the same time, if what has been said above is true, I cannot pretend that I myself am an impartial and neutral observer without any preconceptions or cultural baggage of my own. That is why in this study there is a good deal about the observer (the author of this book) as well as about the observed (the scientists and their aides at the Institute). It is an account of what happens when someone from a completely different sub-culture gains entrance to and observes a group of research scientists, in an attempt to understand what they are up to.

It is also a necessarily selective and partial account in that it is simply not possible to deal with everything and everyone in that group. Again, my study is relative to a given time in the history of the Institute. For example, during my period of field-work the Institute was going through a phase of rapid growth, and it was also changing directions in significant ways as well as moving into a new home.

The construction of knowledge

My approach to the community of scientists at the Institute has been guided by a certain view of scientific knowledge which sees it not just as a passive reflection or registration of the facts of Nature, but rather as the result of making, construction, manufacture, fabrication by scientists. Just as a community constructs (over a long period of time) a language like English or Hindi or Basque, so also a scientific community constructs the corpus of knowledge we call high energy physics or molecular biology. At first blush, this goes so radically counter to the received view of science that I must say something about it.

The common idea of scientific knowledge is that it is based upon direct and immediate observation of the world. Scientific general-izations (like the gas laws and the atomic theory of matter) are built up on the basis of those direct and immediate observations and are ultimately shown to be either true or false in terms of them. Einstein's esoteric and elaborate theory of special relativity was in the last resort shown to be true in terms of some modest and hum-drum observations made with the aid of a telescope during an eclipse of the sun. The basis of this naïve view of science is then that there is a clear-cut distinction between observation (based upon direct sense perception) and the generalizations (laws and theories) that we build up on the basis of the observations. However, it is not difficult to show that this apparently common-sense distinction is fraught with all kinds of confusions. First of all, the observation of the external world requires that we selectively attend to or focus upon a restricted set of the phenomena that flood in upon us when we open our eyes and deploy our other senses (hearing, touch, taste, smell etc.). If we did not focus our attention in this way, we would not see anything at all. Seeing, and observing in general, is very much more than merely opening one's eyes and letting the phe-nomena impinge. Unless, then, we approach the external world with some kind of expectations, some kind of general framework, some principle of interpretation in the back of our heads, observation would be impossible. In other words, the kind of pure, uninterpreted observation that the common-sense view of science relies upon is an absurdity. And that means that the idea that there are pure 'data' is likewise incoherent. What we call the 'facts' or the 'data' are a product of the meeting between a framework of ideas, expectations, principles of interpretation on one hand, and the observable world on the other hand, so that what the scientist observes is a 'construction'—something that is made up out of elements from our side, so to speak, and elements from the side of the external world.

An historical and social dimension was introduced into this constructivist theory of scientific knowledge through the work of the American historian/philosopher of science, Thomas S. Kuhn. In his celebrated work, *The Structure of Scientific Revolutions*[9], Kuhn argued against the idea that science progressed or evolved in a continuous and linear way—Galileo begot Newton who begot Planck who begot Einstein—so that Einstein could be seen as the culmination of a process of discovery begun by Galileo and Newton. According to Kuhn, when we actually look at the way science has developed we find that it is a story not of linear evolution, but of revolutions. It is a history of discontinuous epochs or phases rather than a continuous and cumulative process. Each great epoch in science has its own dominant view (supported by the scientific establishment) of what good and relevant science consists in, and that view functions as a model or 'paradigm' against which all scientific activity is measured. Thus, the areas of scientific research that are thought to be interesting and important, the issues that are considered to be 'problems' and those that are not, the style of scientific research, even what is considered to be scientific 'fact'—these are all, in a sense, dictated by the paradigms or models of science that are adopted at any one time.

An important part of Kuhn's thesis is that the new way of doing science, which emerges after the overthrow of the old paradigms, has to be accepted and endorsed by the scientific community. What is defined as 'science' at any one time is what the scientific community as a whole chooses to accept as science. (Note that Kuhn assumes that there is uniform acceptance of a paradigm by the scientific community instead of what might be called a 'dialectical' situation in which competing attempts to establish paradigms are vying for supremacy.) In this sense the definition of science that prevails is the result of tacit negotiation between scientists; it is a social invention just as much as, say, the idea of marriage in our society is a social invention. Put in another way: scientists do not perceive nature directly; rather they perceive it through the spectacles provided by the paradigm or model endorsed by the scientific community at a particular time. Kuhn, it may be noticed, is not merely saying that science is a social enterprise in the sense that it takes place in a social context; he is making the more radical point that scientists themselves form a distinct community or sub-society which in effect defines what is and what is not to count as 'science'.

Recent developments

Kuhn himself did not elaborate upon the social construction of science thesis that was implicit in his theory. However, since the 1970s there have been various developments, which have all proposed that scientific knowledge is shaped and legitimated by social and cultural factors.[10] For example, it is argued that the categories, or interpretive schemas, or frameworks of meaning imposed upon the observational data (that in fact make the observational data possible) derive from the general Western European capitalist culture of which science is part, or from the culture of science as a whole at any one time (à la Kuhn), or from the sub-culture of a particular scientific discipline (e.g. biology), or even from the micro-culture of a particular institute or laboratory. Thus, at the most general level it has been claimed by some neo-Marxists that there is a correspondence between the style (and even content) of modern science and the socio-economic structures of capitalism. Some have even seen the scientist as a kind of capitalist amassing and exploiting property (scientific knowledge) which in turn gives him or her more power. However, while it is no doubt true that science has flourished within the culture of Western bourgeois capitalism, it has been formidably difficult to show in any concrete way that science (or a particular form of science) is a product of the culture of bourgeois capitalism. (Marx himself says almost nothing about the shaping of science by the dominant social and economic forces, although strictly speaking science ought to be seen, like the other elements of what Marx calls the 'superstructure', as being 'determined' directly or indirectly by those forces.)[11]

At the level of the general scientific culture, some have claimed that the advent of big science in the 1950s—big in the sense of being based upon very large-scale funding from government and private bodies such as the Rockefeller Foundation; big also in the sense of relying upon large-scale and expensive equipment such as the multi-million dollar linear accelerators used in high energy physics; and big in the sense of involving large numbers of scientists (as in the Manhattan Project set up to devise the atom bomb during the Second World War)—has created a new cultural environment for science. The influence of the Rockefeller Foundation in shaping the direction of post-war biological science in the United States has also been emphasized. Thus it has been claimed that the Rockefeller Foundation program in scientific medicine which led to the 'rise of the molecular biology establishment' was the expression of an ideology used by 'the dominant classes of the major industrialised nations' seeking to 'generate the technical expertise required to run the new business corporations, to administer new government institutions and to supply new, more scientifically-oriented hospital-based forms of medical care ... The managed, scientific programme of donation by such Foundations was intended to stabilise and consolidate the corporate state'.[12]

At the disciplinary sub-culture level, Pnina Abir-am, Evelyn Fox Keller and others have claimed that the emergence of the 'new biology' in the 1950s reflects a radically new view of the life sciences, largely brought about by the migration of scientists, such as Delbrück, Szilard and others with a background in physics, into biology after the Second World War. The ideology of physics was, it is argued, imported into biology and the quite new, but immensely powerful, discipline of molecular biology emerged. Again, it has been claimed that this ideology encouraged the development of biomedicine as a commercial enterprise governed by commercial values.[13]

Finally, at the institute and laboratory micro-culture level, a number of studies have attempted to show how particular groups of scientists construct their scientific knowledge. Thus the celebrated study, *Laboratory Life*, by the French anthropologist Bruno Latour and the English sociologist of science, Steve Woolgar, shows how the group of endocrinologists at the Salk Institute at La Jolla, California, negotiate with each other by means of 'inscriptions' (tables of data, graphs, papers etc.) and how certain of those inscriptions come to be accorded the special status of 'facts'. Or again, the American anthropologist Sharon Traweek has attempted to show how the peculiar micro-culture of high energy physics shapes both the form and the content of the science done in this field.[14]

This then represents the general theoretical framework with which I approached the community of immunologists at the Institute and within which my observations of them were made.

Debunking science

Many people are suspicious of, and resistant to, anthropological and sociological accounts because they think that they are necessarily

debunking or reductive; that is, they explain things away or reduce them to other terms. Thus some social scientists, following
Durkheim, explain the role of religion as a means of securing and
maintaining social cohesion. People in a particular culture may
firmly believe that there are gods and that certain rituals must be
performed to gain access to them. But the social scientists know
better, for in reality, according to them, the function of those
religious beliefs and practices is to keep the group together. Religion
is thus reduced to being a mechanism for ensuring social solidarity.
The religious devotees then are deceived about the true meaning of
their beliefs and practices. Only the anthropologist or sociologist
knows what that true meaning is.

There is no doubt that a good deal of social science has been of
this debunking kind, but it does not necessarily follow that all social
science understandings or explanations must be like this, and it
certainly does not follow that anthropological and sociological
accounts of science must inevitably be exercises in 'muck-raking'. It
is possible to show science as a cultural construction, like language,
without thereby explaining it away or reducing it to other terms. An
anthropological approach to science may well have a demystifying
effect upon science and scientists in that it shows that science is
man-made and not god-given, culturally contingent and not a
necessity of nature, and in that it shows up the limits of science. But
to demystify science is not necessarily to debunk it. It is possible to
see science as one of the most astonishing and powerful creations of
the human spirit, without seeing it as the be-all and end-all.[15]

At all events, it certainly has not been my intention here to
'expose' the Institute scientists nor to wash whatever dirty linen they
might have in public. One of the main conclusions to emerge from
my investigation is in fact the unremarkable observation that they
are remarkably human.

The spectre of relativism

A further objection to an anthropological or sociological account of
scientific knowledge is that it leads inevitably to a form of pernicious relativism which radically devalues scientific knowledge. Thus
it is argued that if scientific knowledge is socially and culturally
'constructed' then it must be wholly relative to the particular cultural
circumstances that give it meaning. And this implies in turn that
none of the findings of science—from Boyle's Law to the Crick and
Watson theory of DNA—have any universal or trans-cultural

validity. What we call 'science' is simply an expression of a particular, Western European, culture, just as the use of oracles is an expression of Azande culture, and rain-making rituals are an expression of Australian Aranda culture.

There is a sense no doubt in which anthropological and sociological accounts inevitably 'relativize' what they investigate, since by definition they show things related to, or relative to, a given social and cultural whole. But this kind of relativity does not necessarily lead to the absurd form of relativism which would deny value to the findings of science. Once again, the analogy with language is helpful. Thus the fact that the English language is constructed and 'relative' does not have any perniciously sceptical consequences, as though we could not think and express true propositions in English but merely 'English' propositions and truths. 'Great Britain is an island off the coast of Europe' is not just an *English* truth with no universal or trans-cultural import; it is a *true* proposition. So, while anthropological and sociological interpretations certainly show the relativity of science, this does not lead to an 'anything goes' kind of relativism. 'Relativity, yes: relativism, no!', must be the slogan of the anthropologist of science.[16]

The anthropology of science: relevance and use

What is the use of an account such as this to scientists themselves? Will it provide them with insights into what they are doing and will those insights make them better scientists? In the past, anthropologists and sociologists have for the most part not been concerned to make their accounts either accessible to, or useful to the 'subjects' of their enquiries. In a quite deliberate way, the social scientists did not write their books to be read by the subjects of their research, but rather for their scholarly peers and the educated public back home. Evans-Pritchard did not expect the Sudanese Nuer to read his book about them and to gain insights from it which would help them to live better, and Margaret Mead did not write her books on Samoan culture for the Samoans themselves to read and inwardly digest. Certainly the Bororo people in the Amazon jungle in Brazil were not expected to study Lévi-Strauss's *Tristes Tropiques*! Curiously, the 'subjects' of social science research have been precisely the ones who were denied access to the fruits and benefits of that research. They have been, in effect, precluded from any enlightenment that such research might bring and it was other people, back in England, or the United States or France, or in the universities and academies, who were expected to profit from reading *The Nuer* or *Growing Up in Samoa* or *Tristes Tropiques*. This whole attitude was of course bound up with the 'colonialist' or exploitative attitude of 'studying down' which we discussed before.[17]

One has only to make this situation explicit in order to see how bizarre it is; and yet it was a situation that prevailed in the social sciences (both anthropology and sociology) for more than 100 years. However, there are now welcome signs that social scientists are becoming more aware of their responsibilities to their 'subjects'—responsibilities to make their research findings available to those they study and to avoid that kind of scholarly exploitation which makes their 'subjects' into 'research fodder'. Some Australian Aboriginal groups have given warning that they no longer wish to be objects of scholarly exploitation, and there is a (possibly apocryphal) story that one group has put up a notice on the borders of its country saying 'Ph. D. students keep out!'

How can social science enquiry be done so that it does not exploit or make into 'objects of research' those who are going to be studied? And how can such enquiries be done so that they help those being studied by making them more reflective and self-conscious, and less mystified about what they are doing? One obvious answer is that the research findings must be presented in a way that is accessible to the subjects, and that in turn means forsaking the technical language of the social sciences which is intelligible to professional practitioners but to no others. It is astonishing to note how much social science is written strictly and exclusively for social scientists and for no one else. Many anthropologists and sociologists seem to have made a deliberate decision to write only for the twenty or thirty of their professional peers.

But there is a deeper philosophical reason for social science findings being accessible to their 'subjects'. It is a consequence of the recognition, discussed above, that any social science account is a mutually negotiated business between the anthropologist or sociologist and his or her subjects, and that such an account be accessible to, recognizable by, and in a sense validated by the subjects. It is not just a matter of 'talking down' to the subjects by presenting one's account in simplified and popular language, as though there were two versions, one a really scientific and professional account expressed in technical language and directed to, and fully accessible to, one's peers (but not to the subjects), and the other a simplified and bowdlerized version expressed in popular terms and intelligible to the subjects. There may of course be linguistic and other practical difficulties (lack of interest due to cultural factors, inability to read etc.) which stand in the way of an account of the life and culture of a group of people being intelligible and accessible to all the members of that group. But in principle it ought to be accessible since this is an intrinsic part of social science explanation and understanding. My subjects at the Institute ought in principle to be able to say to me, 'Yes, we see now that this is what we are up to. This makes sense of what we are doing'.

In this present study then I have attempted to present my account of the sub-culture of the group of scientists at the Institute in a way that might be accessible and intelligible to them and to other scientists. Like any other professional group, scientists find it difficult to stand off from what they are doing and to reflect about the larger context within which they work. Perhaps then an unfamiliar perspective on what they are doing will provide them with a basis for reflection and critical self-examination. Referring to Watson of DNA fame, the English scientist Peter Medawar claims that most scientists are historically and sociologically unreflective about their science. They are interested, he says, only in the present state of the art. 'A great many highly creative scientists', Medawar writes, 'take it quite for granted, though they are usually too polite or too ashamed to say so, that an interest in the history of science is a sign of failing or unawakened powers'.[18] Medawar finds this attitude 'natural and understandable'. It goes without saying that the intent of this present study is exactly contrary to Medawar's view. However, whether my findings will really make my scientists more aware or better scientists, I do not know. One can only make the act of faith that reflection on, and self-consciousness about, what one is doing—whether it be sexuality, religion, or art, or science, or anything else—always represents a human gain and is always to the good.

A work of fiction

In a very real sense my account of a community of scientists is a 'story', one account out of a large number of possible and alternative accounts that might be given. Of course, I would want to claim that it is an illuminating story, but I cannot claim that it is definitive—a true and final account. Like the 'life-world' it attempts to portray, it is a construct—a literary construct, an example of a genre of writing which raises certain expectations in the reader. As the American literary theorist, Fredric Jameson, has put it: 'Genres are essentially

literary institutions, or social contracts between a writer and a specific public, whose function is to specify the proper use of a cultural
artefact'.[19]

This book is then a 'cultural artefact' and, in the broad sense, a
work of fiction, just as any anthropological or sociological writing
(no matter how 'realistic' it may appear) must necessarily be an artefact or work of fiction.[20] But it is also fiction in a more deliberate
way in that, while my study is solidly based upon observations of a
particular group of scientists, the personae of the scientists have,
for various good reasons, been disguised by using invented names
and by freely rearranging their words and utterances. Thus when
'Albers' is reported as saying such and such, there is no one specific
person to whom the name 'Albers' refers, and what he is reported as
saying is likely to be an amalgam put together from different
sources. I would contend, however, that what 'Albers' is reported as
saying faithfully gives the gist of what I found through observation
and interviews and putting two and two together. To quote remarks
actually made is, of course, to select—part of choosing *my* story out
of the stories other people have told me. It is then neither more nor
less fictional to attribute to 'Albers' or 'Richmond' or 'Eva Voigt'
things which were said to me, and which seemed pertinent, but
which (usually for obvious reasons) could not be attributed to their
real author. Again, the need to disguise who said something has
sometimes meant that I have put in one mouth what was first said by
several. There are, however, some exceptions to this convention.
The first is the Director who, like God, is unique and so cannot be
disguised; he is therefore reported 'realistically' and in his own per-
sona. The second are the immunoparasitology and molecular biology groups whom it is also not possible to camouflage. However,
for most of the scientists at the Institute, it would not be profitable,
given my fictionalizing presentation, for anyone to try to 'break the
code' and to attempt to find out who really said what and who is
really who. Again, the reader should not suppose that those who
speak 'in their own voice' tell a truer story. There was once an
American police series on television which began each episode with
a voice-over which said: 'The story you are about to hear is true:
only the names have been changed to protect the innocent'.

As has already been remarked, the 'I' who tells the story that
follows is also a fiction since four people contributed to the writing
of this book. Given that this study espouses a 'constructivist' perspective on both science and the anthropology of science, the use of
this fiction shows at least that I/we have the courage of my/our

constructivist convictions! Collaborative writing is, of course, also a social process involving negotiation and compromise. What results is a fifth story, very different from the one each of its four co-authors would have written alone. This is especially so when a conscious effort has been made to find a unified narrative style.

However, I have also tried to bring out the constructed character of this account by deliberately fracturing or breaking up the unified narrative. Thus I have juxtaposed straight descriptions, ethnography, passing thoughts, theoretical analysis and asides on the literature. Observations on the wider research community, the state of play in molecular biology, life at the Institute, interviews and personal anecdote, reactions to preliminary drafts, are all set alongside each other in recognition of the fact that this is a text put together from very diverse materials. Most texts have the appearance of a seamless web, as though the structure and content were simply dictated by the flow and logic of ideas. This is a pretence I have chosen to avoid in favour of constantly reminding the reader that the life-world of the scientist is multi-faceted and can be observed from different points of view. At all events, I hope you enjoy the tale 'I' have to tell.

PART ONE

THE LIFE-WORLD OF THE INSTITUTE

1

Ancestor Worship and Culture Heroes

Aboriginal religion is such that it is hard to separate religious experience from the experience of everyday life. The framework for action and interaction in the everyday world is one constructed in the past by the Dreamtime 'ancestral beings'. Every action has a referent in the 'ancestral past' and a common explanation for behaviour, mundane as well as ceremonial, is that people are simply following the way of the ancestors by acting out a Dreamtime precedent.

Howard Morphy, 'Forms of Religious Experience'[1]

I suppose that what first gave me the bright idea of doing an anthropological study of the Institute was reading Bruno Latour's *Laboratory Life*. So I decide, as an act of piety, before I begin at the Institute, to reread 'Bruno's bible', as my friend Alvin calls it. Latour's general idea is marvellously original—looking at the Salk Institute endocrinologists as though they were a primitive tribe. However, though it is full of powerful insights, the style is quirky and, as I have already discovered, the book is totally opaque to most of my scientists. But the main deficiency of the book is that it gives you no sense of the Salk Institute as the social context within which Latour's scientists carried on their work of 'constructing' scientific 'facts' and making 'inscriptions' (notations of experimental results, scientific papers etc.). For a study that is supposed to be broadly anthropological in method and intent, it is odd that one gets absolutely no sense or feel of the immediate social milieu—the Salk Institute itself. I must attempt, precisely, to show my Institute as a primary social framework within which the scientific knowledge produced there is formed and shaped and without which it simply would not be possible. But how to show this? How to give the sense and feel of this peculiar 'world' or sub-culture? That's the (formidable) question!

****

Entering the Institute

The opening of the new building for the Institute takes place on 8 November 1985. It is a glittering occasion with the Prime Minister of Australia and the Premier of the State of Victoria present, and an assemblage of overseas Nobel laureates and local scientists and their wives and (rarely) husbands. The scientific power-brokers are also there and one can almost physically feel the weight and force of the scientific 'establishment'.

Ceremonies of this kind are, in a sense, pieces of theatre or per-formance art—like school speech days, ship launchings, graduation ceremonies, funerals and annual general meetings—and no one takes them at their face value. Nevertheless, like religious rituals, they have their own function in reaffirming the basic myths of groups and displaying the power of the relevant 'establishment'. They also have a 'political' purpose in that they present an image of the group to the outside world. If some earnest Ph.D. student wanted a good topic, the rhetoric and displays used on these ceremonial occasions would repay analysis.

I have been studying the annual reviews published by the Institute and I have already attended a number of its official gatherings, so I think I know what to expect. My expectations are in fact fully met during the opening ceremony. First, an optimistic image of science in general, and Institute science in particular, is forcefully presented by the Director. This image, I suspect, has very little to do with the lived reality of science at the Institute, but rather with the politics of immunology and medical research as scientific practices: how a relatively new scientific discipline like immunology gets established and maintains itself, elaborates a mystique and gains popular kudos; and how an Institute of immunological research keeps itself afloat, fights off competitors, attracts funds and popular support, and makes its way in the field of international science. There is, of course, noth-ing disgraceful about playing politics like this: every group (no matter how pure and apolitical it may appear) has to play politics and devise power strategies of one kind or another to give itself legitimacy. If knowledge is power, the getting of scientific knowl-edge and the legitimizing of that knowledge also involve power plays and strategies.

The Director begins with a solemn invocation of the spirit of Macfarlane Burnet, the great ancestor hero of the Institute, and a

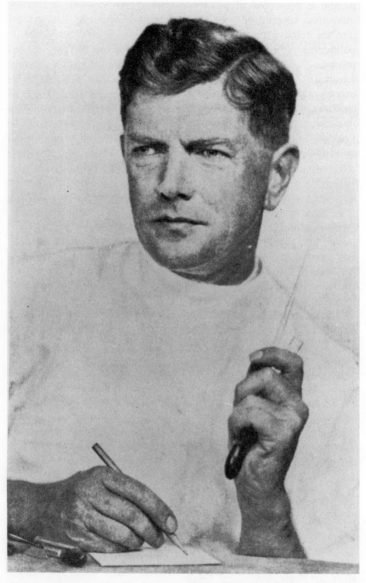

Sir Frank Macfarlane Burnet, Director 1944–65 (photograph taken 1947)

picture is presented of the Institute doing momentous things and more than keeping up with the international scientific Joneses despite the relative paucity of its funding and its resources. For the politicians in the audience there is an assurance that the Institute will produce the practical goods in the form of significant medical advances (a hint is dropped that we are getting closer to solving the cancer riddle and to the discovery of a malaria vaccine). Then, the audience is reminded that the Institute is the flagship of Australian medical science—'The flagship of the jaunty flotilla of proud vessels, large and small, sailing towards a healthier future, which constitute the medical research community of the nation'. Finally, a

Sir Gustav Nossal, Director 1965–

vision of the future of medical science in general is projected—
scientific research moving forward inexorably, solving problems and
conquering new fields, always onward and upward.

On this occasion, the vision splendid of science is presented with
great *brio* by the visiting American Nobel Laureate, Gerald Edelman,
from the Rockefeller University, New York. He describes the
astonishing triumphs of biological science since the Second World
War and gives the impression that the 'mystery of life' will be
solved definitively: all that remains is a certain amount of scientific
mopping up, difficult of course but the end is not really in doubt.
However, understanding the biological basis of the human brain is
the next great challenge and Edelman gives us confidence that that
will also be met and overcome. 'Medical research has already made
it likely that we must soon have a molecular embryology, a
molecular anatomy, and a molecular histology. All of these sciences
will open up an understanding of the morphogenetic bases of higher
human brain functions.'[2] (Consciously or unconsciously, Edelman is
echoing the grand plan for biology of one of the founding fathers of
the new biology, Max Delbrück, with his prediction that the human
mind would be the last frontier for the biological sciences.)[3] Medical
science, says Edelman, is animated by the idea of progress, i.e. 'the
notion of the gradual but definite increase in human knowledge and
... the hope or belief in the continued improvement of the moral or
spiritual state of mankind and humanity'[4]: there is a pre-established
harmony between scientific progress and human progress.

On an occasion like this you become vividly aware of how much
the Institute is a 'world' of its own and how distinctive and closed a
'culture' it represents. I feel rather like Margaret Mead at the beginning of her stay in Samoa, or Claude Lévi-Strauss at his first meeting
with the Brazilian Bororo Indians, or Hunter S. Thompson facing
the Hell's Angels in Los Angeles. How can I gain access to this
'world' and understand the hidden rules and conventions that govern
this sub-culture? It's pretty clear that neither standard questionnaires, nor number-crunching sociology, nor even structured interviews, will help much, any more than they would have helped Mead
or Lévi-Strauss or Thompson. (It is diverting to think of Lévi-
Strauss handing out questionnaires in the middle of the Amazon
jungle!) Even the best and most perceptive of these mainline
sociological approaches—I am thinking of Harriet Zuckerman's
Scientific Elite[5] (on US Nobel Laureates) and Jonathan Cole's *Fair
Science*[6] (on women in US science)—do not really provide us with
an entrée into the scientific 'world'. Despite all the sociological data

we remain outsiders not quite seeing the point of it all. Are we left then with mere subjective and arbitrary intuition, or mere anecdote and gossip? I don't think so. In any case, perhaps there is more to anecdote and gossip than meets the eye. Michelle Rosaldo, for example, urges the anthropologist to take gossip seriously. It is precisely when people are not talking carefully and importantly that one can often learn deep and important things about them.[7]

One obvious way of getting to grips with the Institute is through its history, though one has to distinguish between the chronological record of the Institute's career and the interpretation put upon that record and the symbolic and 'mythical' use made of it within the Institute. That is especially the case with the central figure in that history, Macfarlane Burnet.

Curiously, however, apart from the Director, most of the Institute scientists seem to be profoundly uninterested in its history as such. They view the past of the Institute and of their disciplines as a kind of anecdotal quarry from which *ad hoc* morals and lessons and examples can be drawn as the need arises, but they clearly see little profit in trying to understand the present situation either of the Institute or their disciplines by reference to its, or their, historical genesis. To use de Saussure's famous illustration: if we wish to explain the state of a game of chess at any one stage we can give either an historical account of the past events of the game which have led to the present situation, or we can explain the state of the game in terms of the disposition and inter-relations of the pieces at the present moment. The Institute scientists adopt the latter perspective. As someone says to me: 'A scientist's interest in the past goes back just as far as the earliest paper she or he feels the need to cite'. A rare exception to this is a paper given to a staff seminar by Mitchell, the head of the Immunoparasitology Unit. The paper is entitled 'Ten Years of Immunoparasitology' and Mitchell begins his talk by apologizing for this unusual topic, so much out of kilter with the usual run of Wednesday seminar papers which are severely technical and 'in house'. But, unfortunately, his promise to give an overview of changes in perspective and in conceptual framework and the gradual emergence of immunoparasitology as a discipline or 'field', is not really fulfilled, though he does venture a date (1959) for the 'birthday of immunoparasitology' as a distinct conceptual framework. I make a note to probe Mitchell further on the history of immunoparasitology. Since he was one of the founding fathers of the field it would be history from the horse's mouth.

Later, reflecting on Mitchell's talk, I wonder if he is using the historical genre to vindicate and respectablize immunoparasitology as a sub-discipline? Or is he using the historical mode to explain the lack of progress in immunoparasitology?—it is, he says, on a plateau at the moment. The English philosopher of science Michael Mulkay says somewhere that scientists resort to historical discourse only when things go wrong or are doubtful: usually they speak in the eternal present so as to give the impression that things could not be otherwise.

Macfarlane Burnet

The apparent lack of interest in history evidenced by the present-day Institute scientists contrasts with the lively historical interest of the seminal figure in the story of the Institute, Sir Macfarlane Burnet. The eminent scientist taking to history in his old age to justify his ways to God and his peers is of course a familiar phenomenon. However, while Burnet was to some extent engaged in myth-making, his book, *Walter and Eliza Hall Institute 1915–1965* (published in 1971)[8] is a fascinating attempt to see his own work, and the emergence of immunology as a discipline, in historical perspective. Burnet was Director of the Institute from 1944 to 1965 and was the brightest star in its firmament. In many ways he reflected the older scientific ethos which prevailed before the Second World War—a view which took the history of science (even though it was often very mythologized history) seriously and was also concerned about the philosophical and humanistic implications of science. On the other hand, younger contemporary scientists tend to see an interest in the history and philosophy of their discipline as, in Peter Medawar's phrase, 'a sign of declining powers'.

Burnet was not only interested in the history of the field of immunology, but became himself a central historical figure in the emergence of that discipline and above all, in the development of the Institute as a site of immunological research. In fact, one could say that the history of the Institute *is* Burnet. He also has immense symbolic importance within the Institute and in many ways his ghost still haunts it.[9]

Burnet was a classical scientific hero in the direct lineage of Pasteur and Koch. Like those great figures, he is revered both as an experimenter of genius and as a theoretician of great power. He began studying viruses in the 1920s and 1930s and then became interested in the theory of how our bodies produce the 'antibodies' which protect us against disease from outside. He was interested

above all in the way our white blood cells distinguish between invaders from outside (not-self) and the workings of our own bodies
(self).

Burnet took over the Director's position at the Institute in 1944
and for the next thirteen years maintained the Institute's interest in
virology. But gradually, over that time, Burnet's own concerns, and
those of his colleagues, turned more and more toward immunological issues and in 1957 he decided to radically reorient the
Institute to the study of immunology.[10] From that year onwards
much of the Institute's research was increasingly concentrated upon
the study of the defence mechanisms of the body—how they func-
tioned normally and how on occasions they malfunctioned and
produced 'autoimmune' diseases (the pathology of the immune
processes).

Burnet's fascination with the ability of the immune system to
discriminate between self and not-self led him to see some diseases
(such as rheumatoid arthritis and pernicious anaemia) as being due
to a breakdown in this discriminating ability, so that the cells of the
body are attacked by its own antibodies. As his co-worker Mackay
put it: 'The essence of autoimmune disease is probably the failure at
some point of this power of differentiating between the body's own
material (self) and the foreign material (not-self)'.[11]

The clonal selection theory

The revolution that Burnet effected at the Institute in 1957 was
paralleled in the same year by the announcement of his clonal
selection theory in a brief paper in the *Australian Journal of
Science*.[12] The theory was an attempt to understand what went on in
that 'black box', the immune system, and it turned received immunological ideas upside down. Burnet began by asking how the body
can make so many different and specific antibodies to deal with the
multifarious invaders from outside. (Antibodies are specially
adapted protein molecules that attach themselves to the invading
bacteria, viruses or other foreign bodies and make them prone to
destruction.) A mouse, for example, can through its immune system
fabricate a hundred million quite different antibodies to counter the
myriad hostile antigens that are likely to invade its body.

Until 1955 the 'template' or 'instruction' theory was seen as the
most likely explanation of how the entry of a foreign substance (an
antigen) into the body triggered off processes which eventually
produced a specific antibody which was 'tailor-made' to counter that

specific antigen. According to this account, the invading antigen acted as a pattern or template which 'instructed' the cells of the body to make an antibody of the appropriate pattern. In other words, each antibody is made to order *after* the invading antigen enters the body. In 1949 Macfarlane Burnet and his Australian colleague Frank J. Fenner had pointed to certain phenomena the template theory could not explain: first, the theory could not account for the fact that in the early stages of an immune response the antibodies swiftly came to outnumber their templates; second, the fact that there was an increase in antibody production when the body is invaded by a given antigen for a second time was difficult to square with the template theory; and third, and most importantly, there was the curious phenomenon of immunological tolerance. As it has been put: 'Tolerance keeps an animal from making antibodies against itself and can be acquired for foreign antigens, if the antigens are administered before or at birth. In contrast to immunity, tolerances cannot be maintained unless the antigen persists in the animal. On the subject of immunological tolerances the template theory was silent'.[13]

In 1955 the Danish scientist Niels K. Jerne proposed a radically different model of antibody fabrication (though the model had already been foreshadowed by the German medical scientist, Paul Ehrlich, in 1900), namely that all the millions of different and specific antibodies already existed in the body *before* the invasion of the antigen. The antigen would then 'select' or be matched by one of this vast range of antibodies already being made by the body, i.e. one that happened to 'fit' the antigen. To use a homely analogy, whereas in the template theory it is like going into a tailor's shop and having a suit tailor-made for you, in Jerne's theory it is like going into a tailor's shop and selecting a ready-made suit from the rack. Jerne called his theory 'the natural selection theory of antibody formation'[14], although the name is misleading in that it has nothing directly to do with Darwinian natural selection.

Burnet, who as we have seen had been profoundly dissatisfied with the older account, took over Jerne's basic idea but completely transformed it (as Jerne was to acknowledge graciously later on, 'I hit the nail, but Burnet hit the nail on its head'). Antibodies, Burnet speculated, must be randomly produced during the development of the embryo and each antibody must have a unique pattern. When a foreign antigen invades the body it must sooner or later make contact with and fit into or 'select' an antibody of the appropriate pattern and trigger off further production of the same antibody.

Antibody-producing cells make just one kind of antibody and they have distinctive receptors. An antigen must match its corresponding receptor and it then binds with the antibody-cum-receptor and triggers the cell to manufacture more receptors of exactly the same kind. When a cell is multiplied it produces descendants which in turn all reproduce the same antibody and this 'family' of cells is called a 'clone' (from the Greek word for 'branching twig'). Nossal summarizes Burnet's 'clonal selection theory' in the following way:

Burnet postulated that the different natural antibodies existed not in the blood serum, as Jerne thought, but as fixed molecules on the surface of the lymphocyte (antibody producing cell). The idea was that each lymphocyte carried on its surface a unique antibody acting as a kind of sensor or antenna. Each single cell carried only one specificity. On this theory, all the thousand million lymphocytes of a mouse may look alike, even under the electron microscope but, in fact, they are all very different. Each lymphocyte has locked within it the capacity to form one, and only one, specific antibody. When a foreign antigen entered the body, the great majority of the lymphocytes would display no interest in it. However, a few lymphocytes, those with the right antennae, would be triggered into cell division and antibody formation. The antibody formed would be identical to that originally present on the lymphocyte's surface. The antigen, having encountered its predestined mate in the shape of the cell surface antibody, thus selectively stimulates the formation of antibodies specific against itself.[15]

Burnet thought of the clonal selection theory in metaphorically Darwinian terms in that the antibody-producing cells, just like any organism, undergo mutation and selection, and the fittest survive in the sense that they quite literally 'fit' their specific antigens.

Burnet's bold and ingenious theory encountered both incomprehension and opposition for a number of years. It was, after all, *prima facie* counter-intuitive to suppose that all the antibodies already existed in the body. However, as he put it, 'everyone recognised that it was a good theory in the sense that it could be proved wrong—if it was wrong', and as more evidence accumulated about the structure of antibodies 'it became more and more obvious that the general concept of the 1957 paper must be right'.[16] By 1967 the theory was generally accepted, though by that time Burnet's relatively simple model had become much more complex and intricate. Just as the relatively simple atomic theory of matter eventually led to the incredible complexity of particle physics, so the clonal selection theory led to similarly complex structures and processes of the immune system. Burnet himself believed that there was a funda-

Clonal selection theory

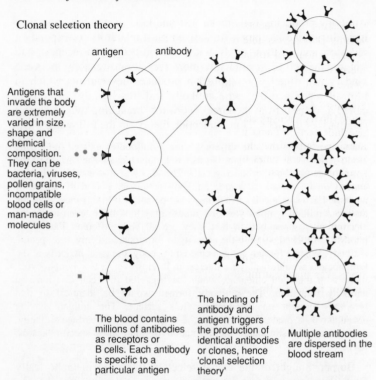

antigen   antibody

Antigens that invade the body are extremely varied in size, shape and chemical composition. They can be bacteria, viruses, pollen grains, incompatible blood cells or man-made molecules

The blood contains millions of antibodies as receptors or B cells. Each antibody is specific to a particular antigen

The binding of antibody and antigen triggers the production of identical antibodies or clones, hence 'clonal selection theory'

Multiple antibodies are dispersed in the blood stream

mental simplicity and economy about the workings of nature in general and the immune system in particular, but that simplicity is certainly not of a naïve mechanical kind. No one could say that the progress of immunology has been characterized by a tendency towards greater and greater simplicity; rather it has been a story of growing intricacy and complexity.[17]

It was crucial to Burnet's theory that one cell produces only one specific antibody. If two different antigens, A and B, are introduced into the body, on Burnet's theory some cells should produce A antibodies and some should produce B antibodies, but none should produce both A and B. If by experiment it could be found that certain cells do in fact produce both A and B antibodies, then the theory must be false. The theory was then 'falsifiable' in the classical Popperian sense, that is, we can think of experimental tests which might possibly disprove it; at the same time it fitted the known immunological facts so well and had been so fertile in suggesting experiments that it was inconceivable that it could be wrong. Burnet was able therefore to hang on to the theory despite a certain amount of initial contrary evidence. Burnet nicely describes the dialectical interplay between theory and experimental evidence in the biological sciences in the following passage:

Scientists who are more interested in experiments than in ideas are liable to quote Huxley's remark about 'the tragedy of a beautiful theory destroyed by one little fact'. I found it of enormous interest, mixed rather often with alarm and despondency, to watch over a decade clonal selection theory being destroyed several times by what appeared to be incompatible facts. Yet, over the same years, virtually every new discovery of general significance made clonal selection seem more and more reasonable. The little 'hard fact' in biology nearly always includes someone's interpretation and interpretations have a tendency to change. No single experiment ever established one biological generalisation or refuted another. Immunology is perhaps one of the most soft-edged of the biological sciences.[18]

A consequence of Burnet's theory was that since antibody formation takes place during the embryo's development, genetically distinct or foreign cells might be implanted and established in the body at this time, and it would then be expected that no antibodies would be developed when that same foreign cell antigen invaded the organism on some later occasion when it was fully developed. In other words the body's immune system would treat the foreign antigen as 'self'. This would mean that 'immunological tolerance' could be acquired. Medawar subsequently did the experiments verifying Burnet's theoretical prediction and they both shared the Nobel Prize for Physiology or Medicine in 1960.[19]

Burnet thought of the clonal selection theory as the one true theory explaining antibody formation. But later developments have suggested that, while the basic structure of the theory remains intact, the immunological mechanisms are much more complex than Burnet thought.

****

Is this account of Burnet's work a kind of 'great man' history? I began by promising a quasi-anthropological account of the Institute and here I am dwelling on an individual scientific genius as though immunology, and the Institute, were all his own work. Isn't this a contradiction? Yes, and no. In one sense, Burnet's individual achievements were very important; but the way in which he has been *used* within the Institute is also important. He is what Pnina

Abir-Am calls a scientific 'culture hero', like Jacques Monod, of the French Pasteur Institute, who has been subjected to 'myth construction' and whose social function is to legitimate 'a certified conception of science'.[20]

****

Burnet as a culture hero

Burnet still has great symbolic importance on a number of levels within the Institute. First of all, he offers a classical model of a great scientist: an individual researcher making momentous scientific discoveries with small and modest means (a little like the great Rutherford in his Cavendish Laboratory). Burnet acknowledged, after his retirement, that the day of individualistic 'small science' was probably past and that future work in immunology would have to be done in large groups and with expensive equipment. Biology, like physics, would eventually have to bow to 'big science'. But, despite this, what he is mostly remembered for at the Institute is his devotion to small scale science and to scientific simplicity. The Director often refers to the economy, even parsimony, of Burnet's approach, although he knows that those days of scientific simplicity are gone forever and that fortune favours the well-funded, the well-staffed and well-equipped. Burnet's example is no doubt used as a reassurance that it is possible for a modestly funded research institute in Australia to compete in the immunological world league, and that small can be beautiful.

Again, Burnet's own work is seen as a kind of Kuhnian 'revolution', standing received ideas about the immune system on their heads. (The Director, who admires Kuhn's book *The Structure of Scientific Revolutions*[21], interprets it in terms of the Institute itself, seeing the various historical phases of the Institute as being dominated by different 'paradigms' of immunological science and viewing immunology as being in a state of 'permanent revolution'.) Burnet's radical restructuring and reorientation of the Institute in 1957 is also seen in much the same light. The invocation of Burnet's ghost reminds the Institute scientists that revolutionary breakthroughs are always possible.

Finally, there is in all of Burnet's writing a calm assurance that there is a pre-established harmony between scientific progress on one hand and human progress on the other hand and that advance in science is *ipso facto* for the good of mankind. The possibility of a conflict between the values of science and social and moral values (as happened, for example, in the recent recombinant DNA debate) is not even envisaged. Another of Australia's world-ranking scientists, the physicist Marcus Oliphant, had his innocence disturbed by the invention of the atomic bomb—here *scientific* progress seemed in flagrant conflict with *human* progress—but nothing analogous appears to have occurred to Burnet. His faith that what is good for science is good for the world—a faith that Burnet inherited from his early scientific education and never lost—is powerfully reaffirmed by his successor, Nossal.

****

I receive an invitation to a symposium on the history of immunology, with special reference to Burnet and the clonal selection theory, at the University of Toronto.[22] Burnet is seen by most of the participants as the hero of early immunology and a good deal of emphasis is given to the prolonged opposition to his clonal selection theory. It was in fact only at the time of the Cold Spring Harbor Symposium in 1967 that the battle for the theory was finally won. David Talmage, who was working in the field at the same time as Burnet, gives an interesting paper on 'The Acceptance and Rejection of Immunological Concepts'. 'Experimental evidence in biology', he says, 'is rarely universally compelling. Evidence that appears to convince one scientist is frequently discounted by another. Thus the wide acceptance of a particular concept depends more on the total framework of accepted and acceptable theories than on the experimental evidence designed to test that particular concept'. Talmage sees the clonal selection theory as: 'the main organising hypothesis of present-day immunology ... developed by a group at the Walter and Eliza Hall Institute in Melbourne, Australia, in the mid-1940s and 1950s'.[23]

In another paper, 'Immunology Old and New: The Beginning and the End', an historian of science, Anne-Marie Moulin, argues that while Burnet's work in the 1940s was crucial for the emergence of cellular immunology, immunology did not emerge as a mature scientific field until the notion of the 'immune system' had been accepted in the 1970s (though the idea had first been put forward at the Cold Spring Harbor Symposium in 1967). Moulin also argues that the idea of 'system' encouraged the hope of establishing linkages between the immune system, the nervous system and the endocrine system, so that eventually immunology might become part of a general overall science of biological information and control—a new 'general biology', the centrepoint of which is the genetic code.[24] As one of the participants puts it: 'DNA says it all'.

A number of the symposium participants comment upon the fact that before the clonal selection theory immunologists could be classified as either chemists or biologists, but that the theory had brought about a marriage of these elements such that no self-respecting immunologist could ignore either. Ironically, of course, Burnet had done just that. According to Nossal, Burnet didn't trust chemists; he 'shunned' them and 'made an enemy of chemistry and chemists'. Eisen (from Massachusetts Institute of Technology) notes that a new book with the title *Molecular Cell Biology* exemplified what would have been impossible in the 1950s and early 1960s—a commitment to a joint biological and chemical approach in immunology.[25]

What emerges from a number of the papers at the Toronto Symposium is that, while the acceptance of the clonal selection theory and its role in furnishing a theoretical framework for a 'mature' immunology provided a triumphant finale to Burnet's career, his younger collaborators and successors at the Institute were much better placed than he was to capitalize on the new directions in immunology. Burnet's rather strange antagonism to chemistry and to high technology in science made him unsympathetic to the combination of biology and chemistry that his theory helped bring about. It also made him suspicious of the technique-dominated biology that was emerging in the 1960s. Like a scientific Moses, he was not to enter the Promised Land to which he had led others.

****

Nossal

Nossal, Burnet's successor, was fortunate in that he had another mentor in Joshua Lederberg whose commitment to the new biology and to high technology in science provided him with an entirely different model from that espoused by Burnet. Lederberg was visiting the Institute when Nossal began his work and it was to Lederberg's laboratory at Stanford that Nossal went while he was still working on his one cell/one antibody project which was important in the clonal selection theory gaining acceptance.

Nossal was Burnet's own choice of heir-apparent as Director of the Institute (the story is that Nossal was the only applicant for the post) and there is, *prima facie*, some cause for puzzlement about this since their personalities and scientific outlooks were poles apart. The older Burnet was austere and reserved while the much younger Nossal (he became Director at the age of thirty-five) was enormously vital and enthusiastic and extroverted. Again, Burnet was committed to small and individualistic science using modest resources and eschewing elaborate scientific technology, while Nossal on the other hand embraced big science and recognized the need for group research and new scientific technology.

One might have thought that Burnet would have found Nossal's personality and scientific style completely antithetical to his own. That, on the contrary, he selected and designated Nossal as his successor reflects credit on Burnet. Of course, Nossal had, through his own research, vindicated Burnet's clonal selection theory, and then again he had the powerful support of Joshua Lederberg who was then beginning his career as a scientific entrepreneur and power broker.

Burnet and Gajdusek

A number of those who knew Burnet personally give the impression that he was a rather difficult character, very conscious of his own worth as a scientist and impatient with lesser mortals. Again, despite his carefully cultivated apolitical stance, he also favoured conservative doctrines such as eugenics. On my return to the Institute after the Toronto Symposium I talk to Stephens (a former member of the Institute) about the great man. He says that a revealing aspect of Burnet's scientific personality is shown in his dealings with the romantic and extraordinary American scientist, D. Carleton Gajdusek, in the late 1950s. Gajdusek had studied with Linus Pauling and Max Delbrück at the California Institute of Technology, and John Enders at Harvard (he used to joke that everyone he studied with eventually got the Nobel Prize!) and in 1957 he came to visit Burnet at the Institute. Gajdusek was a flamboyant character with an extraordinary range of interests, but though Burnet was impressed with his work he did not consider that he was a first-rate scientist.

After eighteen months at the Institute Gajdusek visited Papua New Guinea and there became interested in the mysterious disease called kuru which afflicted the Highlands people. Burnet had also been interested in kuru and viewed the investigation of the disease as an Australian project. When Gajdusek made known his designs to take on kuru as his own research project Burnet saw him as an interloper and a rather frosty exchange took place between the two. As a friend at the Institute wrote to Gajdusek at the time: 'You are most certainly not the white-haired boy down here at the moment! I thought that in the year down here you should have realised that the Boss (Burnet) likes to think out and arrange things himself. You know what a stuffed shirt he is ...'.[26] Gajdusek, however, was able to show that kuru was a slow virus disease and that it was transmitted through the practice of cannibalism. Burnet, despite his initial pique at Gajdusek invading what he (Burnet) considered as Australian scientific territory, generously acknowledged the latter's success. Gajdusek was awarded the Nobel Prize in 1976 for what was a classical piece of scientific discovery and detective work.

Gajdusek subsequently published a collection of letters and field notes which cover his relations with Burnet during the kuru episode. In her preface, the editor of the collection, Judith Farquhar, makes a revealing remark about scientific territoriality:

These letters record more than the medical thinking and the field and laboratory investigations that formed the foundation of slow virus studies. They also betray something of the professional and national territoriality that often affects the course of scientific research. The medical importance of kuru escaped no-one's notice, and much of the early 1957 correspondence directly concerns the allocation of research rights over the problem. The tacit rules that govern the scientific division of labour and the competitive pursuit of significant research findings can be seen at work in these pages, though some would say that they are evident more in the breach than in the observance.[27]

The mythical Burnet

Burnet is then a many-faceted figure who is 'used' within the Institute for a variety of mythic purposes. He represents the golden age of the simple experiment and the grand theoretical insight and scientific 'breakthrough'. He also represents 'small' (antitechnological) science as against 'big' science and shows that small science can win the ultimate prize. He is also a symbolic founding father who mapped out immunology's territory and legitimized immunology as a discipline. And he exemplifies the conviction that there is some kind of pre-established harmony between scientific progress and human progress. As I said before, he is a kind of culture hero who serves the purposes both of the discipline of immunology as a whole (as witness the Toronto Symposium) and of the micro-culture within the Institute.

Although Burnet takes an historical view, what is a little strange about his 1971 account of the rise of immunology as a scientific discipline is his lack of reference to the larger world of the new biology. Perhaps because Burnet was unsympathetic to the molecular approach to biology, Crick and Watson receive only cursory reference and there is no hint that a revolution had occurred. If, however, we are to get an idea of the small world of the Institute we must first get some idea of the big world of biology from 1960 onwards.

2

The Emergence of the New Biology

In the 1920's the new fieldworker-theorist brought to completion a powerful new scientific and literary genre, the ethnography, a synthetic cultural description based on participant observation. The professional ethnographer was trained in the latest analytic techniques and modes of scientific explanation. This conferred an advantage over amateurs in the field: the professional could claim to get to the heart of a culture more quickly, grasping its essential institutions and structures. A prescribed attitude of cultural relativism distinguished the fieldworker from missionaries, administrators, and others whose view of the natives was, presumably, less dispassionate, who were preoccupied with the problems of government or conversion. In addition to scientific sophistication and relativist sympathy, a variety of normative standards for the new form of research emerged: the fieldworker was to live in the native village, use the vernacular, stay a sufficient (but seldom specified) length of time, investigate certain classic subjects, and so on.

James Clifford, *The Predicament of Culture*.[1]

The new turn in biology

The relatively simple and tranquil scientific world in which Burnet grew up was to undergo momentous changes in the 1940s, with the introduction of a new ideology into the biological sciences, and again with the beginnings of molecular biology in the 1950s and 1960s. As I have said, immunology is a little world within the larger world of biology and it is inevitably affected by changes and developments and 'revolutions' within the latter, though often after a considerable time-lag.

The 'new turn' in biology is usually associated with the discovery of the structure of DNA as the key to genetic replication by Crick

38

and Watson in 1953. But that remarkable and dramatic event was the culmination of developments set in motion in the 1940s. The participants in that revolution in biology, and many of the historians of science who have written about it, make it all seem inevitable, as though the new biology simply developed to accommodate the discovery of a new 'field'. In other words, the emergence of the new discipline mirrored or reflected the discovery of a new set of phenomena which were objectively 'there' waiting to be recognized. There were of course a few scientists, such as Erwin Chargaff and Barbara McClintock, who resisted the new way of doing things and who suggested that things could have been otherwise, but they are, so it is claimed, exceptions who prove the rule. In fact, so the public relations people for the new biology say, the development of biology has been necessary and inevitable and it is idle romanticism to wish to go back to an older style of biological science. One of my scientists, Richmond, for example, dismisses Chargaff and his doubts about the present course of the biological sciences as the gripes of an old-fashioned and embittered biologist who just didn't make it.[2]

The emergence of the 'new biology' was, however, anything but inevitable or necessary. Biology could have taken a number of different directions in the 1940s and that it took the course it did is due to all kinds of accidental and contingent and 'political' factors. The rhetoric and the 'public relations' used by the scientists involved in the new movement (and also by their sympathetic and compliant historians like Judson and Olby[3]) was also a major element in this development. As someone has remarked, Crick and Watson and their allies instructed us how we should view them; they made sure that they would be given a good press. In a sense Watson's famous book *The Double Helix*[4] is almost as significant a part of their success as their actual discovery of the structure of DNA (announced in two impersonal pages in the scientific journal *Nature*).

For physicists in the 1930s and 1940s biology was viewed as a kind of Third-World scientific territory, mainly descriptive in its orientation, imprecise and woolly and with very little theoretical power or ambition. Compared with the triumphs of quantum mechanics in physics, biology was still largely in the older tradition of 'natural history' typified by patient observation and description and low-level theory. McClintock was very much in this tradition and so was Burnet. Ingenious as the clonal selection theory is, it does not have the radical character or the supreme explanatory and unifying power of the theories of quantum physics. The latter could claim to have uncovered the secret of matter, but no biologist could claim to have discovered the secret of life. As Max Delbrück, one of the pioneers of the new biology, put it, in the 1940s he had as a physicist found biology to be in a rather 'depressing' state since often 'analysis' (in biology) seems to have stalled around in a semi-descriptive manner without noticeably progressing towards a radical physical explanation'.[5] After visiting laboratories working on animal viruses, one of Delbrück's younger colleagues reported that it had been a 'sad and discouraging' experience revealing 'the lack of a proper quantitative approach', and he complained of the 'unconvincing character' of the approaches, methods and goals of animal virology as then practised.[6]

What was even worse was the lack of ambition on the part of biologists. No biologist in the 1940s would have thought it decent to claim that biology was concerned with solving 'the secret of life', i.e. seeking a fundamental and final explanation of that which differentiates living from non-living beings. To physicists such as Delbrück and Szilard, fresh from their triumphs in quantum mechanics, the classical biologists were curiously uninterested in such a fundamental question. They were happy to admit that life was a 'mystery', a 'secret', which did not admit of any final explanation. The older materialist and reductionist theories of Haeckel and Loeb, that life could be explained in physico-chemical terms and that biology could be reduced to physics and chemistry, were seen as just so much idle speculation, and it was mostly assumed that life was an irreducible datum with its own peculiar laws. As Leo Szilard said, the classical biologists before 1940 'lacked the faith that things are explainable'.[7] Instead, they remained content with what one commentator has called 'a certain reverential pleasure ... in contemplating the mystery of living things, and almost preferring the mysterious to remain mysterious'.[8] Szilard saw the 'faith' that everything could be finally explained, so that nothing would be left as a mystery or a secret, as the crucial difference between classical biology and the new biology which arose in the 1940s and 1950s and whose most dramatic fruit was the Crick and Watson model for DNA. According to Szilard what he brought to biology was

not any skills acquired in physics, but rather an attitude: the conviction which few biologists had at the time, that mysteries can be solved ... If secrets exist, they must be explainable. You see, this is something which modern biologists brought into biology, something which the classical biologists did not have. They often were astonished, but they never felt it was their duty to explain. They lacked the faith that things are explainable and it is this faith ... which leads to major advances in biology. An example is the Watson–Crick model for DNA, a model which immediately explained how DNA can duplicate. Everyone knew that DNA can duplicate, but nobody asked how it does.[9]

****

It occurs to me that the new biology transforms the phenomena of life processes into something that can be *read*. The genetic mechanisms are, precisely, a *code*, an information system. Genetics and biology thus become part of the 'linguistic turn' that has dominated 20th-century thought for the last fifty years—Saussurean linguistics, Lévi-Strauss's attempts to 'read' cultures as though they were languages, the interpretation by Barthes and other semiologists of various kinds of human behaviour as though they were texts, Wittgenstein's 'language games', Foucault's emphasis upon the various 'discourses' that govern the way we think and exercise power. The linguistic model or metaphor is so pervasive that we are entitled to call this the Age of Language. In a sense it has succeeded the 18th- and 19th-century Age of the Machine when the mechanical model or metaphor reigned supreme.

****

The new scientific ideology

This change in scientific ideology, as one may call it, came about mainly through the influence of a number of remarkable emigré physicists, the Austrian Erwin Schrödinger (1887–1961), the Hungarian Leo Szilard (1898–1964), the German Max Delbrück (1906–81) and the Italian Salvador Luria (1912–). Schrödinger was one of the founding figures in quantum mechanics and Delbrück and Szilard had also had brilliant careers in physics. They were all convinced that quantum physics was, as Delbrück put it, 'the final word' on the 'behaviour of atoms'. Biology then offered a chance to do something new. If one could use the same approach in biology that had proved so successful in physics then perhaps something could be done about the dismal and depressing state of the life sciences. One could also, perhaps, assuage some guilt for the use made of physics in producing the atom bomb by showing that its approach and spirit could serve in the investigation of life processes. (That was certainly a powerful motive in Szilard's switch from physics to the despised biology.)[10]

The introduction of this new scientific ideology in which the attitudes and 'faith' of quantum physics to physical problems were carried over into the investigation of life phenomena, created a radical change in the latter realm. The kind of questions that were now asked in biology, the way problems were conceived, the modes of experimentation used, the research programs adopted, the way biological science was organized at the laboratory and institute level, all changed. It would, perhaps, be extravagant to call this change a 'revolution' of the Kuhnian kind, but it did bring about a new spirit in biology. One has only to contrast the 'macho' scientific style of the heroes of the new biology, Crick and Watson, with the more modest and patient style of 'old-fashioned' biochemists and biologists such as Chargaff or McClintock, to see what that difference meant.

Crick and Watson's theory of gene replication was of course the most dramatic vindication of the new approach. Watson described his discovery as: 'perhaps the most famous event in biology since Darwin's book'.[11] But the new biology also prepared the way for a new scientific discipline, molecular biology (the investigation of the ultimate units of the living cell in the same way that physicists and chemists investigate the ultimate units of matter). Since the 1960s the successes of molecular biology have, so it is claimed, changed our conception of life: 'By revealing the ultimate nature and universality of the molecular mechanisms underlying the diversity of life forms, molecular biology challenged evolution as the central problem of biology'.[12]

The attitude of the pioneers of the new molecular biology—Crick, Monod, Stent and others—was based upon an extra-scientific, philosophical, commitment to materialism and reductionism. As Crick put it in 1966, 'the ultimate aim of the modern movement in biology is in fact to explain *all* biology in terms of physics and chemistry'.[13] Consciousness itself is, in principle, explicable in the same way. 'The soul is imaginary and ... what we call our minds is simply a way of talking about the functions of our brains.'[14] The workings of the human brain are themselves explicable in terms of 'the nature of the hereditary mechanism that constructs the nervous system'.[15] Again, Jacques Monod claimed in 1971 that molecular biology's explanation of the genetic mutations that drive the process of biological evolution destroys the 'anthropocentric illusion'which pervades all Western religion and philosophy—the idea that life, especially human life and its evolution, is guided by some purposive force.[16]

These philosophical, almost religious, views of the significance of molecular biology no longer have much persuasive force among contemporary scientists in this field. But there is no doubt that they played an important part in the establishment of the new scientific discipline.[17]

The emergence and legitimation of this new conception of biology has resulted in a new multi-disciplinary 'field' involving resources from a number of traditional disciplines. It also required the establishment of new kinds of institutional organization, university courses, programs of education and training, journals, conferences, networks. This has been to some extent a 'political' process. New scientific fields have to be accepted by the scientific establishment and they frequently face conservative resistance from within the establishment, resistance which has to be neutralized by 'political' means. In this case part of that politicking has involved the *ex post facto* construction of the history of biology showing how inevitable and irresistible the supplanting of classical biology by the new biology has been. As I remarked before, the founders of the new biology not only made revolutionary discoveries in biology but also instructed us how to view them. They provided both scientific results and an ideological interpretation or representation of those results. Thus Crick and Watson not only discovered how genes replicate and laid down the foundations of molecular biology, but also succeeded in representing this discovery as being 'the central dogma' within the whole of biology and also as a final explanation of the 'secret of life'.[18]

An important part of that quasi-political work of representation was the myth-making construction of a 'history' of the new biology showing how it had its sources in quantum physics, especially through Bohr and Schrödinger, and how its eventual triumph was prefigured.[19] The use made of both Niels Bohr and Erwin Schrödinger is extremely interesting in this respect. The impression was given that the general approach of quantum physics was directly translatable to biology, thus enlisting the prestige of Bohr and Schrödinger for the new enterprise. However, it was not so much the scientific substance of what Bohr and Schrödinger said that was of interest to the scientist historians of the new biology, as the scientific attitude and style and 'faith' that their work illustrated. Thus Delbrück interpreted Niels Bohr's famous 1932 lecture 'Light and Life' (which in fact rejects the reduction of biology to physics) as legitimizing his move from physics to biology.[20] Delbrück had been present at Bohr's lecture and, according to Rosenfeld, he was 'so excited about the prospects it opened up in the vast field of biology that he there and then decided to take up the challenge'.[21] Bohr made it respectable for quantum physicists such as Delbrück to enter the hitherto despised territory of the life sciences.

It is, however, Erwin Schrödinger's little book *What is Life?* (written during his exile from Nazi Germany in Dublin) which is usually given pride of place in most of the 'constructed' histories of the new biology. According to Stent, Schrödinger's book 'became a kind of *Uncle Tom's Cabin* of the revolution in biology that, when the dust had cleared, left molecular biology as its legacy'.[22] However, the actual content of Schrödinger's little book is difficult to square with its reputation. As the English historian of science Edward Yoxen says, 'The archaic style, the abstruse argument and the elaborate, dated message of Schrödinger's book seems a curious sort of inspiration for the threat and power of molecular biology'.[23] Abir-Am, however, argues that there were 'political' motives behind the annexation of Schrödinger by the molecular biologists.

As a founder of quantum mechanics, an innovation which upset the classical order in physics and by implication in science, Schrödinger had acquired the aura of a revolutionary who had become respectable, since by the 1960s quantum physics, once a threat to classical physics, had become part and parcel of a redefined physical discipline. It is precisely this image of being respectable revolutionaries that molecular biologists sought to convey: revolutionary in order to attract newcomers; respectable in order to gain acceptance by the prevailing scientific order and obtain recognition and legitimacy as an autonomous new area of research and teaching. Claiming kinship to Schrödinger, even though by oblique and undocumented means, was instrumental in acquiring legitimacy for their conceptual and socio-political claims, thus reducing the resistance they encountered on the part of the traditional order in science in general and biology in particular.[24]

However it was not the content of Schrödinger's book that was important to those who invoked him; rather it was, as Crick put it, the assurance that 'fundamental biological problems can be thought about in precise terms, using the concepts of physics and chemistry'.[25] Crick used Schrödinger's name and reputation to legitimate his reductionist approach to biology and to help him represent his theory of gene replication as the solution to the secret of life. Just as Shakespeare's plays, so it has been argued, were a kind of legitimation of the new Tudor regime, so also Schrödinger's book was used to legitimate the new biology in the face of opposition in the 1950s and 1960s and the power struggle over the definition of the biological field or realm between the new molecular biologists and the older cell biologists, organismic biologists and biochemists. As

Abir-Am puts it:

This interpretation is the only one which can explain why molecular biologists discovered Schrödinger only in the 1960s when his topicality was already obsolete in their own terms and thus he could have had no conceptual function. His invocation was a subtle means to gain legitimation for certain definitions of biology both among molecular biologists and vis-à-vis the scientific order at large.[26]

This kind of historical construction of the emergence of the new biology was not just confined to the scientists themselves; it has also had powerful support from popularizing writers such as Horace Judson in his best-seller *The Eighth Day of Creation: The Makers of the Revolution in Biology*[27], and historians of science such as R.C. Olby in his book *The Path to the Double Helix*.[28] Both Judson and Olby offer a 'Whig' interpretation of the history of biology. Judson largely identifies the history of the new biology with Crick (also a convert from physics) and Monod, and his book is in many ways a popular version of the 'official' history. Similarly, Olby's compendious (500 pages) work identifies the new biology with the Crick and Watson discovery and presents that discovery as the necessary outcome of two coverging 'schools', each of which produced one of the two co-discoverers. Both accounts are 'internalist' in that they describe the history of scientific developments solely in terms of ideas, discoveries, scientific geniuses and 'great men'. Social and political factors are excluded and the whole process of development is seen to be necessary and inevitable, as though it were impossible that it might have been other than it turned out to be. Recalcitrant and inconvenient critics and objectors such as Chargaff are presented (and dismissed) as eccentrics.[29]

This then is the overall context that immunological scientists in general, and the Hall Institute scientists in particular, find themselves in. Although it is generally agreed within the Institute that the future lies with molecular biology, there are still residues of the older views of biology. For example, one of the scientists at the Institute, Stephen Wade, after acknowledging that molecular biology has brought new rigour into immunology ('a lot of the stuff that goes on in the field is very sloppy' he says) also laments the fact that it has led to a cult of technique. He claims that there are a lot of whiz kids about with the latest sophisticated techniques but who know little about cell biology. On the other hand, Richmond says that 'biology *is* molecular biology, full stop'. But the scientific ideology introduced by the new biology is taken for granted by everyone, namely that the same scientific rigour is possible in the life sciences as in the physico-chemical sciences. The old materialist and vitalist debates about whether life is reducible to physico-chemical terms are now dead as a doornail and it is assumed that the mystery of life is no longer mysterious. The 'secret of life' has been unravelled and all that remains is a kind of mopping up operation, though that may take several decades.

James Rainer at the Institute even says that he can envisage the exhaustion of immunology as a distinct scientific field in that in the foreseeable future most of the main mechanisms will have been explicated and it will only be a matter of filling in the detail. In many ways immunology is in the phase of what Kuhn calls 'normal science', i.e. working out the consequences and implications of the 'revolutionary' shift that took place in the life sciences in the 1960s, a shift which established new models or 'paradigms' and, as remarked before, introduced a new ideology or 'faith' (to use Szilard's term). There are still, of course, exciting discoveries to be made and Nobel Prizes to be won in immunology but no Kuhnian 'revolutions' are in the offing.

Burnet and molecular biology

As I said before, Burnet was profoundly suspicious of molecular biology because of the complicated and expensive experimental technology involved, and the 'arrogant' reductionist program it espoused. Thus one of his colleagues remarks that Burnet had a deep rooted 'distrust of sophisticated apparatus and machines. In his own work he employed the simplest of tools and instruments'.[30] And another, referring to the portrait of Burnet in King's Hall, Canberra, notes that it 'shows him with his tools of trade—a Pasteur pipette, test tubes, Bunsen Burner etc.—nothing more complex than a microscope'.[31]

This made him slow to respond to the equipment needs of younger scientists at the Institute who had been trained in the new techniques in the United States. In fact, it was not until 1961 that the Institute had an ultracentrifuge, bought for G. L. Ada's research on the influenza virus. Ada's work was really the only molecular biology done at the Institute prior to Burnet's retirement in 1965.

Again, Burnet reacted against the reductionist program of the molecular biologists who argued that, in principle, all phenomena studied by chemists can be explained in the terms of physics: in other words, cellular, bacterial and viral biology can, in principle, be fully understood in molecular terms. If biology is defined as the chemistry of the nucleic acids, and those nucleic acids are defined in physical molecular terms, both biology and chemistry become second-class sciences. As Burnet confessed:

I am positively schizophrenic about molecular biology. I find myself fascinated at the way the Watson-Crick formulation of the structure of DNA was able to compass all the important requirements for a chemical basis for genetics ... On the other side of the ledger I find myself resenting the arrogance which defines biology as the chemistry of the nucleic acids, thus eliminating almost all those aspects of the study of life and its appreciation which have come my way.[32]

In 1965 Burnet was still claiming that 'however fascinating it may be as a scholarly achievement, there is virtually nothing that has come from molecular biology that can be of any value to human living'. Indeed, he suspected it contained 'tremendous possibilities of evil'.[33] Again, as late as 1968, he was maintaining that 'even with all the new knowledge of molecular biology, I can see no way even in theory by which it can be turned to benefit by preventing or treating cancer'. 'Overall', he concluded, 'its human implications are sinister rather than promising'.[34]

Burnet's schizophrenic reticence about molecular biology and the spirit of the new biology is a fascinating illustration of a scientist painfully caught in a culture shift or transformation. Formed in an older scientific culture where biology had a certain autonomy, Burnet, like Erwin Chargaff in the United States, remained sceptical about post-DNA biology even while seeing its enormous possibilities.

Yoxen and the capitalizing of biology

Harking back to my observation that molecular biology transforms the phenomena of living processes into something that can be *read*, I come across an interesting article by Edward Yoxen.[35] Yoxen claims that 'at the centre of molecular biology in its developed state lies the principle that genes (which in concrete form are sections of double-helical DNA molecules located within more complex structures in cell nuclei known as chromosomes) can be thought of as instructions'.[36]

Yoxen then argues that this new way of looking at the gene—'the idea of a genetic program as a major organising principle in the life sciences[37] and 'the attempt to apprehend nature as programmed'[38]— chimes in with the post-war attempts by Western capitalism to 'incorporate' the biological sciences and subject them to centralized State control. Warren Weaver, head of the Division of Natural Sciences of the Rockefeller Foundation in the 1930s and 40s, is seen as the central figure in this move to 'managed science'. 'What Weaver did', so Yoxen says, 'was to develop a system of patronage and direction of research and to bring modern management to science'.[39] This in turn led to the development of State-funded and State-controlled biological science through the National Institutes of Health in the United States and the European Molecular Biology Organization. Finally, this kind of biological science lent itself to the interests of the biotechnology industry, controlled by pharmaceutical, chemical and agricultural corporations, which is one of the central developments in contemporary capitalism.

The connections that Yoxen sees between (a) the idea of the genetic code as the organizing principle of the new biology, (b) the idea of 'managed science' developed by Weaver, (c) the idea of State-controlled and 'incorporated' science, and (d) the idea of biological science in the service of contemporary capitalism, are no doubt very interesting. But, while there are affinities between these various ideas, it is difficult to see that molecular biology represents a 'capitalizing' (a 'capitalist' interpretation and exploitation) of the biological sciences.

****

The Director of the Hall Institute places great stress upon 'family spirit' and collegiality among the staff, and morning and afternoon tea are viewed as voluntary/compulsory occasions. One is expected to show one's face and to look collegial, and most members of staff turn up. It is, of course, an ideal opportunity for me and I do some gossip-research over tea. On informal occasions like this, one can often discover a lot about the formal structure of a group. People often ask me over tea how the project is going and it is very interesting to observe the different attitudes that they have to this cuckoo (me) in their nest. I suppose that the anthropologist has to take account of the natives' reactions to his or her presence as an observer, and that these reactions ought to from part of his or her anthropological 'data'. At the Toronto Symposium Nathan Reingold said that historians of science should view scientists as their guinea pigs: but I am also one of the guinea pigs—a kind of meta-pig! In other words I, as observer, and the project itself must also be an integral part of my study. (Anthropologist, anthropologize thyself!)

I fancy that the older and more senior scientists think that my project is a passing enthusiasm of the Director (the Director is whole-heartedly and very publicly in support of the enterprise), and more or less a waste of time and effort, indeed even possibly dangerous in that it could—if it publicly washed the dirty linen of the Institute—jeopardize funding. Some of the younger scientists are, however, sympathetic and see my interests as chiming in with some of their own views about the way science is done. A few even think that it might help them to become more reflective about what they are doing as scientists and even, as a bonus, be good public relations as far as the general public is concerned.

****

I show John Rolland, one of the scientists at the Institute, a draft of this chapter and he reacts very critically. He is clearly offended by the idea that the development of the new biology was in some way historically constructed. Any analysis of biological systems, he says, ends up in DNA. This is, biologically speaking, the bottom line. Proteins, cells, biological systems, individuals, even societies are biologically constructed, at different levels of complexity, out of DNA and it makes no sense to speak of DNA, and the biology in which DNA has paradigmatic status, as being 'constructed' by social factors. To a biologist, Rolland says, it is nonsense to argue that the new biology could have taken a different direction. 'I cannot imagine', he says, 'that a DNA sequence of a gene would be different depending on who determined it, or when it was determined'.

The structure of DNA, he goes on, is a typical scientific fact if ever there was one and it seems perverse to explain it as a 'social construct'. Our belief that DNA is a double helix is simply a result of DNA being structured that way in reality. Further we have good reasons to back this claim. On one hand, there is no reason to doubt it, since there is no competing alternative theory, no controversy, and there are no unresolved problems. On the other hand, knowledge of the structure of DNA has led to successful application in many areas like genetic engineering. If there ever was any 'social' element in the establishment of the structure, it has simply been winnowed out, leaving only the facts which correspond directly to what is there in nature.

This is indeed a formidable argument for denying the 'social construction' of DNA and affirming its reality as a fact. However the power of the argument is a consequence not so much of the argument itself but of the effectiveness of scientific knowledge-making techniques. In order to be able to see those techniques at work we have to go back to the period when the structure of DNA was uncertain and a matter of controversy. Since we cannot gain access to reality directly, when we make our first tentative efforts to work out the structure of a particular piece of it there are always differing views and bewildering bits of evidence whose importance or significance no one is certain of. Moreover, any process of establishing an accepted answer always requires the input of skills and techniques from a wide range of people, as well as a variety of contingently available materials and instrumentation. Thus the accepted structure is the product of a process which is social in two important ways: it involves human choices or selections and it is necessarily collective. The structure that is finally accepted results from a chain of selections of approaches, techniques, data, theory and instruments which reflect the inputs, relations and strategies of all the workers in the field.

In 1951 it was not clear that the form of DNA was helical at all; or, if it was, whether it was a double or a triple helix. Crick and Watson got their model to work, i.e. to fit with the known data, after a protracted process in which they were competing with those like Pauling who was anti-helical but who was also the most advanced in the field and hence most likely to come up with an answer. Equally they needed input from others, such as the biochemical advice of Donahue and the X-ray crystallographic work of Franklin (who also held that it was a triple not a double helix). Subsequently a process of solidifaction took place, and the double helix structure of DNA became built into a network of practices and is now thoroughly entrenched. The social factors involved in this gradually becoming accepted as a 'fact' have been forgotten, and they can now only be revealed by a very problematic reverse process of deconstruction.

For this reason any problems with the structure of DNA, such as those about how the helices unwind themselves in the process of replication, have simply been put into the 'acceptable anomaly' basket, especially in light of the failure of the alternative models like the 'warped zipper' to mount a credible counter-argument.

That DNA is now the basis of much of our biological understanding tells us only that it is instrumentally effective within the constraints of the network of practices we have established on the basis of that structure. In other words, it works. But even if the structure of DNA has become relatively well established, its role and function is less certain and is undergoing constant transformation.

There is, for example, no fixed agreement about what a gene is and how genetic control works. It is perfectly possible that, if a different view prevailed—for example, that the nucleus of the cell does not control all the processes of heredity but has a dialectical relationship with the cytoplasm—a different understanding of the role of DNA might emerge. If this were to happen, it would not be unreasonable to anticipate a radical modification of the structure of DNA. In other words, if the European views on cytoplasmic inheritance had prevailed, DNA might well have been other than it is. I put all this to Rolland, but he remains unconvinced. 'DNA is DNA is DNA', he says.

3

The Institute's Setting

No society consists of anonymous eccentrics bouncing off one another like billiard balls, and Moroccans, too, have symbolic means by which to sort people out from one another and form an idea of what it is to be a person ... The selves that bump and jostle each other in the alleys of Sefrou gain their definition from associative relationships they are imputed to have with the society that surrounds them. They are contextualised persons ... As individualistic, even wilful, as the Moroccans in fact are, their identity is an attribute they borrow from their setting.

Clifford Geertz, *Local Knowledge: Further Essays in Interpretive Anthropology*[1]

The Institute is a small world of its own with its own material and economic base and organizational structures. It also has a place within international science and measures and defines itself against its institute peers in Basel, Palo Alto, Berkeley, Washington and London. All these factors constitute a complex framework or context within which the Institute scientists do their science.

People

The Institute numbers roughly 310 people, of whom eighty are scientists, fifty students and the rest support staff. Only about sixty of the scientists have completed their Doctor of Philosophy degree which is an essential rite of passage in becoming a research scientist. Eight or ten of these are post-doctoral fellows spending two or three years at the Institute. These fellowships are a path to becoming a research scientist, though the young scientist's apprenticeship and socialization is usually a long and arduous one, before he or she finally makes it. (As Lambert says to me: 'It's a bit like becoming a top actor: you have not only to make it, but you have to keep on making it'.) Although teaching is not the primary focus of the Institute's work, there are quite a few students around—twenty-five or so. Nearly all are undertaking their Ph. D. apprenticeship. More than half of these students arrive with a B.Sc. (Hons.) in hand. The rest have completed medical degrees and usually have spent a couple of years working in a hospital.

Apart from a few visiting scientists, the rest of those working at the Institute are support staff. There are some fifty technical assistants (mostly women) who usually work with a particular scientist. Most of the remaining support staff are occupied in providing technical services—preparing experimental media and reagents, cleaning, washing glassware, maintaining and breeding experimental animals (mostly mice), providing computing, library, audio-visual, engineering, catering and specialist analytical facilities. The rest supply administrative services—accountancy, fund raising, purchasing, stores, word processing, secretarial assistance and reception. The technical and support staff usually get left out of accounts of science and scientists and I will clearly have to look at the role they play in the Institute. I am reminded of Bertolt Brecht's poem on the forgotten workers:

> Who built Thebes of the seven gates?
> In the books you will find the names of kings.
> Did the kings haul up the lumps of rock?
> And Babylon, many times demolished
> Who raised it up so many times? In what houses
> Of gold-glittering Lima did the builders live?
> Where, the evening that the Wall of China was finished
> Did the masons go? Great Rome
> Is full of triumphal arches. Who erected them? Over whom
> Did the Caesars triumph? Had Byzantium, much praised in song
> Only palaces for its inhabitants? Even in fabled Atlantis
> The night the ocean engulfed it
> The drowning still bawled for their slaves.
>
> The young Alexander conquered India.
> Was he alone?
> Caesar beat the Gauls.
> Did he not have even a cook with him?[2]

****

Some time ago I heard a lecture by Steven Shapin, a historian of 17th-century science, on the 'invisible technicians' who made Boyle's air-pump and other scientific discoveries possible. The technicians—variously called 'laborants', 'operators', 'domestics', 'servants'—did the dirty and often dangerous work for the 'experimental philosophers'. But it was the latter who claimed authorship and scientific authority and, because they were 'gentlemen', guaranteed that the testimony on which their findings were based was trustworthy. The relationship between the experimental philosopher (who was 'knowledgeable') and the technician (who was 'skilful') was based on 17th-century views of the master-servant relationship. Thus Hooke was 'Boyle's man'. Shapin wants to show how important the 'invisible people' who make things work in science really are, and that science is the result of the collective work of all the people who make it possible—from bottle-washers to Institute Directors and from experimentalists to the publishers of scientific journals.

****

Organization

The Institute is organized into eight Units: Cellular Immunology, Cancer Research, Clinical Research, Thymus Biology, Lymphocyte Differentiation, Immunoparasitology, Molecular Biology, and Transplantation.

These Units vary in size, the larger ones being subdivided into Laboratories. The Molecular Biology, Immunoparasitology and Transplantation Units were once Laboratories in other Units but expansion and/or research success (and in some cases internal politics) led to a change in their status. The names of Units and Laboratories alter too, as their research interests and responsibilities change.

The Director spends a great deal of time thinking about the organization of the Institute. He is very critical of some United States and European scientific institutes which take a laissez-faire approach to organization. ('All you have to do is to gather together a group of bright and ambitious young scientists and let them go to it.') There *must* be, he says, a better way of organizing scientific activity. In a relatively small institute with limited funds, organization and management are necessary if it is to keep up with its larger and more affluent international competitors. The Director sees himself as fighting for a place for smaller and peripheral countries such as Australia against the domination of North American and European science. He also sees himself as being responsible for the 'guiding scientific philosophy' of the Institute which includes the following main elements: seeing immunology in an international context with research being undertaken on a world-wide stage; recognizing that scientific research is a collaborative and collegial and interdisciplinary enterprise; understanding biomedical science as a 'knowledge revolution'; seeing 'pure' and 'applied' (or basic and clinical) research as mutually interactive; viewing state of the art technology as essential to biomedical science and recognizing the need for 'technique cross-fertilization', that is 'where a new technique derived by one person can rapidly and efficiently be applied to a wide variety of problems, many of them almost unrelated'. The Director is a true believer in big science and the need for sophisticated technology in science. His view of the scientific process is poles apart from that of his great predecessor, Macfarlane Burnet, whose emphasis was upon classical simplicity and economy of means.

Research fields

In the Director's view, there are four broad 'themes' to the Institute's work. First, the Cellular Immunology, Thymus Biology and Lymphocyte Differentiation Units are chiefly occupied in the fundamental immunology for which the Institute is famous, examining at the cellular and molecular level the way in which our bodies defend themselves against invading substances and organisms.The second theme is cancer—leukaemia being studied by the Cancer Research Unit's investigation of the control of blood cell development, differentiation and function. A group in the Clinical Research Unit investigates the body's natural killer cells as a mechanism for control of cancerous cells. The Molecular Biology Unit's focus is on genetic causes of cancer (the so-called oncogenes). The third theme is the Immunoparasitology Unit's study of how the body's natural acquisition of some immunity to parasites might be exploited to produce vaccines against a number of diseases, but principally malaria. Fourth, there are the clinically oriented studies. The Clinical Research Unit is interested in how and why our immune system sometimes goes awry and attacks the very body it is supposed to protect, leading to 'autoimmune' diseases like diabetes and arthritis. It is also interested in the opposite problem, where the immune system fails catastrophically, leading, for example, to the scourge of AIDS. The Transplantation Unit is trying to develop a novel treatment for diabetes. This involves transplanting into sufferers cells

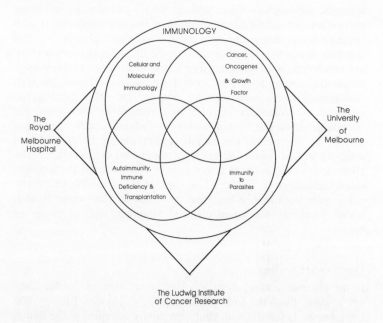

Venn Diagram of the Walter and Eliza Hall Institute of Medical Research

which will, it is hoped, eventually secrete the insulin which diabetics lack. Finally, there is a small group in the Cancer Research Unit working on the inherited disease thalassaemia. The Director has produced a 'Venn Diagram' which attempts to show how the four areas are inter-related and overlap and how the Institute is linked to the University of Melbourne, the Royal Melbourne Hospital and the Ludwig Institute. It gives the impression that there is a systematic connection between all the various parts of the Institute's research and that there is a great degree of common ground between the four main areas. While there is a good deal of collaboration between scientists in the various areas, many of the scientists themselves, however, see the Director's Venn Diagram as a piece of innocent public relations, an attempt to put an *ex post facto* veneer of order and system on the disparate and anarchic reality of scientific activity at the Institute. 'We should, of course, have more to do with each other', Short says. 'But we don't have the time or the will. In any case, the mentalities and approaches of the various groups are very different, even if they are all dealing with immunological issues.

I suppose it's a bit like the differences within a university sociology department between the "hard" number-crunchers and the "soft" anthropological interpreters.'

In one of his speeches, the Director says that the Institute rejects the simplistic idea of pure research leading to applied research which in turn leads to technological development and then to the manufacture of products.

Rather, we regard the world of ideas as somewhat of a bubbling cauldron— we believe passionately in fundamental research, as deeper knowledge of normal life processes is critical to any understanding of disease and hence to rational prevention or treatment. But we also realise that the many tragic experiments of nature, the diseases themselves, feed back vital clues to the pure scientist. For example, looking closely at cancer has taught us an enormous amount about how normal cells divide ... So basic and clinical research interact dynamically and continuously. Furthermore, both compartments are now heavily dependent on advanced technology and particularly on automated scientific instruments. The Hall Institute thus seeks to occupy the full spectrum from basic research to clinical research and patient care, infusing its endeavours with 'state of the art' equipment and techniques.[3]

How much this ideal vision of the Institute's work controls what is actually done at the laboratory level is, of course, another question.

Government

The Institute is a private organization governed by a Board. However, since its foundation, the Institute has been linked to the Royal Melbourne Hospital and the University of Melbourne, each of which has two representatives on the Board. Again, since 1968, the Institute's major funding source, the National Health and Medical Research Council (NH&MRC) has also had two representatives on the Board. The Walter and Eliza Hall Trust (the original donors) also appoints two Board members, and the Board itself appoints a further three members. The Institute constitutes the Department of Medical Biology within the Medical School of the University, its faculty consisting of the Director as Professor of Medical Biology and the Unit Heads, who hold honorary positions which enable them to supervise students. The Clinical Research Unit has close links with the Royal Melbourne Hospital, which provides a ward for its patients.

The Walter and Eliza Hall Trust now contributes a mere 0.1 per cent of the Institute's annual income. The NH&MRC, however, provides approximately half the Institute's income in the form of a block grant. In return, the Institute submits to a quinquennial review by an external expert committee. These reviews can lead to substantial increases in funding, and the criticisms they offer the Institute's research projects are treated seriously (if not always accepted) as a result. There is, however, some polite scepticism about the reviews since the reviewers are usually 'members of the club' who are well known to the Director and the senior staff who also act as reviewers for other institutes. So there is a certain amount of a 'you scratch my back and I'll scratch yours' attitude about the quinquennial reviews. In any case, the Institute scientists are pretty self-confident about their status. As Fuller, a critic from another Australian institute, puts it: 'The Hall Institute scientists have a well-developed superiority complex'.

The Director reports to the Board, but in matters of scientific policy, organization and management, the Board's approval is really a rubber stamp. The Director consults a good deal with his scientific staff, and meets regularly with the Unit Heads. Nevertheless, the final decisions are his. What is astonishing is the almost universal acceptance within the Institute of the Director's style of 'guided democracy'. In any large organization there is bound to be a certain amount of anti-authority grouching and oedipal hostility towards father figures. But there is extraordinarily little of this spirit at the Institute. 'He talks too much', says Amos, 'but he runs this place superbly well'. Thus, the Director is seen as being admirably even-handed in managing the competing interests for funds and staff from the various sections within the Institute, and his entrepreneurial skills in 'bringing home the bacon' (in the shape of funds) and keeping the Institute's image to the fore on the international scene are recognized by everyone. The only complaint I have heard so far (from some of the younger scientists) is that he is not ruthless enough in purging the Institute of scientists ('burnt-out cases') who are no longer doing productive research and who are resting on past laurels.

Mice

The Institute requires mice, rats, rabbits, sheep, guinea pigs, toads and chickens for its experiments; however, mice are by a long way the principal experimental animal. In a sense the Institute runs on mice. Since infections can affect biological functions, it is absolutely necessary to have healthy mice to ensure consistency of response in experiments. By the beginning of the 1970s some of the Institute's work required mice whose immune system was genetically deficient or had been deliberately damaged by surgery, drugs or radiation. These immunosuppressed mice which were bred at the Institute's conventional Animal House in the nearby University Veterinary Precinct were very prone to infections. What was needed was a facility designed for breeding and maintenance of germ-free and specific pathogen-free (SPF) mice, and the Clive and Vera Ramaciotti Laboratories were established in 1973 in a separate location to meet this need.

I visit the 'Mouse Hilton', as the technicians call it, and I am struck by the extraordinary precautions—the laboratory under air-pressure, ingenious airlocks, autoclaves, disinfectant showers etc.—that are taken to ensure that the mice are kept germ free. The mice behind the pathogen-free barrier are living artefacts—scientifically 'ideal' mice—in the sense that no mice in the real world live as the Ramaciotti mice do. In a sense they are an essential part of the 'machinery' needed by the Institute scientists to produce their data: no mice; no data; no science. One could even say that the *style* of science done at the Institute is *dictated* by the fact that the mouse is the favoured experimental animal. I make a note to study further the history of experimental techniques in immunology since, pretty obviously, immunology depends on the techniques available at any one time. This is one of those obvious things that are usually left out of account. The French philosopher of science, Georges Canguilhem, says that the big breakthroughs in science often come about through the construction of new instruments and the use of new techniques of detection and measurement and manipulation. There's clearly a lot in that.[4]

The quest for germ-freeness goes to rather macabre lengths in that new strains of mice are introduced into the laboratory by the 'caesarian' process, i.e. the mice are bred outside the barrier and just before the mother gives birth she is killed and the sac containing the litter is then taken from her and transported into the germ-free section. The baby mice are next put in the care of a foster mother who has been bred behind the barrier. This process takes a lot of nice timing and luck: if the babies are taken too prematurely they will die, and if the foster mother does not accept the babies she will eat them. The laboratory produces something like 170 000 mice a year, 125 000 of which are used at the Institute; 45 000 are kept in stock at any one time. A complete stock of lines not being used currently is kept in the form of frozen mouse embryos—a kind of mouse bank on ice!

Extraordinary measures are taken to ensure that laboratory conditions—air-pressure, humidity, temperature etc.—will be maintained in the event of a power failure. The machinery plant looks like the engine room of a small ship and it has a complete back-up generating plant in case of power failure. Even though the bomb should fall, the mice will be safe! Equally stringent precautions are taken against the possibility of infection getting behind the barrier and wiping out the mice population. In effect, the entire stock is duplicated and the two sections are kept separate.

During my time at the laboratory I kept on thinking: what if observers from Mars were to come across the Ramaciotti laboratory? What would they make of it? Here is a large, rather space-age looking plant with elaborate machinery designed to produce thousands of pampered, so-called 'germ free' mice lovingly cared for by a number of white-coated servants—mice that will eventually be sacrificed by people in another place to produce what they call 'science'. One can, of course, see why the germ-free mice are absolutely necessary for science at the Institute but, as I have noted, the mice that the Institute scientists experiment on are artefactual or 'ideal' mice. It is a good exemplification of the paradoxical point that Karen Knorr-Cetina and other sociologists of science make, viz. that science is not directly concerned with the real and ordinary world, the world of ordinary mice. (It also brings out the point that for scientific research to be possible immense amounts of time, energy and money have to be invested in order to sustain this 'artificial' world).

I put this point to Peter Jameson at afternoon tea. Jameson argues that I am making a philosophical mountain out of a very trite molehill. 'Of course', he says, 'we can't use "the mouse in the street" when each one may be dying from a different illness or being eaten by a different predator or poisoned by a different bait. Laboratory mice are a useful model and are "typical" only of the luckiest "real" mouse. What you fancifully call "ideal" mice are simply healthy mice!'

Services

The Institute is a highly integrated organization and the research laboratories can only function because of a great number of ancillary services. Most floors are provided with rooms where the mice are kept, and where most procedures on live animals are done. There is also a central facility which prepares more than 2000 litres a month of saline, buffer, anti-coagulant solutions, and bacteriological and tissue culture media for use in the research laboratories. Cultured mouse tumour cell lines are also maintained and distributed. The same department is responsible for decontamination, cleaning and sterilization of glassware and laundry (everybody wears white gowns or coats) used in the laboratories. There are several laboratories which provide specialist services or analysis: histology, electron microscopy, protein sequencing, cell-sorting, X-radiation, and radio-isotopes. There is a library and visual aids section. The engineering department has to maintain and repair a great deal of sophisticated equipment and cope with plumbing breakdowns, and it also manufactures special equipment to scientists' specifications. One has the impression of a relatively small number of research scientists at the front line being supported and maintained by a large and complex supply line and commissariat at the rear. The older idea of the scientific process, personified in Burnet, where the individual scientist worked away with test tube and pipette in virtual isolation, is gone forever.

Funds

In 1987–8 the Institute's operating cost was almost $A14 million. Some of this money came from the Institute's accumulated endowment of some $A10 million, some came from investments, but over half came from the Australian Federal Government. The vast bulk of this money comes through NH&MRC's block grant, which directly supports 120 of the Institute's staff. The Victorian State Government's contribution, about $A600 000, is specifically ear-marked to support 'housekeeping' or infrastructure costs. The Institute also receives about $A1 million in overseas funding, and attracts about $A300 000 in public donations annually.

If we measure the Institute's output in terms of the papers produced by its scientific staff, we can say that in 1987–8, $A14 million bought 160 scientific papers. This is, of course, a very crude measure, but it means that the production of each scientific paper cost something like $A50 000. Science at this level does not come cheaply!

The Institute and Australian biomedical research

Apart from the biomedical research that is done in university medical schools and cognate science departments, and also in hospitals, there are sixteen institutes of medical research in Australia. The largest, the John Curtin School of Medical Research, is something of a hybrid between an institute and a university. Established in 1947 as a postgraduate and research School within the Australian National University (ANU), its involvement in teaching is greater than that of any institute. But, like the institutes, the Curtin School's staff are all engaged in full-time research.

There are also the Sydney and Melbourne branches of the Ludwig Institute for Cancer Research, which are directly funded by a Swiss-based charitable organization. The Sydney branch of the Ludwig Institute focuses on research in cancer therapy, whilst the more recently established Melbourne branch works on tumour biology. Having been established as a result of the Director's lobbying for a share of the philanthropist Daniel K. Ludwig's largesse, the Melbourne branch has always enjoyed a close working relationship with the Hall Institute (especially the Cancer Research Unit). The Hall and Ludwig Institutes between them are now almost equal in size to the John Curtin School.

Half the NH&MRC's funds are distributed as individual project grants, and many of the institutes attract such grants. The Queensland Institute of Medical Research (QIMR) and several institutes in NSW receive five-year program grants to support groups working on a common theme. The Hall Institute, the Howard Florey Institute of Experimental Physiology and Medicine, and the Baker Medical Research Institute each receive substantial block grants.

The NH&MRC justifies the block grant arrangements by claiming that the Hall, Florey and Baker are 'world class' institutes which 'continue to make internationally recognized contributions in their respective fields'. Nonetheless, the disproportionate NH&MRC funding of institute research in Melbourne results in some predictable envy elsewhere, especially in Sydney. In particular, the Hall Institute comes in for a good deal of bitchy criticism. One Sydney scientist, for example, describes it as 'Gus Nossal's sheltered workshop'! The Director's frequent references to the Institute being the 'flagship' of Australian science also provoke some hostile comment from other scientists in other places.

Ranking the sixteen Australian institutes of biomedical research is not straightforward. Judging by sheer size and level of funding, the

John Curtin School would be first, and the Hall Institute second. However, there is no doubt that the international scientific community sees the Hall Institute as having pride of place. As the most recent quinquennial reviewers put it:

The Institute enjoys a very high international reputation. It belongs with a handful of great institutions of medical research abroad which include the US National Institutes of Health, the French Institut Pasteur, the UK National Institute of Medical Research and a few others. By scientists in relevant areas abroad it is perceived as the premier institute in Australia.

The Institute and international biomedical research

The international focus of the Institute is clearly shown by its pattern of collaboration in that very nearly two-thirds of the collaborative projects listed in its 1984–5 *Annual Review* were with foreign institutions.

How can one measure the value of a scientific institute? One can of course get some kind of rough 'objective' measurement by looking at the reputations of its scientists. Reputation is very important in science in that it increases opportunities and facilities for scientists and puts them in a more favoured class. As the American sociologist of science, Robert K. Merton, notes:

The process provides differential access to the means of scientific production. This becomes all the more important in the current historical shift from little science to big science, with its expensive and often centralised equipment needed for research. There is a continuing interplay between the status system, based on honour and esteem, and the class system, based on differential life chances, which locates scientists in differing positions within the opportunity structure of science.[5]

Merton also refers to what he neatly dubs the 'Matthew effect' in science (from the passage in St Matthew's Gospel: 'To them that hath more shall be given') which consists in 'the accruing of greater increments of recognition for particular scientific contributions of considerable repute and the withholding of such recognition from scientists who have not yet made their mark'.[6] Opportunity to make one's way in science is then far from being equal. Those who have an established research reputation have, as might be expected, greater opportunities than others and more is given to them that already hath.

Another way of measuring the value of scientists and their institutes is by looking at citations of their scientific papers. Between 1965 and 1978 more than a million scientists published more than five million papers in specialist journals. A large proportion of these papers were written by a small fraction of the scientists. Even among this prolific minority, some had more impact than others. One useful measurement of the relative significance of a scientist's work is the number of times other scientists refer to it in their own papers. These references are called citations, and it turns out that the thousand most cited scientists (around 0.1 per cent of the total) average more than ten times as many citations as the average author whose work is referred to by others (which by no means all scientists manage). Indeed, Eugene Garfield, head of the Institute for Scientific Information which publishes the *Science Citation Index*, argues that membership of this select band of 'most cited scientists' indicates that a scientist is of Nobel Prize winning class.

The *Science Citation Index*, from which these data come, records citations in more than 4000 scientific journals regardless of their national origin or the language in which they were published. Yet 996 of the top 1000 scientists are from Western bloc countries—736 from the USA alone. Of the remaining four, three scientists are from Eastern bloc countries, only one of them from the Soviet Union. The USSR ranks with France in total number of articles published, yet France has twenty-six scientists among the 1000.

If, instead of counting the number of citations *scientists* receive, we count the number given to *journals*, we can obtain a rank order which measures their relative prominence in the scientific community. Such a ranking of 1984 citations reveals the nearly total dominance of the English language journals. Of the top 100 journals, all but four are published in English alone. Two German, one Russian and a Japanese journal are in the top 100, but all four are published in English as well as non-English editions—and they are ranked respectively, 73rd, 92nd, 88th and 100th. (Note that the *Science Citation Index* counts *all* citations, not just those in Western and English language journals.)

Ninety per cent of all scientific articles are now published in English. The negative effect of having a national language other than English on participation in so-called 'international' science can be shown by the comparative placement of scientific articles in national and transnational journals. Considerably more than half of the scientists working in Australia and New Zealand place their work in journals published elsewhere—at the Institute during 1984–5, only ten out of 161 scientific papers were published in Australian journals. In sharp contrast, virtually all French and Japanese, and most German scientists' work is published in their own national journals. There is little doubt that this is one main reason why, despite having a techno-scientific sector enormously larger than Australia's, Japan actually has one fewer member in the top 1000 scientists (11 versus 12).

Numbers and percentages can be rather eye-glazing, but a subjective flavour of the relative significance of English as *the* scientific language can be gained from Mitchell's reply when I asked him if he could remember the last time he needed to read an article written in a language other than English, and what the language was. He said, 'Yes, it was in Russian, and five or six years ago. It was also the only time'.

National attitude has as much to do with these things as does national language. French science was recently demonstrated to have a diminished impact internationally because of the national tendency to publish in France and in French. The reaction of a former French Prime Minister, Michel Debré, was to suggest that such a conclusion threatened 'the existence and permanence of the French nation' if it encouraged French scientists to publish in English. In contrast, the Swedes are distinctly more relaxed about the effects of English linguistic imperialism on their culture. As a result, they rank third after the USA and UK in the top 1000 list, with nearly twice as many representatives as fourth-ranked France.

The language factor then suggests that citations as a measure of scientific merit have to be treated with great caution. Australia ranks eighth (after Canada, West Germany and Switzerland) in the 'most cited scientists' list. Its twelve representatives come from six institutions—four universities, the Australian National (2), Sydney (2), Adelaide (1) and Monash (1); the Anglo-Australian Observatory (1), and the Hall Institute (5). This certainly supports a view of the Institute as being the pre-eminent scientific group in Australia. Its representatives in the top 1000 were Ian Mackay, Don Metcalf, Jacques Miller and Gus Nossal. However, it makes little sense to compare scientists in one speciality with scientists in another. Clearly such comparisons are worthwhile only when like is being compared with like; for example, Australian immunologists with other immunologists. Six of Australia's twelve representatives in the list of 1000 (four at the Institute) were among the 128 immunologists (the largest single category) who featured among the most cited scientists. Metcalf was the most highly cited of twenty-two haematologists in the list.

The Institute scientists are, however, pretty sceptical about the value of citations as an index of scientific worth. For one thing, it is much easier to publish, and to be cited, in some areas than in others. Talking to Salmon, one of the younger Institute scientists, I remark that biomedicine seems to be very experimental in orientation as compared, say, with physics. Big new theories, like Burnet's clonal selection theory, are fairly rare and one gets the impression that theoreticians are not really encouraged and that the way to fame lies in experimental work. Salmon agrees with me. To some extent, he says, it is bound up with publication. There is a good deal of stress at the Institute on publishing scientific papers and scientists who are theoretically inclined, but not otherwise productive in publications, are not favoured.

****

So that I can establish a link with the Institute scientists and keep them informed of what I am doing I decide to produce a simple *Newsletter*. One of the scientists sympathetic to my project, Jack Balfour, had told me, a little cynically, that if I wished to keep the scientists happy I should produce some figures and diagrams. 'We suspect anything that is not in quantified form', he says. I decide, rather foolishly as it turns out, to include in the *Newsletter* a simple graph of scientific output measured in terms of papers produced by Institute scientists over the last fifteen years. The graph shows that a large number of papers were produced by Institute scientists between 1970 and 1973, but that there was a notable dip in output immediately after 1973. I hadn't really wanted to draw any very momentous conclusions from this fact but almost immediately some quick and sharp reactions come from a number of the Institute scientists. The 1970–3 period, they all point out, included a large number of papers, written by a small number of scientists whose experimental work was rather poor. Almost all the work they reported could not be repeated and this had slowed up subsequent progress. Manners, a senior figure at the Institute, gives me a severe lecture: he was astonished, he says, that I had assumed that the mere quantity of scientific papers meant anything. The quality of scientific work cannot be judged in quantitative terms and it was utterly naïve to think that simply counting up the numbers of papers produced showed anything about the health and respectability of science at the Institute. My approach, he went on, was in fact positively dangerous in that those who determined funding for science were likely to be influenced. I feel suitably chastened. At the same time I am surprised at the extreme sensitivity shown about funding and the way in which, it is imagined, the Institute's funding might be jeopardized by my innocent if incautious little graph.

Some time later I come across an article by Otto Larsen on the funding for the social sciences by the US National Science Foundation. Larsen is a well-known power-broker in the social sciences in the US, and is a major figure in the NSF bureaucracy. He is very pessimistic about scientists' perceptions of the social sciences and says that 'social science today is held in the same disesteem that marked its beginning'. Scientists, he says, are very sceptical about the social sciences and apprehensive about their 'political trouble-making capacity' which they fear can jeopardize science funding and support.[7] After my curious experience I can say 'Amen' to that!

****

Commercial science

About 7 per cent of money spent on research and development the world over goes to the health sector (this compares with around 24 per cent for national defence). The majority of the research, especially non-clinical research, is done in the West. The USA is by far the largest spender, followed by Western Europe and Japan. Each of the three major settings in which Australian biomedical research takes place has its counterpart in the Western bloc; and each has the same place in the overall scheme of things. But there is a fourth major area of biomedical research which is of little importance in Australia—the commercial/industrial sector. Until very recently, practically the only commercially oriented research in Australia was done by the Commonwealth Serum Laboratories (CSL). For most of its existence the CSL was not permitted to develop drugs, and it is still mainly involved in vaccines. Apart from some clinical trials, little pharmaceutical research is done in Australia by indigenous or multinational commercial firms. However, following the advent of recombinant DNA technology in the later 1970s, several commercial biotechnology firms have been established. It is still a small-scale industry, mainly located in Sydney (a curious state of affairs given the Melbourne dominance in molecular biology). But there are signs that the traditional suspicion of commercial involvement among medical researchers is beginning to weaken. Collaborations—such as that between the Institute, Biotechnology Australia Pty Ltd, the

CSL and the QIMR on malaria vaccine (on which, see later)—are being established. The Hall Institute is also engaged in collaborative projects with a number of foreign companies. The projects involve the Institute scientists coming to terms with commercially interested firms and with their lawyers.

There is something of a clash of cultures between the two groups with their vast differences in attitudes and expectations and time scales. Some of the scientists seem a little uneasy about the restrictions that these commercial arrangements might place upon their research (for example, delaying publication of results until the commercial possibilities of a piece of research are worked out), but most seem unworried. Biomedical science overseas is now thoroughly commercialized and the pure and disinterested pursuit of scientific knowledge for its own sake is as old-fashioned as amateur tennis. Frank Dubinskas at MIT in Cambridge, Massachusetts, has done some work on biologists and entrepreneurs in the US biotechnology industry, and I would like very much to study the interactions between the Hall Institute scientists and the commercially oriented companies interested in developing the malaria vaccine when it is finally achieved. I ask the Director if I can sit in on the discussions of the future production and marketing of the vaccine. However, my request is politely refused and I decide not to press the point.

In contrast with the position in Australia, private pharmaceutical and biotechnological research is a very large sector of Western biomedicine. Even though their work tends more toward the applied end of the spectrum, a number of the world's most highly cited scientists are employed by private companies. Industry does nearly 40 per cent of health research in the USA where pharmaceutical concerns like Wellcome, Dow Chemical and Hoffman-La Roche support their own research institutes to develop new drugs. The Swiss multinational Roche not only dominates Basel—the country's second city, and the firm's headquarters—it also supports research by paying the whole cost of two institutions—the Basel Institute for Immunology and the Roche Institute for Molecular Biology in the USA. And yet the cost to Roche is an insignificant fraction of its total research budget.

Another major commercial biomedical research arena is the burgeoning biotechnology industry. Though it has yet to justify its early promise in terms of profit, the biotechnology industry has nevertheless attracted very large sums of high-risk venture capital. The US biotechnology firm Genentech had, as a result, a research budget in 1984 of US$42 million—about the same as the NH&MRC.

To date, the most biomedically significant product of genetic engineering is the manufacture of large quantities of antibodies to specific
antigens. (The two scientists who first devised this so-called
'monoclonal' technique shared a Nobel Prize in 1985.) In addition to
the many offering monoclonal antibodies, journals such as *Nature*
are crowded with advertisements offering biochemicals, assay kits,
DNA libraries, reagents, buffers, and an array of laboratory
equipment. A recent number of *Nature* carried a review of the
products of what it called 'the immunology industry'. Forty separate
product lines were discussed, among which monoclonals were prominent. One firm took a full-page advertisement seeking monoclonal
antibodies which had been discovered by scientists for inclusion in
its immuno-assay product line.

The Australian Government has recently decided to jump on
the biotechnology bandwagon and has set up a company—the
Australian Medical Research and Developmental Consortium—
which it hopes will encourage research and development in a field
that could be a big dollar earner. (The company had US$80 million
of sales in the last six weeks of 1987.) The US company Genentech
claims that a new bio-engineered substance for dissolving blood
clots has a potential market of US$500 million a year, so large
rewards are clearly expected from this new industry. When traditional exports like wheat and wool are declining in value in Australia,
biotechnological exports look very inviting.

In some ways this tendency represents a return to the nationalistic
spirit in science that was so strong in the 19th century when French
and German and English scientists vied with each other and the
awarding of a Nobel Prize (supposed to be a recognition of international standing) was seen as a national honour. It also represents
an intrusion of alien values into science—entrepreneurship, an emphasis on useful and dollar-earning research, the dictates of 'the
national interest'. What is astonishing is that there is so little debate
about these issues. Hugh Niall, a former Melbourne scientist who
has made good with Genentech, gives an interview on a visit to his
Alma Mater. Singing the praises of the vast and lucrative new biotechnology company, he says that the scientific staff are strongly
committed. 'It's the norm to work extremely hard and for long
hours, on evenings, and at weekends. Generally, the ethic is to get
the work done in the knowledge that it's a highly competitive situation and the success of the company depends on everyone's
efforts.' Niall goes on to explain that because the scientists employed by Genentech can buy Genentech shares at reduced cost,

they benefit financially as the company succeeds and makes larger and larger profits.[8]

This is a view of scientific research so alien to the traditional view that one would think there would be intense soul-searching about it by bioscientists. But none of the scientists at the Hall Institute seem unduly concerned.

A bioscience-watcher, Susan Wright, claims that as soon as genetic engineering was seen as a promising investment prospect 'a fundamental deviation from traditional scientific practice occurred and a movement toward a corporate standard took over. The dawn of synthetic technology coincided with the emergence of a new ethos, one dominated by concerns external to science'.[9] The same author notes, for example, the increase in secrecy regarding scientific results, and she cites Paul Berg: 'No longer do you have this free flow of ideas. You go to scientific meetings, and people whisper to each other about their company's products. It's like a secret society'. Dewitt Stettin, former Deputy Director of science at the US National Institutes of Health (NIH), is also quoted as saying that scientists 'simply will not tell their friends and neighbours what they are doing or what they intend to do. Both teacher and student have schooled themselves to be tight-lipped lest the competitor discovers the name of the new product or the means to its production'.[10]

Comparisons with other institutes

Among the peer group of the Hall Institute referred to by its Quinquennial Reviewers, I have already noted how incomparably vast the US NIH intramural program is with its budget of US$4000 million. Its counterpart in the UK, the National Institute for Medical Research, with a scientific staff of around 200 and a recurrent budget of £9 167 826 in 1983–4 is rather more than twice the size of the Hall Institute. And this is, on the whole, the pattern.

The more noteworthy medical research institutes in Western Europe and the United States tend to be considerably larger than the Hall Institute, as well as more diverse in their interests. The Research Institute of Scripps Clinic in La Jolla, California, for example, had 126 senior staff members and 173 postdoctoral fellows in 1985. These 300-odd scientists spent more than US$43 million on their research. At the Hall Institute some eighty scientists, fifty students and support staff make do with about $A14 million. The Scripps Institute has Departments of Basic and Clinical Research, Immunology and Molecular Biology. With more than 160 senior staff, even its Department of Immunology dwarfs the Hall Institute. The Sloan-Kettering Institute in New York, another major American body, has divisions of molecular biology and virology, cell biology and genetics, immunobiology, and developmental therapy and clinical investigation. The immunobiology division, with around 110 senior staff, is about twice the size of the Hall Institute.

The Hall Institute is still very largely an immunological institute, though there has been a discernible broadening in its interests in the last decade or so. Of the Western world's leading biomedical research institutes, only the Basel Institute for Immunology is as focused in this area. The Basel Institute is a young place: it commenced operations only in 1971, and few of its workers are senior, tenured people. Most are at the senior postdoctoral level, and are there only for a couple of years. The Hall and Basel Institutes have always enjoyed a close fraternal relationship, with a particularly high level of collaboration and exchange (Macfarlane Burnet and the Basel Institute's foundation Director, Niels Jerne, were co-discoverers of the modern-day basis for immunology, the clonal selection theory.) Size is not all—indeed there are important diseconomies of scale such as difficulties of communication between institutes and a loss of a sense of community. The significant social group for the scientists of most leading institutes is the laboratory or department. At both the Basel and Hall Institutes, however, there is some sense of belonging to the Institute as a whole.

The Hall Institute is, in Australia, a big fish in a small pond. Internationally, as we have seen, it is quite small scale. But its performance is, none the less, creditable. In a scientific world where the publication of original research is the main measure of achievement, one way of discounting sheer scale is to look at the average number of publications per scientist that an institute produces per annum. At the Hall Institute in 1984, this was exactly two. In the same year, the Basel Institute's scientists averaged about one each; the immunologists at the Scripps Institute 1.7 each; those at the Sloan-Kettering Institute 1.8. The other main Australian immunology centre with an overseas reputation, the John Curtin School of Medical Research, conducts research in this area in several of its Departments. Its overall average rate of publication in 1984 was 1.2.

Again, Hank Thurow's experience confirms these so-called objective measures (which can sometimes be quite misleading). Hank is a new American postdoctoral fellow in the Cellular Immunology Unit and on his first day at the Institute, the Director introduces him to me at morning tea. I ask him why he has chosen to come to the

Institute. Well, he replies, it had been traditional for American Ph. D.s in immunology to do a postdoc overseas. However, as the USA became more and more dominant in the field, the tradition had begun to fall into abeyance. Nevertheless, as an old-fashioned person, he had decided to follow it. That being so, there appeared to him only two choices, the Hall Institute and the Basel Institute. But someone had told him that Basel was a boring town, so he chose the Hall Institute and Melbourne!

During August 1984, I was able to attend the 17th International Congress of History of Science at the University of California, Berkeley. That gave me an opportunity to find out first-hand just what the Hall Institute's international reputation was, as well as to compare the place with similar institutes overseas. I asked the Director to nominate a select peer group. On the American west coast, he nominated the Salk Institute and the Scripps Clinic and Research Foundation, both near San Diego at the southern end of California, together with the Stanford University Medical School at Palo Alto. On the opposite side of the USA, he suggested I visit the Memorial Sloan-Kettering Cancer Center and the Rockefeller University in New York, the Wistar Institute in Philadelphia and the National Institutes of Health in the Washington DC suburbs. In Europe, the Director recommended the Basel Institute for Immunology, the Imperial Cancer Research Fund Laboratories in London, the International Institute for Cellular and Molecular Pathology in Brussels and the Max Planck Institute for Immunobiology in Freiburg. The Director provided a generous letter of introduction to smooth my path when I sought permission to visit the various institutes. No doubt because of this, with one exception, each institute readily granted permission, as well as offering assistance in finding accommodation. The exception was the Salk Institute.

Frederic de Hoffmann, the Director of the Salk (whose first language is not English) was very firm:

> I regret that I have to inform you that we have had several requests at this time and have made it a policy to turn down requests of this kind which dilute from the point of view of the scientists working in the laboratories on various scientific subjects. It so happens that I am a physicist by profession and, therefore, I cannot help but be reminded of Heisenberg's statement that under well-known circumstances 'observation perturbs the measurements.' In this case, I am not concerned about perturbing the measurements, I am only concerned about 'interfering' with the measurements.

The Salk Institute's refusal derived perhaps from the fact that they had already had their own 'anthropologist' of science, Bruno Latour, who had spent nearly two years there pioneering the ethnographic study of the 'tribe' of scientists. His book, *Laboratory Life*, had an introduction by the then Director, Jonas Salk himself, famous for developing an oral polio vaccine. Though that introduction had been cautiously positive, Salk had admitted that he and his colleagues might find parts of it 'slightly uncomfortable or even painful in places'. Evidently one such experience had been enough. I wondered again what my own 'tribe' would make of what I had to say about them when the time came.

Institutes specializing in biomedical research are the third most important organizational locus of such work, after universities and hospitals, but they enjoy a number of advantages over the other two. (The first professional medical research institute in the world was the Pasteur Institute founded in 1891. It was followed soon after by the Lister Institute in London, the Robert Koch Institute in Germany, and the Behring Institute also in Germany.) The principal, if not the only function of a biomedical institute is, of course, research. Universities' primary function is to teach; hospitals' is to heal. Their respective structures are largely determined by their functions.

In order to provide an adequate scientific education, universities have to teach the whole range of the sciences, but few are so well endowed that they can excel in research in most, let alone all. Similarly, general hospitals must support clinics in a full range of medical specialties, but do not usually perform first rank medical research in them all. Furthermore, hospitals' research is, for obvious reasons, strongly biased toward the development, in the short to medium term, of cures for the diseases with which they must deal. Biomedical institutes are able to concentrate and excel in a few areas and, if they choose, to work in basic as well as applied areas.

Specialization means that biomedical research institutes can guarantee a 'critical mass' of workers, providing a sustained flow of good, leading-edge science. Many university biology departments will have a virologist or two, each with a couple of postgraduate students. Institutes working in this area often have dozens. However, it is not only a question of breadth, but also of flexibility. Universities simply do not have the capacity to eliminate a Biochemistry Department in favour of establishing a Department of Molecular Biology. Nor do hospitals have the capacity to eliminate geriatric care and research in favour of a maternity centre. The most that either usually can do is to seek to emphasize one area at the expense of others.

Biomedical research institutes can respond to advances in theory and technique by quite radically altering their focus. The Hall Institute provides a good example of this. During the years following the Second World War, almost everyone there was engaged in one way or another in studying the biology of influenza. But Macfarlane Burnet was also developing an interest in immunology. By 1958, the Institute had become almost entirely in immunological research institute.

This also illustrates the peculiarly influential role of Directors in scientific institutes. It is not only a question of power, but also once again one of scale. Universities are simply too big for their Vice-Chancellors to completely reorient them single-handed. On the other hand, a charismatic Director is able to turn an Institute around. For example, in 1957, when Hilary Koprowski came to the Wistar Institute of Anatomy and Biology in Philadelphia as its new Director, it was moribund. The large collection of skeletons gathering dust and cobwebs meant that the dead outnumbered the living. With Koprowski came a half-dozen young scientists he had persuaded to help him revitalize the place. The skeletons were sold and the space they occupied filled with laboratories. Anatomy was replaced by study of viral degenerative and malignant disease. By 1984, a total of 300-odd scientific and support staff consumed a budget of more than US$17 million—80 per cent of it derived from competitive grant awards. The Wistar is very much Koprowski's Institute. He created it.

The biomedical research institutes and their directors are, in some ways, an exclusive international club. Whilst I was at the Wistar, the Director of the Basel Institute of Immunology, Fritz Melchers, was also present, taking an annual break from his duties to do some hands-on research. The Director of the International Institute of Cellular and Molecular Pathology in Brussels, Christian de Duve, is also a full Professor at the Rockefeller University in New York. (The Rockefeller Institute for Medical Research was the first medical research institute in the US, having been founded in 1901. The change from Institute to University took place in 1965, in recognition of its substantial, but subsidiary role in training Ph. D. students.) The President of Rockefeller, Joshua Lederberg, was at Stanford when I visited, doing research. Directors of biomedical research institutes all serve from time to time on each other's governing boards and scientific advisory councils.

One could easily multiply examples of the central importance of these directors. The Swiss Basel Institute, established in 1968 by the giant pharmaceutical firm Hoffman-La Roche, is an institute for immunology because its founding Director, Niels Jerne, was an immunologist. Jerne was awarded a share of the 1984 Nobel Prize for Physiology or Medicine for his theories concerning immunological specificity in the development and control of the immune system.

The Basel Institute is unusual in that most of its scientific staff are either visiting on sabbatical leave from their permanent institutions, or are rising young stars on non-renewable short-term contracts. As a result many Hall Institute immunologists spend time in Basel. The two places are of a roughly comparable size, too—which makes them both considerably smaller than most of their peer group of leading international biomedical research institutes. Consequently, they share an institute-level *esprit de corps*, having common rituals like eating lunch and drinking morning and afternoon tea together. Every scientist at the Basel Institute has a personal technician assigned to assist her or him. In this, too, the Basel and Hall Institutes are similar.

Most biomedical research institutes have some feature or other which distinguishes them from all, or most, others. At Basel, it is the sharp focus on immunology, the short stay of most scientific staff, and the generous private funding by Roche—which means that no one need ever make a grant application. Other institutes also achieve this freedom from outside granting agencies, but in different ways. At the Imperial Cancer Research Fund (ICRF) Laboratory in London, for example, all the research is financed by donations. Cancer research is comparatively easily supported because the public are far more worried about cancer than, say, heart disease—even though they are much more likely to die of heart disease than cancer. Thus, in 1984, the ICRF had an income of more than £24 million, almost all from legacies and donations.

The world's richest granting agency, the US National Institutes of Health, has its own internal research program, mostly on-site in the suburbs of Washington, DC. Ironically, those who work in this 'intra-mural program' are directly funded and so do not have to apply for grants. This is reminiscent of the John Curtin School of Medical Research at the Australian National University which, like the ANU itself, is funded directly by the Federal Government. This precludes them from applying for grant funds, exceptional circumstances apart.

There are some important organizational contrasts between the Hall Institute and US biomedical research institutes, such as the Scripps and the Salk Institutes on the west coast, or the Sloan-

Kettering and Wistar Institutes on the eastern seaboard. Their organizational model—like US science—dominates Western biomedicine. Though still specializing in only a few areas, these places are usually so large that they bear comparison with smaller universities. Often—for example at both the Scripps and the Sloan-Kettering —institutes have their own research hospital.

This greater size means that the institute itself is not as important a social unit as it is at the Hall or Basel Institutes. Instead, the department or laboratory takes its place. Thus one finds departmental tea and lunch rooms, and people can even be discovered eating in the laboratories—something I have never seen happen at the Hall Institute, and (having taken on board some of my tribe's values) was actually shocked by.

At the Hall Institute a laboratory is typically composed of one, two or three scientists, maybe a postdoctoral fellow or two, or a research assistant, as many technicians as there are senior scientists, and a couple of Ph. D. students. In all, half-a-dozen to a dozen at most. An American biomedical institute laboratory very rarely has more than one permanent researcher at the full or associate Professor level. Perhaps there will also be one or two untenured Assistant Professors. Often they are the heads of their own, smaller laboratories. In US laboratories postdoctoral fellows are the largest group of workers, outnumbering Ph. D. students. Technicians play a much smaller role. If there is some key piece of equipment, such as a cell-sorter machine, it might have a technician in charge of it. Since the laboratories are frequently very large, there might well be a laboratory manager. The postdocs do their own bench work, so only the laboratory head and any other senior scientists have a personal technician.

There are two reasons for this smaller number of technicians than is common in Australia or Europe. Firstly, postdocs combine greater theoretical understanding with the technical expertise they learned as Ph. D. students and, secondly, biomedical research institutes cannot match the salaries pharmaceutical laboratories can offer a trained technician (postdocs are not particularly well paid, and Ph. D. students are on even less generous scholarships).

Leading American institute laboratories are commonly a couple of dozen strong, almost all Ph. D. students and postdocs. There are some with upwards of fifty. Competition is pronounced between laboratories in the same institution. Each tenured senior scientist works largely independently of his or her colleagues. There is little inter-laboratory collaboration, except at the technical level. Thus, one laboratory may well help another out by making equipment available or providing reagents, but they will only rarely engage in a common research project since it is difficult to decide how to allocate credit for any resulting papers, and the allocation of credit is crucial because of the intense competition for tenure.

Used as I was to the very collaborative atmosphere that prevails at the Hall Institute, I was quite taken aback when told by a scientist working on AIDS at the National Institutes for Health that his collaborator, in another laboratory there, would only tell him of some of his results, keeping the rest secret prior to publication. These American laboratories resemble feudal fiefdoms headed by a liege-lord to whom all owe allegiance. Provided only that the liege-lords can find the grant funding, they can organize their laboratories pretty much as they wish.

Dr Jonathan Sprent, of the Department of Immunology at the Scripps Institute, explained to me how grants from the NIH work (Sprent did his Ph. D. under Jacques Miller at the Hall Institute). The applicant asks for, say US$100 000. This is for direct costs. Above all it pays some or all of the salaries of those involved in the research, including the laboratory head. If the scientist is successful, the NIH also pays the scientist's institution an additional amount for indirect costs—overheads such as electricity, maintenance and so on. This is negotiated with each institute separately, but will certainly be at least 50 per cent of the direct costs, and sometimes as much as 100 per cent.

There is, here, a noteworthy difference between the NIH and the Australian NH&MRC, which does not provide any funding for indirect costs—even to recipients of block grants, such as the Hall Institute. There, the Victorian State Government's contribution has traditionally been ear-marked to cover overheads. In US institutions—including the leading universities—NIH indirect funding underpins research, and enables places like the Scripps to exist with an endowment supporting only around 5 per cent of its activity. Indeed, many institutes normally expect not to have to pay any of the salary of their scientists.

Grant-based research is criticized as occupying large amounts of scientists' time in the preparation of grant applications, and for encouraging projects which are likely to produce quick results rather than important basic work which has a higher risk of failure. On the other hand, scientists working on grants must regularly be assessed by their peers, and this helps make sure that the research they do is worth doing and well done. Institutes which do not rely on project grants—like the Imperial Cancer Research Fund Laboratories, the NIH intra-mural program, the German Max Planck Institutes, or the Hall Institute (with its NH&MRC block grant)—are able to do riskier and longer-term work. But the lack of annual peer review leaves them open to the accusation of harbouring unproductive research workers and 'burned-out cases'.

Most directors and scientists to whom I spoke admitted that you probably had to put up with a few burned-out scientists. But, in institutes which are based on the granting system, they are not such a problem since, without grant support, their institution is likely to give them little more than a salary and a broom closet for a laboratory.

How, then, is the Hall Institute regarded by its peers? Among the comments I heard from those whose research lay in areas covered by the Institute, those of Dr Irving Weissman, of the Stanford University Medical School, are fairly representative. In Weissman's opinion:

It is quite clear that all the way through the sixties and certainly into the mid seventies the Hall Institute scientists were the leaders in immunology and haematology. They are now joined by a number of other leaders, but it is not that you just read a few papers from the Hall Institute; they are among the leaders.

In the sixties and seventies when things were so exciting, the Hall Institute produced probably the best group of graduate students who went on to become post-doctoral fellows elsewhere—because Gus [Nossal] sent them everywhere. They were the standard for the best postdocs you can get—we had Graham Mitchell [Immunoparasitology Unit Head] here for a while, Jonathon Sprent, Marc Feldman; there were lots of them.

There must have been something in the organization of the Hall Institute that allowed the scientific enterprise to prosper both from the point of view of research, from the excitement about the research, and the training of good people.

But Weissman did add a note of caution:

I think, however, that they have not produced as many great scientists in the past several years. Nevertheless they are still leaders in my field, lymphocyte haematology, and with the new immunoparasitology enterprise, they are rapidly becoming leaders in that area too.

The large scale, co-ordinated, goal-oriented research undertaken by the Institute immunoparasitologists into malaria especially, but also other tropical parasites, is unusual. The work of most biomedical institutes' laboratories is not internally co-ordinated, let alone co-ordinated with other laboratories in the same and other institutions. A laboratory's work will be sufficiently in a single area for the head to be able to supervise the progress of each project. But that is about the extent of it. The Director is clearly backing a hunch about the future of the organization of biomedicine.

The 'sub-culture' of the Hall Institute

What has emerged so far? Well, we have a group of scientists whose attention is concentrated upon a particular area of enquiry, the human immunological system, working within the broader context of the biomedical sciences and very much a part of the astonishing revolution that has taken place (is still taking place) in that domain—a revolution that has been legitimized by a long and well-run 'political' campaign. Again, this group works within an Institute that has its own distinctive history and 'mythology', largely centred around the career and work of a scientific 'hero', Macfarlane Burnet, whose posthumous and ambiguous presence is still very powerful. The Institute has its own peculiar organizational structure which is partly a result of its history and partly a result of deliberate design, and its own very complex infrastructure without which its specifically scientific activities would not be possible. (To consider only one element of that infrastructure—the 125 000 experimental, specially bred, germ-free, quite 'artificial' mice which are used each year are a *sine qua non* of the Institute's scientific activity. If past history has been, as Zinnsner put it, largely a matter of rats and lice, science at the Institute is largely a matter of mice.)

Our group at the Institute is caught up within the broader network of Australian science, relating to and competing with other Australian research institutes. The Institute sees itself as the 'flagship' of Australian science, but some other local institutes and scientific groups see it as a pampered child getting much more than its fair share of government research funds. At the same time, however, as a scientific body with international status and prestige, the Institute is also a part of the larger world of international immunological science. The Institute's scientists see their real peers as being in Switzerland, France, and the US, so that in some respects the real 'community of interest' is an international one. Allan, one of the younger Institute scientists, says that he has much more in common scientifically with Schwarzer in Lausanne or Colin in Paris than he has with other Australian scientists—more indeed than he has in common with many of his colleagues at the Institute. Finally, the

Institute has begun to be affected, and will be increasingly affected by the demands and politics of the new biotechnology industry.

The micro 'world' or 'culture' of the Institute is then not tightly and strictly structured—but is, so to speak, 'multi-cultural' or pluralistic in that the various units, and even some of the laboratory groups within the units, have their own distinctive outlook and ethos. And yet, despite this, I believe that there is a genuine—if loose and flexible—community here with its own distinctive 'subculture'. At the moment, this is an intuition or an act of faith: time and further research will tell whether the Institute is a genuine community, with its own multi-cultural culture, or whether it is merely a convenient location for a number of quite discrete groups—a 'scientific transit camp' as Peters, one of my confidants at the Institute, calls it.

****

I am asked to give a report on my research at the Institute by a seminar group of social scientists at a local university. I try to explain my methodology, such as it is, and I am met with a barrage of objections from my hard-nosed colleagues. 'You claim you are using an interpretive method', Fogel says, 'but how do you validate interpretations: why is one interpretation better than another; why should I accept *your* interpretation of what your scientists are up to; why should I accept what *you* have chosen to see as significant (why, for example, fix on the experimental mice, or on the Institute's morning and afternoon teas as being worthy of your sociological attention)?' Deller also weighs in: 'You have assumed', she says, 'that what is important is how your scientists *see themselves*, and that it is not your business to judge whether what they are doing is good or bad, socially desirable or undesirable and needing to be changed'. (I had remarked in the discussion that I had enough trouble *understanding* the world of my scientists let alone trying to *change* that world.) 'One can', Vance says, 'become absorbed in what is of interest and importance to the members of the group one is studying: it is all too easy to become co-opted by them. The fact that you are allowed to enter the group and to observe them implies that you are seen by them as non-threatening and not likely to rock their boat'. 'Remember', he goes on, 'that social science research is always a political activity: it is easy to denounce positivism at the theoretical level and then proceed in one's research in a completely positivistic manner as though all one had to do was to observe in a neutral value-free way what the scientists are actually doing. Remember also that your research findings will be used by others— by the scientists themselves, by their enemies *et al.*, for their own purposes. I once did some work on schools', he says, 'and I tried to be as honest as I could about them, but my report was used by the educational powers-that-be to justify closing two of the schools in question'.

I must say that I feel rather depressed at the end of the seminar, but I remind myself that it must be possible to do what I am trying to do. Geertz on the Javanese, Stanner on the Australian Aborigines and Evans-Pritchard on the Azande have all shown how to understand and sympathetically interpret the exotic 'worlds' of their subjects and it must be possible for me to do the same *vis-à-vis* my subjects. I derive some comfort from an observation by Henry James on the force of imagination of the authentic novelist. He envisages a young woman brought up in cloistered circumstances passing by a military barracks and overhearing through an open window a snatch of conversation between two soldiers. If she were a true novelist, James says, she would be able, by imagination and intuition, to recreate the whole atmosphere and feel of army life from that momentary incident.

4

Socialization and Social Structure

*Over the years, anthropologists have developed a series of analytic
tools which enable them to label the alternative ways in which a
particular society copes with the organisational problems which con-
front it. For example, if descent is traced through the male line for
some purposes, the descent system is labelled 'patrilineal' in that
respect, if through the female line, 'matrilineal'. If, after marriage, a
couple normally resides with the husband's relatives, the residential
rule is said to be 'patrilocal', if with the wife's relatives, 'matrilocal'.
For modern social anthropologists, what might be termed the 'structural situation' of a given society consists in the combination of
behavioural options employed by that society. That is, if one says that
a society has a patrilineal descent system and a matrilocal residential
rule, one will have specified part of its 'structure'.*

Ian Langham, *The Building of British Social Anthropology*[1]

The people who work at the Institute form two quite distinct social
groups—the scientists and the support staff. The divide between the
two is profound. Perhaps the closest analogy is that between officers
and other ranks in the armed services. It is not impossible to become
an officer after having joined up as a private soldier, it is just uncommonly difficult. Technicians can become scientists, and occasionally they do. But it is a rare event. Indeed, few trainees taken on
at the Institute make a life-long career there even as formally qualified
technicians.

Support staff

The support staff comprises several separate groups. There are the
technicians, who may be further divided into animal technicians and
laboratory technicians and who are recruited and trained separately.

Both groups of technicians consist of trainees and qualified staff, each at defined levels of seniority. Another group working in the research and service laboratories, but ranking beneath the technicians, are laboratory assistants—known to all as 'wash-up and tea ladies'—since they also double as catering staff. Along with the cleaning staff, the 'wash-up ladies' have little social contact with other groups. The cleaners, in common with the higher status technical staff of the Engineering Department, are usually men. Finally, the support staff includes various clerical workers (mainly female) who form another distinct social grouping.

Social stratification and rank at the Institute is clearly illustrated by the morning and afternoon tea rituals. It is an unwritten law that everyone attend morning and afternoon tea in the cafeteria. This ritual is seen as having a socially binding effect, encouraging people to see themselves as a part of the Institute, and not just their Unit or Laboratory. And so it does, to a degree, though in the very act of affirming their unity, the staff of the Institute assert their social diversity and rank.

Angela Manners, one of the technicians, advises me to study the places the various groups occupy in the cafeteria. The first year trainee technicians are simply never seated at the same table as the Manager, Instrument Officer and long-serving senior technicians, who usually take their tea together. Whilst the technicians tend to sit with one another, they can also be seen at tables made up of the scientific staff of their own Laboratory—which is the commonest arrangement among the scientists themselves. There is also a temporal and spatial distribution. Thus the lower ranking social groups (who start work earliest) arrive first and sit at the rear of the room. Next come the technicians working in animal and service areas, again sitting at tables toward the rear, followed by the laboratory technicians. Their arrival overlaps with that of the scientists, who occupy the tables towards the front. There is some mobility within these arrangements—especially among the scientists taking the opportunity to button-hole people working in other Units. However the social structure of the tea room is rigid enough for people who don't fit neatly into any of the groups to find the tea ritual a most uncomfortable experience. Only the Director has no home base, moving from table to table with ease.

Laboratory and animal technicians are recruited when they are about seventeen years of age, at the end of their secondary schooling. Trainee technicians are overwhelmingly women. The former Manager, whose job was to recruit and train technicians, preferred women, believing them both more tractable and more tolerant of routine than men. This attitude apart, the idea has long been inculcated into young Australian women that, of the sciences, biology is the most suitable for them. Consequently most of the applicants for the six to eight positions available annually are women. The Manager also believed that applicants with a talent for animal care are distinguishable from those with laboratory work talents. Trainees are therefore recruited specifically for one or the other job. Animal technicians have a different social existence from laboratory technicians. They work mostly with other technicians in breeding and holding facilities rather than as the personal assistants of scientists.

I interview four trainee technicians beginning work at the Institute and ask them how they came to be there. Each says she had first wanted to study medicine, but had not achieved good enough results in the public examination at the end of secondary school to enter this very competitive field. Each of them had then unsuccessfully sought entry as a trainee technician working in a pathology laboratory. It was only as a third choice that they answered the Institute's advertisement.

Technicians receive their practical training on the job, but they are all required to enrol part-time in courses leading to Certificates or Degrees in Applied Science. Carrying a half-time course load, they take at least twice as long to complete their courses as full-time students—six years in the case of those studying for a Degree. This long-drawn-out post-school education, undertaken on top of a full-time job, makes major inroads on the trainee technicians' social life. It becomes plain very soon that the job requires something of a vocation.

From the point of view of the Institute, there are advantages in recruiting technicians in this way. On-the-job training is essential to equip technicians with the skills and work practices needed in the Institute's laboratories. A qualified but inexperienced technician (having studied full-time) would still need to learn these skills and practices before she would be of value in the laboratory. And she would have to be paid a much higher salary than a first-year trainee. Of course one would expect such a qualified person to pick up the Institute's routines quickly. The real monetary saving arises from the fact that the Institute employs far more trainees than qualified technicians. At the time of the 1984 Quinquennial Review there were fifty-six support staff working in the Institute's laboratories, thirty-six of them trainees. There were only eleven qualified technicians, two technologists and seven research assistants. The last category includes university graduates. Research assistants are recruited as (generally experienced) graduates as well as being promoted into the position. They usually work without close super-vision, and are often treated as junior colleagues.

Senior Technical Officers are paid about twice the salary of a first-year trainee. Trainees, like apprentices, receive low initial salaries on the assumption that they are largely being carried by their employer. As each year passes, and they become more skilled, they receive increases supposedly commensurate in payment. At the Institute, a trainee spends her first six months in a circuit of basic service facilities—wash-up and sterilization, media preparation and mouse rooms. There she learns some basic skills and, in doing so, relieves the permanent staff of the more unpleasant and tedious tasks. The trainees are then placed in one or more laboratories for up to another six months' experience before being given their semi-permanent assignment to a scientist.

By the end of their first year at the Institute, trainees are able to make a real contribution to work in a laboratory. The learning curve is very steep early on, since it is in the interests of scientists to train technicians quickly. After six months or so with their assigned scientist, learning his or her peculiar techniques, a trainee rarely needs close and constant supervision. Indeed, I observed one trainee who, after only a matter of months with her first scientist, was left with six weeks' work to do during his absence overseas—and she coped admirably. Long before they graduate as formally qualified technicians, trainees are fully qualified in practical terms, yet they are still paid at a lower rate.

Curiously, the Institute does not expect its trainee technicians to make their careers there. There is a natural attrition rate as trainees find they don't have a vocation for the demanding work. But even those who do finish are not encouraged to stay unless it is felt they have some special potential. Once there was no real problem since most technicians left to get married and raise families. However, young women now expect to remain in the workforce after marriage, and they have children later in life. Moreover, once having been trained and qualified at the Institute, a technician does not have an unrestricted choice of occupation elsewhere since her technical training is quite specialized. Someone trained at the Institute would have to look to another biomedical research laboratory for work. For these reasons the Manager finds more of her technical staff than she would prefer wanting to stay on at the Institute after they qualify.

Nevertheless, the Institute still depends on its high proportion of trainees to qualified and senior technicians in order to keep its labour costs down. Salary costs are the single largest burden on research funds and constitute some two-thirds of the Institute's expenditure.

Another advantage in having a high proportion of comparatively junior female technical staff is that they are prepared to take a properly respectful attitude toward junior scientists—especially Ph. D. students. Students at the Institute are not allocated a technician as a personal assistant, but it is the technicians who teach them many basic skills. (New Ph. D. students are mostly considered worse than useless by technicians.) The attitude the technicians adopt to the Ph. D. students is rather like that sergeants have traditionally adopted toward officer cadets.

The job of ordinary laboratory technicians is becoming steadily more demanding. In Burnet's day a technician was just an extra pair of hands at the bench since even senior scientists did much of their own experimental work. But today the official policy is as follows:

In the execution of a research project the investigator formulates the questions to be answered, chooses the technology most suitable for the purpose and designs the experiments which will provide the answers to his or her questions ... The young investigator must, of course, develop skills and learn the limitations of the techniques available but, although it is Institute policy for all investigators to get their hands dirty in the production of the results they publish, it is not an efficient use of time and skill for trained investigators to perform all manipulations personally, especially when the techniques used are standard ones. Instead, specially trained technicians and technologists carry out experiments under direction.[2]

Officially, postdoctoral fellows are not assigned a technician as a permanent personal assistant, but they are often given such help unofficially or for specific purposes—as are visiting scientists. Every other scientist at the Institute has a technician as a personal assistant and, increasingly, that technician does almost all the routine bench work. Whereas once the scientist and technician worked at the bench together, more and more the scientist is desk-bound most of the time.

A couple of large laboratories have technologists, whose job includes organization and supervision of their technical staff, and increasing use is being made of research assistants, whose work is supervised less closely. But many junior, though experienced, technicians work quite independently. Such independent work requires much more than mere technique, and the technicians' grasp of research tactics—sometimes even research strategy—is often remarkably high.

One major bone of contention among technicians is authorship of papers. This is a complaint I hear from many of them. When technicians were mostly engaged in closely supervised routine work, the question of whether they deserved to be one of the several co-authors of the resulting papers rarely arose. With the increasing sophistication of their role, the question is much more insistently asked—by technicians, as well as scientists. Using the standard often employed by younger scientists—does a technician who has contributed towards producing the results understand the article in which they are announced?—many do deserve co-authorship. And, it should be said, more are receiving this acknowledgement of the importance of their role in research. Audrey Blonden tells me that the issue came to a head at the Institute a couple of years back when one young scientist went a step further and argued that a technician should be given the prized, first-named co-authorship of a paper. Some of his colleagues strongly disagreed. In the end the matter was taken to a Unit Heads' meeting. They decided that technicians could be named as co-authors if their involvement was sufficiently prominent, but that they were not to be first-named co-authors. A Solomonic judgement!

The former Manager, having begun her own scientific career as a technician, always had a protective, even motherly, attitude toward the technicians. She told me of one young technician who tested as over-exposed to radiation on several occasions. (All technicians who work with radioactive isotopes wear a small square of film which is regularly developed to check that exposure had been within safe limits.) The Manager took the technician to task for sloppy safety practices. However she was even more severe on the scientist concerned, since she regarded him as having failed in his duty to give proper instruction and supervision to his technician.

However, young women are becoming less tractable and submissive. As a result, technicians are beginning to see their position at the Institute in industrial terms and the Manager is now approached by disgruntled groups of them as employer rather than as mother-figure. Anthea Boss, an experienced Institute technician, informs me that one issue on which there is simmering unrest is mouse allergy. Mouse allergy is the commonest chronic industrial health problem associated with working in the laboratories and animal breeding and maintenance facilities at the Institute. It can usefully be compared with repetition strain injury (RSI) in the office. Like RSI, mouse allergy can blight or destroy a career and, also like RSI, though it affects both senior and junior workers, it is the junior workers who are in the weakest position to deal with the problem.

Mouse allergy is, ironically enough, an immune system problem which arises when the body reacts hypersensitively to particular antigens called allergens. Those who work with mice can develop an allergic response to mouse antigens (for example, mouse hair). The symptoms, which can be quite severe, are somewhat similar to hay fever, a common allergic response to pollen. Unlike pollen, the levels of which fluctuate with the season, mouse allergens are constantly present in even the most meticulously cleaned facility. Consequently those who work with mice, and are susceptible to mouse allergy, will suffer from it chronically unless the symptoms are suppressed with drugs. Indeed, such constant exposure to mouse allergens can lead to a steady increase in the severity of the hypersensitive reaction.

Laboratory technicians and scientists who work with mice often develop mouse allergy after many years of trouble-free exposure (in the same way as people can quite suddenly begin to suffer from hay fever). Scientists have a good deal of personal autonomy. They are able to respond to developing mouse allergy by changing the nature of their research, and the techniques it requires, to eliminate or minimize mouse work, or they can use technicians to perform procedures involving mice. But, says Anthea Boss, the position is different for technicians.

In the past the former Manager took the view that technicians who develop mouse allergy should resign and seek a position in a laboratory elsewhere which has nothing to do with mice—for example, a hospital pathology laboratory. Technicians in this position point out that it is easier said than done. Pathology laboratories use techniques which they do not know, and have no use for many skills which they do have—such as those involving mice, for example.

Faced with this situation, Anthea Boss simply put up with the effects of anti-allergy drugs. However, even though she used the drugs constantly, when she went into a mouse room symptoms would still develop. So the scientist for whom she worked volunteered to do his own mouse work.

The technicians are inclined to regard themselves as mere 'hewers of wood and drawers of water'. And, speaking to some of the scientists, you could easily get the idea that the technicians' work is little more than repetitive routine. There is no doubt that scientists do unload repetitive work on to technicians whenever they can. Nonetheless, repetitive tasks often need to be performed precisely and are, accordingly, very exacting. Following a number of technicians through their daily round of jobs I have been enormously impressed by the number, range, and level of the skills involved.

Because technicians constantly work with one scientist, their relationship with him or her is critical. The Manager tries to match temperaments, and to change assignments which do not work out. She also tries to avoid having technicians form too close a bond with one scientist by moving them from time to time.

Technicians certainly learn all the foibles of the scientists for whom they work. Nonetheless, the younger technicians do tend to look up to scientists, taking pride in their successes, and being personally wounded by their failures. And, with the more experienced technicians, a productive and enduring working relationship is forged. It may not be the norm, but neither is it exceptional for a technician to follow a scientist to a new appointment, or even halfway round the world for six months' sabbatical leave. Scientists, too, can become very dependent on a particular technician who, after many years, has learnt all the special variants of technique and reagent which, though each is a small thing, together amount to producing experimental results which are reliable and replicable. Having to train a new technician is an unwelcome prospect which may mean substantial delays in scientific research.

At the Basel Institute of Immunology, technicians have very much the same role as they do at the Hall Institute. But in most US institutes things are quite different. There are relatively fewer technicians, and they are usually engaged either in skilled work or in genuinely routine and repetitive tasks. They are difficult to retain once trained because the commercial sector offers substantially higher salaries. The leading American institutes therefore rely on large numbers of Ph. D. students and postdoctoral fellows and it is they, not the technicians, who do the great bulk of the bench work.

Rare though they are, there are examples of technicians becoming scientists. As one would expect of women who have made their way in a world which certainly was, and still largely remains dominated by men, they are exceptional people.

Postgraduate students

The Western world over, entry to science is as a postgraduate student. The Institute accepts small numbers of students doing the final year of an Honours Bachelor of Science degree, and the Bachelor of Medical Science degree undertaken part-way through a medical education by those who want to find out if biomedical research is for them. Even more rarely, someone—usually a technician or research assistant—will be doing a Master of Science degree. But the licence to practise science is the Doctor of Philosophy (Ph. D.) degree.

Novice scientists enrol in a Ph. D. at the Institute from one of two backgrounds. They will either have a first degree in a biological science (majoring in fields such as microbiology, biochemistry or genetics), or medical training and qualifications. Those with a science background will typically have been at university four years, those with a medical background five or six—generally followed by one or two more working in a hospital to qualify for practice. Both groups must bring their own funds to the Hall Institute in the form of scholarships. These come from different sources. Science students will have the usual Commonwealth or University postgraduate research awards that all non-medical Ph. D. candidates compete for. Medicos compete for NH&MRC postgraduate research awards. These provide a more generous emolument in recognition of the considerably greater potential earnings foregone by young doctors. However, neither group is well paid by any means. Both earn less than a junior trainee technician for the whole three years it will take them to get their degree.

If technicians at the Institute bear comparison with valets, for Ph. D. students the best analogy is apprentices. Indeed, the whole process of scientific education has a striking resemblance to that of the medieval art and craft guilds. In the guild system a boy was indentured for as many as seven years as apprentice to a master. The master undertook to teach the apprentice his craft; in return the apprentice undertook to serve his master for little more than his keep. At the end of his term, an apprentice might be required to submit one or more 'masterpieces' before he could be admitted to the guild as a master. If he could not afford the considerable outlay involved he would hire out his services to a master as a 'journeyman'. After an apprenticeship, sometimes a period as an 'improver' was required and occasionally a journeyman might be compelled to wander for a time before settling down as a master.

Commentators on medieval guild education emphasize that one of the great advantages of the apprenticeship system over the academic education provided by schools and universities lies in the individual approach. Schools and universities give classes or lectures, but the apprentice enjoyed the benefit of an exclusive tutor for seven years on end. The result was a skilled craftsman with an extremely high degree of accomplishment. The benefits of this system were mutual since the master received value from his apprentices, the more so as their training advanced, and they were always cheaper than journeymen. Apprenticeship is essentially a practical rather than a theoretical system of education, well suited to the acquisition of tacit knowledge, secret recipes and techniques.

At the Institute, apprentice scientists—Ph. D. students—are 'indentured' for three years. They arrive scientifically literate, but with little or no experience of the practice of science at this level. Their 'master' is their Ph. D. supervisor. He or she will teach the novices their craft and, in return, the student will serve his or her master as junior researcher. As the students bring scholarships with them, the only cost to the Institute is their research materials and equipment. Places at the Institute are extremely competitive, and students are chosen on merit as judged by their academic performance to date. But they must be willing to fit into the laboratory's present research work.

At first, like apprentices, Ph. D. students are of little use. They must pick up basic skills and knowledge before being allocated a share of the work. This is not a job for the master. Just as the medieval apprentice turned to his fellows and the employed craftsmen, so the student will rely on the technicians, other students and junior scientists. After a while, and very much under advice from his or her supervisor, the student will first be given small-scale tasks, then finally a problem of his or her own.

This problem, when solved and written up as a dissertation, constitutes the student's masterwork. Along the way, she or he will have a part in several publications, jointly authored with others in the laboratory, announcing the results of their work. These, too, are masterworks, a critical learning experience. The papers which eventually appear with the student as first-named co-author (and which he or she is likely to have literally written) will be the basis of the thesis.

Obviously, the relationship between a supervisor and student is crucial to a successful Ph. D. candidacy, as is the ability of the supervisor to teach the often hard-to-articulate arcane arts of good experimental science. A difficult or poor relationship is always a problem when people work so closely and constantly together, and can be catastrophic. A good relationship can set a scientist up for a triumphant career.

A good Ph. D. candidate—as most at the Institute are—will become a valuable member of the research team long before he or she graduates. This is where the senior, supervising scientists benefit from training their apprentices. Many large American laboratories have few scientists occupying positions intermediate between the laboratory head and a host of Ph. D. students and postdoctoral fellows—the scientific journeymen. In science, one is required to spend several years as an 'improver'—a two-year postdoctoral fellowship certainly, another senior postdoctoral position quite commonly.

Postdoctoral fellows, like Ph. D. students, bring their own money with them. With their doctoral experience behind them, they are an especially valued source of skilled but cheap labour. These 'improvers' are always in fixed-term positions. Unlike the Ph. D. students, many of the Institute's postdocs come from foreign countries—they are, quite literally, journeymen and journeywomen. Indeed, the Institute expects to send even its very best Ph. D. graduates wandering for at least one postdoc. And this is the norm everywhere. The circulation of postdocs and postgraduate students is an important feature of international scientific communication. Postdocs are sent off as emissaries and spies; they are sent to learn new experimental methods and techniques; they are acquired to import new skills and knowledge. Clearly they play an important function in binding the scientific enterprise together. Postgraduate circulation is also important of course for students as a way of making international contacts.

This resemblance of scientific training to medieval craft guild education is no accident. For becoming a scientist—unlike studying science—requires a great amount of practical experience, not just acquiring a knowledge system. Scientific knowledge includes a great deal of tacit knowledge and the many recipes and techniques—even if not exactly secret (and sometimes, perhaps increasingly, they are secret)—certainly cannot be learned by simply reading the technical literature.

Though there are many similarities and continuities between the apprentice and the journeyman or journeywoman scientist, there is also a profound difference between the two. The doctoral dissertation is a rite of passage in the scientific culture in that it marks a qualitative change in social status, a scientific coming of age. Students come to the Institute to *become* molecular biologists or cellular immunologists, or whatever. Postdocs come to the Institute *as* (relatively junior) molecular biologists or cellular immunologists.

While Ph. D. students have comparatively little intellectual autonomy, postdocs pursue their investigations with the help of more senior scientists certainly, but not at their direction. But, in gaining this independence, postdoctoral students also lose the protection of a supervisor, the tribal elder who is responsible for making sure that the rite of passage is successfully negotiated. In a way, they are still on trial; but the test now is of how well they can make their way in open competition with their peers.

Mitchell recalls his doctorate apprenticeship with Jacques Miller: 'Miller taught me what scientific method was all about; the honesty required, the precision and attention to detail required. We had our fair share of luck too—but I think the relation between luck and effort is rather direct. We had a struggle, we made a major discovery, and I learned the methods of research'.

Miller and Mitchell had discovered that the two lymphocyte subgroups, T-lymphocytes and B-lymphocytes, interact collaboratively in the production of antibodies. As a result, by the time Mitchell had finished his Ph. D. and was looking around for an overseas postdoctoral, his name was known internationally and he was offered a postdoc from Stanford University Medical School in California. The postdoc was a resounding success. As he puts it: 'My publication record kept going, and I spent two years working up a new system. It was easy, in a way, going into a laboratory that was well established and flourishing. I just grafted my expertise onto theirs, which is what they wanted'.

That was 1969. After two years in Stanford, Mitchell went on to a second postdoc at the National Institute for Medical Research, Mill Hill, London. A third, prestigious short-term position followed as a member of the Basel Institute for Immunology before he returned to the Hall Institute in 1973.

The experience of doing a Ph. D. involves a good deal more than simply acquiring a body of specialist knowledge and a set of techniques. At the Institute, a novice also learns what life is like at the leading edge of biomedicine. It is very demanding. Most scientists at the Institute are workaholic personalities. They put in long hours, and the hours are erratic. Experiments have their own logic which demands when the next stage must be performed. Ball tells me that he recently started work each day at 4 a.m. just to complete his experimental work. If you are in the international league, he says, you need to have more than a touch of monomania.

This competitive internationalism imposes another burden on young scientists particularly. As I noted before, the circulation of postdoctoral fellows between laboratories plays a crucial part in diffusing new ideas and techniques through the biomedical community. Naturally they, too, benefit in professional terms from the experience. But the journeyman/journeywoman phase comes in the mid-twenties and extends to the late twenties—just the period when most people start a family and acquire a mortgage. It is not until their early thirties that scientists can expect to find a well-paid and permanent job. Again, most people take it for granted that they can live and work in their native town and country. But a career in international science means that you have to be footloose—like it or not.

Eggers, for example, left Australia aged twenty-eight, and returned to the Institute four years later at thirty-two. In that time he had no fewer than eight postdoctoral fellowships of various kinds which saw him working in the United States, the United Kingdom, Israel and Switzerland. As commonly happens, he met and married his wife whilst overseas. In support of his career, his wife left her native New York and followed his postdoctoral meanderings, finally coming back to Australia with him. She has her own independent professional life and Eggers says this is important in enabling him to take the time he needs for research without generating domestic tension.

****

One of the main figures in the sociology of science is the English scholar Michael Mulkay, and I receive his latest book *The Word and the World*[3] with much interest and speculation. Mulkay is concerned with the 'discourse' of scientists, i.e. how they talk about science, talk to each other about their scientific projects, and talk to people outside the world of science. He thinks that in this way it is possible to see how scientists 'construct' science. He says that his book is a study of 'the textually constructed character of the social world of natural science'. At the same time he is also concerned with the appropriate style for a sociological account of science which allows for a reflective dimension, i.e. where the sociological observer sees himself or herself as also a part of the 'field' being studied—where the observer is observing herself observing. The usual style of scientific monograph—the 'empiricist monologue' as Mulkay calls it—does not allow for this, and he argues that it is necessary to look for alternative styles of sociological accounts. Mulkay cleverly uses dialogues, exchanges of letters between scientists, transcripts of tape-recorded discussions, Borges-type fantasy, and a parody of Nobel Prize presentation to make his point.

I read the book avidly since the question of style—how to write up this project—preoccupies me. But while it is full of illuminating points, it is rather meta-sociological in style and would, I think, be accessible only to sociologists. Certainly I can scarcely imagine any of the scientists here at the Institute understanding it or even being interested in it. What I must do is to find a style that will enable me (a) to give an account of the scientific life; (b) to include myself as observer in that account; and (c) to present such an account so that it will be accessible to the scientists themselves.

Reading an account of the work of the great French anthropologist of the 1930s, Marcel Griaule, I find this engaging description of the ethnographer who must combine 'the art of being a midwife and an examining magistrate'.

By turns an affable comrade of the person put to cross-examination, a distant friend, a severe stranger, compassionate father, a concerned patron, a trader paying for revelations one by one, a listener affecting distraction before the open gates of the most dangerous mysteries, an obliging friend showing lively interest for the most insipid family stories—the ethnographer parades across his face as pretty a collection of masks as that possessed by any museum.[4]

PART TWO

THE SUBJECTIVE SIDE OF
SCIENCE

5

The Myth of Objectivity and the Impersonal Scientist

The fabrication of a scientific voice was, not surprisingly, one of the conditions for the entry of the discipline (anthropology) into the academy. This required a number of steps. First, the anthropologist or fieldworker has to be separated from and set in opposition to the arm chair anthropologist. This was done primarily by stressing the experimental dimension of the anthropologist's work ... The second element of this strategy is the textual suppression of the first. From Malinowski on, a double step of founding the anthropological authority of the outhor on the 'I was there' credential is accompanied by a suppression of the inevitable dialogic construction of anthropological knowledge ... the anthropologist establishes his unique authority by showing that he was there and then disappears from the text. The reason the anthropologist can do this leads us to the scientific rhetoric appropriated by modern anthropology ... The third element in this story is the rise of a theory of 'culture', one assuming that there is a unified Dogon or Balinese culture out there and that representing it is relatively unproblematic.

Paul Rabinow, 'Discourse and Power: On the Limits of Ethnographic Texts'[1]

If a scientist attempted to explain how he had come by his ideas, the great Russian theoretical physicist, L. D. Landau, would say disdainfully, 'That is only an item for your autobiography'.

Every culture has its own sustaining myths or stories which it uses to legitimate itself. These kinds of myths are not meant to be taken as literally true and in a sense everyone knows that they are not factually true. (Like poetry, they involve as Coleridge puts it, a 'willing suspension of disbelief'.) Their function is, rather, to express the ideal image that a society or group has of itself and to provide a framework of meaning or a 'map' within which the beliefs and activities of the group can be located. They are also used to justify developments that have to establish a place for themselves and fight for recognition. One could say, perhaps, that they are *functionally* true in that they serve a necessary social function.

Pure science

The scientific sub-culture has its own myths: the myth of 'pure science', for example, plays a central part in that culture. According to the myth there is a sharp distinction between the domain of science, which is morally and politically neutral or 'value free', and the domain of moral and social values. In itself science is neither good nor bad, save insofar as knowing the truth about the world is good. The scientific investigation of nuclear fission is one thing: what other people do with the results of that investigation is not the interest or the responsibility of the scientist as such. No matter how the results of pure science may be applied by wicked politicians or others, the scientists' hands are always clean. Harry Truman must bear the blame for Hiroshima, not the scientists of the Manhattan Project who made the Bomb.

The myth of 'pure science' is closely linked with another myth about the 'objectivity' and 'disinterestedness' of science. Science is characterized by the fact that scientists adopt a completely impersonal attitude. Their own personal (subjective) feelings, emotions, motives, intentions, attitudes and wishes have nothing to do with their scientific activity. In this view the ideal scientist approximates as closely as possible to the status of a pure instrument: the scientist is, as it were, an instrument whose task it is to read other instruments—a pure observer, the whole of whose personal and interpersonal side is left out of account as irrelevant. 'Pure science' is uncontaminated by the personal and subjective. It may be that in the social sciences—the 'soft' sciences—personal and subjective factors play a part in the scientist's mode of theorizing, in the selection of an area of research interest and in dictating the style of research; but in the 'hard' sciences, so it is claimed, these factors have no place. According to the myth, the natural sciences have no real flesh and blood history and the scientist qua scientist has no biography. This impersonality is also reflected in the peculiar style and rhetoric of scientific monographs. To the non-scientific outsider the prose style of the standard scientific paper gives the impression that the paper has in some curious way not been written by a human being! Once again, everyone knows quite well that, as Medawar has said, the scientific paper is 'fraudulent' in that it misrepresents the scientific thought that has gone into it.[2] But the myth persuades us to suspend our disbelief.

This view is emphasized very clearly in the work of the great and enormously influential 19th-century physicist, Ernst Mach. For Mach every scientific statement can be translated into statements about the scientist's sensations, but these sensations are seen by Mach as being physical reactions of the same kind as those that occur in scientific instruments. They are not attached to a self or ego; as Mach put it, 'The ego must be given up'.[3] In reality, of course, as everyone knows very well, personal and subjective factors play a very large part in scientific activity, just because it is a *human* activity. But the myth of scientific objectivity and impersonality demands the suppression or screening out of the scientist's ego or personality and prevents us from adverting to these factors.

Philosophically, the idea of scientific 'objectivity' is, of course, linked to a realist theory of knowledge according to which we know what there is in reality in a direct and unmediated way. Scientific knowledge is simply the faithful reflection or mirroring of what there is 'out there' and we do not contribute anything from our side. Essentially the scientific knower *discovers* or reads off what is there and does not interpret or invent or construct. The scientific mind mirrors nature and tells it 'like it is'. The 'facts' completely determine or necessitate the theories the scientist advances so that they could not be other than they are. Scientific knowledge is then separated off from the person who knows. Knowledge is, as it were, disembodied or depersonalized.

This paradoxical idea goes back a long way in our cultural history. Thus for Descartes, for example, the knowing subject or *cogito* is quite disembodied: it has no flesh and blood history or biography. Similarly for Hume's empiricism the knower is also depersonalized and we are forbidden to take personal factors into account. Again, the distinction that the influential 20th-century philosopher of science, Hans Reichenbach, makes between the context of discovery and the context of justification, also reflects this dichotomy between knowledge and the knowing subject. For Reichenbach any information about how the scientist discovers some truth is totally irrelevant to justifying whether that 'truth' is really true or not.[4]

In this view then the subjective side of science is completely devalued. Of course we all know that scientists are human and have their foibles and temperamental quirks, but this, so it is claimed, has nothing to do with their science. Thus the unflattering personal portraits of Crick and Watson that emerge from Watson's book *The Double Helix* have really nothing to do with their discovery of the structure of DNA. The brouhaha caused by *The Double Helix* stems in part from the shocking discrepancy between the ideal image of impersonality and self-effacement on the part of the scientist required by the myth of objectivity, and the actuality of the two brash and opinionated, win-at-all-costs, scientists revealed by the book. It is interesting, by the way, to compare the image projected by the fathers of DNA with the image that emerges in Sir Macfarlane Burnet's book on the Hall Institute. In the preface to the book Burnet refers to 'the rather intensely personal approach I have adopted'. But in fact nothing at all emerges about the personal and subjective side of either himself or his colleagues. All that we get, between the lines, is a picture of an austere and reserved, almost clerical, personality—the self-effacing and humble servant of the scientific truth.[5]

By and large, I think that most of the scientists at the Institute would subscribe to Landau's dismissal of 'autobiography' as having anything to do with the validity of their scientific ideas. They have been socialized to believe that 'subjective' factors are irrelevant, just as artists on the other hand have been socialized to believe that autobiographical factors are supremely relevant in explaining why they paint or write or compose as they do. The interesting question is why there should be this difference. Why should scientists be taught to screen out their autobiography? I read recently an intriguing paper by the English anthropologist Mary Douglas on what she calls 'socially structured forgetting' or 'structural amnesia': that is, how a particular 'social order' prevents people from thinking about certain things and makes certain kinds of thoughts impossible.[6] Clearly the lack of interest in the subjective side of science is precisely an instance of 'socially structured forgetting'.

Within the context of this view of science there is therefore no proper place for any study of the subjective conditions of science and the work of scientists. Since the psyche or subjective self is not as such involved in scientific knowledge there is no place for analysis or discussion of the scientific psyche. As a result there has, until recently, been very little done in this area. However, if I am to investigate the scientific life-world, the whole subjective side of science has to be taken into account. In the next two chapters then I will be concerned with various aspects of scientific subjectivity, first in a general way and then with respect to the Institute scientists in particular.

The scientific temperament

There were, it is true, some early 19th-century studies of scientific temperaments. For example, Wilhelm Ostwald claimed that most of the great scientists could be characterized as either romantics or classicists. The scientific romantics are, according to Ostwald, the revolutionaries who bring about radical changes in science and become the founders of schools. The classicists, on the other hand, regard their work as a private, personal vocation and they work slowly and painstakingly on a narrow front.[7] Ostwald's classification of scientists is obviously not based upon any real psychological research and does not tell us a great deal. Disappointingly, the same must be said of a more recent study by the American psychologist, Abraham Maslow.[8] Maslow is on the side of the angels in that he insists very strongly upon the personal and subjective aspect of science, but at the same time he implicitly accepts the idea that science has a special and privileged status, and his characterizations of the psychology of scientists are largely idealized and a priori. Here is part of Maslow's summing up:

I was confronted again, as so many other investigators have been, with the temptation to differentiate the contrasting types which have been called by so many names, tough-minded and tender-minded, Apollonian and Diony-sian, anal and oral, obsessional and hysterical, masculine and feminine, controlled and impulsive, dominating and receptive, suspicious and trusting, etc. For a time I used the designations x character and y character, defining these as the common elements in all these pairs of antonyms. At other times I used the words 'cool' and 'warm' because neither of these is invidious or insulting, and I thought also that the 'physiognomic quality' of these words was better than more explicitly defined words in the present state of knowledge. For the same reasons I have also tried the 'blue-green' (end of the spectrum) and contrasted it with 'red-orange-yellow' people.

Maslow then offers the 'impression' that those he thought of as cool or blue-green or tough-minded in character and outlook tended to be concerned with the establishment of law, of regularities, of certainty, of exactness.

They spoke of 'explanation', and by this they clearly implied the tendency toward parsimony, and economy, the simple, the monistic. The moment of reductiveness, i.e. of a reduction in the number of variables, was a moment of triumph and of high achievement. By contrast I felt that the 'warm' people, the red-orange-yellow, the intuitive ones (who came closer to the poet-artist-musician than to the engineer-technologist), the 'tender-minded' and 'soft-nosed' scientists tended to speak glowingly of the moment of 'understanding' as the high spot and the reward of investigation![9]

In my view, Maslow's 'impressions' are little more than intuitive ('red-orange-yellow') guesses and once again have little to tell us. I cannot help wondering why, as a psychologist, he did not feel the need to examine the character of the scientific mentality (or mentalities) in the same close and detailed way as, say, the religious mentality has been examined by William James and others.

A rather more factual approach to the psychology of scientists has been taken by social psychologists such as Roe and McClelland. In her book *The Making of a Scientist* Anne Roe reports that scientists (especially physical scientists) tend to be loners as children, to have weak social interests and skills and even to avoid contact with others.[10] Similarly, D. C. McClelland, in an article entitled 'On the Dynamics of Creative Physical Scientists', reports that 'young scientists are typically not very interested in girls, date for the first time late in college, marry the first girl they date, and thereafter appear to show a rather low level of heterosexual drive'. Again, he finds that 90 per cent of a group of eminent scientists see in the 'mother-son' picture used in the Thematic Apperception Test, 'the mother and son going their separate ways'. This is a relatively unusual response to the picture. McClelland claims that scientists, both male and female, typically have a distant relation to their mothers, and that for most the father is the parent of primary emotional and intellectual importance.[11]

Most of the scientists at the Hall Institute whom I have spoken to about these findings think that they are rather banal, or even comical. But, in any case, it is doubtful whether these findings about the scientific *psyche*, based as they are on a sample of American physical scientists in the 1950s and 1960s, are generalizable to other kinds of scientists (e.g. biologists) in other societies at other times. The idea that young creative scientists exhibit 'a rather low level of heterosexual drive' certainly does not seem to apply to many of the young active scientists at the Institute.

A more imaginative attempt to provide some kind of insight into the nature of the scientific *psyche* is that of Lewis S. Feuer in his curious book *Einstein and the Generations of Science*.[12] Feuer adopts a psychoanalytical approach and gives an account of 19th- and 20th-century physics in terms of generational conflict; that is, in terms of conflict between the young and their fathers and elders, or in other words, conflict between innovators and the tradition-bound establishment. The Einsteinian generation is seen as being motivated by 'Oedipal' feelings towards the preceding generation of 'classical' physicists. Feuer also claims that the scientific community has devised means for containing and neutralizing this conflict: 'Only in the sciences has human society devised a means for resolving the conflict of generations. The scientific community has undergone basic reconstructions of ideas without suffering the equivalent of social revolutions. Fundamental theoretical changes have been made in a rational, constitutional spirit; a common loyalty to scientific truth has overridden divisive generational, national, political and religious forces'.[13] Some of Feuer's Freudian analyses of classical physicists may seem rather bizarre. However, I certainly don't think that they should be dismissed out of hand. Any approach that throws any light on scientific subjectivity ought to be welcomed, no matter how outlandish it may appear at first sight. At the same time, I don't think I have the courage to attempt Freudian sessions with any of the Institute scientists!

With the questioning and criticism of the realist theory of scientific knowledge (science directly mirrors nature) in the 1960s and 1970s, and the emergence of 'constructivist' accounts of various kinds (scientific knowledge is the product of observational data filtered through interpretive frameworks), a space has been made, so to speak, for studies of the subjective conditions of science. If scientific knowledge does not merely mirror 'the facts' and the structure of reality, or put in another way, if the facts do not totally constrain or determine scientific knowledge, then we need to look for other factors, both subjective and social, to explain why scientific knowledge in any specific area is as it is. (The proponents of the social construction of science assume that only *social* factors are, so to speak, let in by the underdetermination of scientific theories by scientific data. But clearly other factors, such as those discussed below, may also have a part to play.)

A book that has always impressed me is that by the American social psychologist, Ian Mitroff: in my view it is one of the most ambitious and systematic attempts to investigate the subjective conditions of science. Mitroff's study is entitled *The Subjective Side of Science: A Philosophical Inquiry into the Psychology of the Apollo Moon Scientists*[14] and it examines the attitudes, beliefs and practices of the group of scientists (forty-two geologists, geophysicists, geochemists etc.) engaged in the Apollo moon rock project of the late 1960s and the early 1970s. Mitroff's ulterior purpose is to critically assess the 'norms of science', i.e. the ideal institutional standards (proposed by Merton and others) considered necessary to ensure the rationality and the basic characteristics of scientific knowledge. His main enemy is what he calls 'the Storybook Image of Science' which stresses that 'science is a passionless enterprise performed by passionless men, and that it has to be (so) if it is to be objective'. According to this view, scientific objectivity involves emotional neutrality on the part of the scientist. 'The scientist must be impersonal, dispassionate, disinterested, detached, ready to think coldly.'[15]

Mitroff's strategy is to show, through his study of the attitudes and practices of his forty-two moon rock scientists, that scientists do not (and in a sense cannot feasibly) conform to 'the Storybook Image of Science'. I will return later to Mitroff's work.

Over the last ten years there has been a steady stream of studies of the subjective side of the scientific process. Thus, for example, there is H. F. Judson's vast work, *The Eighth Day of Creation*, which is a deliberately personalized account of the emergence of the new biology; Daniel Kevles' work, *The Physicists*; Harriet Zuckerman's book, *Scientific Elite*, on the work and professional and institutional power of a number of American scientists who have won Nobel Prizes; Russell McCormach's *Night Thoughts of a Classical Physicist*, a psycho-social study of a German physicist through a fictional recreation; June Goodfield's psycho-biography of a young woman scientist, *An Imagined World: A Story of Scientific Discovery*; and Philip J. Hilts's popular book, *Scientific Temperaments: Three Lives in Contemporary Science*.[16] The anthropologist Sharon Traweek has written a comparative account of groups of high-energy physicists in Stanford and Tokyo, and Pnina Abir-Am, Donald Fleming and Evelyn Fox Keller have studied the development of the new biology, emphasizing the importance of the personal style and ethos of the new breed of hard-nosed biologists who came into the biosciences after the Second World War. In her book, *A Feeling for the Organism,* Fox Keller presents the American geneticist and Nobel Prize winner Barbara McClintock as exemplifying the older 'natural history' approach to biology and as representing a totally different kind of scientific mentality from that of Crick and Watson and the new biologists who claimed to have solved the 'secret of life' by discovering the mechanism by which DNA replicates.[17]

Gender and science

The emergence of interest in the influence of gender upon science has also affected the study of subjective factors in science. Some feminist writers have argued that the view of science that has prevailed so far, with its emphasis on objectivity and rationality and rigour, is associated with an aggressive and exploitative male patri-archalist world-view. That is why science has been, and remains, predominantly a male preserve. Easlea, for example, argues that science is motivated by a 'phallic dream: to expose, pierce, penetrate and thereby to dominate Nature'.[18] Evelyn Fox Keller in *Reflections on Gender and Science* also claims that science has so far been linked with a male ideology and she explores 'the emotional sub-structures underlying the conjunction of science and masculinity'. Through such a quasi-psychoanalytic approach one can, so she claims, be led to envisage the possibility of a new way of doing science that would transcend gender stereotypes.[19]

On a less theoretical level, a good deal of research has recently been done on the performance of women scientists. Although women are grossly under-represented in the ranks of research scientists, it is not at all clear that this is due, as commonly supposed, to the restrictions imposed by marriage and family life. Thus in a striking paper entitled 'Marriage, Family and Scientific Publication', Harriet Zuckerman and Jonathan Cole look at what they call 'a myth of modern science', namely that marriage, family, and science are incompatible.[20] 'This myth appears *centrally* in all discussions of women in science. The argument goes as follows: a scientific vocation, like a religious one, requires superhuman commitment and dedication. Married women with children inevitably have a divided commitment. Therefore, they are less creative and publish less. Women who do achieve, the Madame Curies, are either super-women or achieve at the expense of their personal and family lives.' Women, then, are 'forced to choose between productivity and repro-duction'. However, Zuckerman and Cole show that there is no firm evidence for this view. In fact, all the evidence goes to show that marriage and motherhood are not incompatible with scientific research productivity. Indeed, some research indicates that married women are more productive than single women. 'Yet the myth persists. In the interview material, older scientists, both men and women, express the belief that domestic life is incompatible with productive science. Younger scientists also hold that marriage, family, and science are incompatible. They still believe that motherhood marks the end of productive careers for their female colleagues. These beliefs, largely unsupported, serve as bases for decisions about women's careers and thus tend to yield outcomes perceived to be consistent with the myth'.[21]

Unfortunately Zuckerman and Cole do not carry their analysis further by asking why this myth persists. Might it, for example, be based on male envy of female reproduction and a determination to keep scientific production a male preserve?

In an article entitled 'High Energy Physics: A Male Preserve', the US anthropologist Sharon Traweek discusses the 'gender gap' in the high-energy physics community.[22] She estimates that there are about 1000 active high-energy physicists in the world at the present time with an 'elite core' of about 400. Women scientists constitute only 3 per cent of the general high-energy physics community with a mere handful in the core group. Traweek claims that the traits required for gaining entry into this exclusive community—'aggressive individualism, haughty self-confidence, and a sharp competitive edge'—are traits that are 'typically defined as masculine by our society'. As the physicists say, 'Only blunt, bright bastards make it in this business', and women typically do not have these qualities. Physicists are heavily socialized during their undergraduate, graduate and postdoctoral training (a process which takes around fifteen years); they are taught to revere the (exclusively male) scientific heroes of the past; they work under male supervisors, and during their postdoctoral period they are closely watched and eventually selected for qualities that are (in our culture) typically male—'the preferred style is confident, aggressive and even abrasive'. Above all, they have to be good at promoting their own work and denouncing the work of others. Since women are socially conditioned to get on well and smoothly with others, they find it difficult to display the degree of 'social eccentricity, disdain for others and careful insubordination' required at the postdoctoral stage.

Interestingly, Traweek notes that the personality characteristics associated with success in the US high-energy physics culture and which are identified in US culture as masculine—aggression, individualism, competitiveness—are perceived quite differently in Japan. (Her control group is in Tokyo.) In Japan the traits of individualism, aggression etc., are associated with successful *women* and not with men! Thus in the Japanese high-energy physics community 'women physicists ... are seen as not sufficiently schooled in the more masculine abilities of consulting, negotiating and reaching consensus!' Traweek concludes that 'there is nothing consistent cross-culturally in the virtues associated with success in the high-energy physics community. Yet both societies have reserved the higher status for the behaviour displayed by males'.[23]

Professionalization

A further component of what I have been calling the subjective conditions of science is the professional formation of scientists. There have been many studies of professions and the ways in which their members are 'professionalized' in law, medicine, business, and the military. For example, Donald Light's fine book, *Becoming Psychiatrists: The Professional Transformation of Self*[24], is concerned with 'what kinds of people choose to become psychiatrists, how their training experience alters their sense of illness, treatment, and responsibility, how they cope with suicidal patients and how they overcome the uncertainties of their work. Underlying these lessons is the organisation of the [training] program, the moral transformation it puts the residents through, and the tendencies toward omnipotence it embodies'.[25] Again, the medico-cum-anthropologist Melvin Konner has given an illuminating account of how medical students at Harvard are initiated into the profession.[26] Scientists are also members of a profession with its own distinct and strict ethos and standards and 'ethics' and it is obviously of some importance to see how scientists are inducted into the profession, what kind of 'moral transformation' they undergo, and what part their professional identity plays in the way they do science.

Ethics

Finally there is the ethical dimension. Clearly the scientists' views of the ethical and social implications of their scientific work must have some effect on the way they do science. It may be, of course, that scientists believe that their work has no direct moral or social implications and that, in general, moral and social values are irrelevant. But that position is in a sense also an ethical position, just as the view that science is 'value free' surreptitiously involves an evaluation of science (scientific knowledge is so valuable that it overrides ordinary ethical and social considerations).

There are then a number of factors, ranging from psychological temperament to gender, to ethical commitment, to professional formation, which condition the way in which science is done—the areas of scientific enquiry that are preferred, the style of scientific research, the scientific paradigms set up. The myth of scientific objectivity and impersonality pretends, like Landau, that these factors are strictly irrelevant to science and do not need to be taken into account, unless we are concerned merely with 'human interest' stories about scientists. Autobiography is screened out by a process of 'socially structured forgetting'. In actual fact, however, the subjective side of science is crucial to an understanding of it.

The subjective side of science at the Hall Institute

For people committed to scientific objectivity and impersonality, the Institute scientists talk very frankly, sometimes brutally, about each other's personal traits. Technicians, who have a worm's-eye view of their scientific bosses are, naturally enough, especially sensitive to the latter's personal failings. No one is a hero to his valet, and it is certainly true that a number of the scientists at the Institute are not seen as heroes by their technicians. Betty Askew, for instance, speaks very critically of the arrogance and aloofness of her scientific superior, Angus Pollard. 'When something goes wrong', she says, 'he doesn't speak to me directly about it: he just goes into a sulk and I'm supposed to work out where I have failed. Again, there's no hope of me participating in his work: he simply takes the results and that's that. On one occasion I had left my reports on my desk overnight: when I came in the next morning they were gone. I was rather panic-stricken until I found that Dr Pollard had simply taken them. He didn't see why he should tell me about it. To him I was just a menial'. On the other hand, there are technicians who speak very warmly of their scientists. Alison Bowlby, for instance, is usually included among the authors of the papers that come out of George Munro's group at the Institute. Munro is very much against the traditional device of putting the name of the laboratory head first on all the papers produced by the group. However, the recruitment, training, pay and general feudal treatment of the technicians works against too much democracy and equality. 'It's a hierarchical situation', says Betty Askew: 'I mean there are hierarchs and lower-archs, and we are the lower-archs!'.

Among the scientists themselves the team situation sometimes leads to competitiveness and a good deal of personal friction. Paradoxically, says Peter Marvell, it is when a group is running hot and producing good results that things become difficult. Naturally, you want to have your name first on a significant paper and quite tense feelings can arise over attribution. It's then that personal attitudes reveal themselves and people 'bare their fangs'. In a team, Marvell says, you need to have someone who can reconcile the adversarial passions that emerge in the group and generally to act as a middle-man. 'I'm not a genius', Marvell says, 'but I think I'm a good leader of the group. Bamber tends to be rather obsessive and moody; Cannon wants his "rights" recognized; Allen is extremely bright and is capable of huge conceptual leaps, and so on. In other words, they're a bunch of prima donnas. Someone has to mediate between them, and I'm the one'.

The Director is generally held to be a supreme exponent of this kind of ecumenical leadership on an Institute-wide basis and Marvell says that he takes the Director as his role model. Does he look for team people when he is appointing new staff? Not really: you can be an utterly self-centred individualist and a good scientist, and con-versely you can be a nice friendly guy and a bad scientist. It is a bonus if you get both a good scientist and a team person. Marvell mentions a US scientist, Vassar, who believes that you should appoint bright, aggressive, individualistic, egocentric bastards and let them slug it out! In some US laboratories two Ph. D. students are set the same topic in competition with each other.

However, while there is this recognition of personal faults and virtues and of different psychological types—loners, obsessives, optimists—this is usually completely divorced from the judgements that are made about colleagues *as scientists*. Most of the Institute scientists have very decided and sharp views about who are good scientists and who are not, though the criteria they adduce for these judgements are not always very clear: 'You just know that Alvin is a class scientist', they say; 'You just know that Bloom is doing shonky science'. Baldock, who has done some reviewing of other scientific institutes, claims that he can tell whether a laboratory is any good as soon as he walks into the place. 'A few crucial ques-tions will quickly reveal whether they are up to the state of the art or not'. Ron Nixon is more explicit about his very trenchant judge-ments of the other scientists in his field: 'You must remember', he says, 'that doing science is, among other things, a way of making a living, keeping your family in food and paying off the mortgage on your house, and that is the way many scientists treat it. They have nothing original to say but they keep beating the same old drums at conferences and seminars and manage to give the impression that they are busy and doing useful work. Many scientific seminars and conferences are full of papers given by people of this kind'. It's not even 'normal science' in the Kuhnian sense (tidying up and teasing out the implications of some breakthrough): it's just doing the same old unoriginal thing. (Nixon refers to a recent Institute conference on T cells which, he says, was pretty bad in this respect.) The few people at the forefront of an area of research will know that these people are simply flogging dead horses.

At the other extreme there are the theoretical speculators: just recently at the Institute a debate was held on a big theoretical controversy in German microbiology. But both positions were fantastic constructions fabricated out of very meagre data and Nixon said that he remained unexcited and totally unconvinced. Again, an eminent visitor to the Institute had put forward a very ingenious theory about T cell regulation, but the verification of the theory depended finally on measuring increases in the thickness of the ears of experimental mice. What is more, the measurements were made manually! Once again, Nixon remained unconvinced. One just feels, he says, a bit suspicious of that kind of science: it simply doesn't feel right.

Asked to say whether there are specific psychological types who do better in the biological sciences, a number of the Institute scientists clearly think that there is not any very distinct scientific temperament. You have, of course, to be intelligent and you also have to be lucky, being in the right place at the right time, and you need to be sharp enough to capitalize on your luck. But that's about all the equipment you need. Albert Inkster says, however, that a sucessful scientist needs to have 'a lot of ego'; you must, he says, be confident, even aggressive, and he adds wryly, if you are after a Nobel Prize you need a good deal of self-promotion and the ability to win friends and influence people in the right quarters. The image of the gentle, contemplative scientist gazing in childlike wonder at the workings of Nature (as in that marvellous photograph of Einstein) is strictly for the birds. What you have now with the big post-war funding of science by government agencies and foundations, is increasing scientific entrepreneurship and wheeler-dealing.

Mitroff on the psychology of scientists

I had two interviews with Mark Swayne, one of the young up-and-coming Institute scientists, about 'the subjective side of science', using as a basis for discussion Ian Mitroff's book on the psychology of the Apollo moon rock scientists.

Mitroff's study of the attitudes of the moon rock scientists shows, so he claims, that scientists do not in fact do science in the dispassionate and 'cold' style that the Storybook Image of Science supporters say they do. Mitroff's scientists, for example, lay great stress on emotional commitment and drive, and even aggression. One of them says to Mitroff:

The uninvolved, unemotional scientist is just as much a fiction as the mad scientist who will destroy the world for knowledge. Most of the scientists I know have theories and are looking for data to support them; they're not sorting impersonally through the data for a theory to fit the data.... A good scientist will not be above changing his theory if he gets a preponderance of evidence that doesn't support it, but basically he's looking to defend it. Without commitment one wouldn't have the energy, the drive to press forward, sometimes against extremely difficult odds.[27]

Another moon rock man says:

A scientist has the same wolves biting at his rear end as everybody else, and the same internal wolves biting at him, his ego, his own worth. If you had scientists who were completely psychologically normal, balanced human beings, they wouldn't be scientists. They would be objective then, but would there be real progress? ... The best thing you can do is to raise a kid to be deprived, psychologically and materially, so that he has a tremendous drive for success, will trample over people and work like hell.[28]

I had given Swayne a summary of Mitroff's findings and he had read it through, he said, with a great deal of interest since he had always thought the popular view of scientific objectivity was very simple-minded. At the same time he thought that all that Mitroff was saying was that scientists were, after all, human—surprise, suprise! Certainly most of the people at the Institute would agree that self-confidence and push, and even a kind of tough aggressiveness, were necessary in top science if you were to get anywhere. Getting your ideas accepted often involved a lot of politicking and sometimes depended on the charisma and force of personality of a scientist. Swayne referred to a recent visit to the Institute by a Nobel Prize winner. Swayne thought that his results were very dubious indeed, but he was certainly a saleman and an operator. Fortunately, recent advances in molecular biology techniques had now made it possible to test the Nobel Laureate's theory and it would be very interesting to see if it was anything more than a very ingenious piece of speculation backed up by persuasive talk. *En passant,* Swayne says that this has been one of the great benefits of molecular biology, namely that it enables you to make quite precisely measurable judgements and to cut through vagueness and waffle. By and large, molecular biology had had a cathartic effect on immunology and had to some extent cleansed the stables of charlatans and speculators by forcing scientists to make their ideas testable and operational. On the other hand, he certainly doesn't think that molecular biology is the be-all and end-all of biology. I tell him of Evelyn Fox Keller's account of Barbara McClintock's battle with the early molecular biology establishment ('By God', Joshua Lederberg said of McClintock, 'that woman is either crazy or a genius') and Swayne says that he is pretty sympathetic to McClintock's opposition to the tunnel vision of some of the molecular biologists.

Getting back to the subjective side of science, Swayne says that although the psychology of the scientist is important, Mitroff's whole approach is too individualistic in that it concentrates upon individual scientists and doesn't advert to the differences between *groups* of scientists. Virologists, biochemists, biologists, molecular biologists all have their own 'group psychology' and their own ways of doing things. For example, the controls that biochemists sometimes use look quite crude and odd to an immunologist, and of course the procedures of 'classical' immunology look very sloppy to the molecular biologist. Again, Swayne thinks that national differences are quite important, though Mitroff doesn't say anything about them at all. For example, in Swayne's field Australians are much more free and easy than Americans and don't resent or resist criticism as much as the latter. But then that depends to some extent on cultural factors (the Americans value competitiveness in a way in which Australians don't), and on purely material factors such as security of funding and even security of tenure. If your job is secure, no matter what, you can afford to be relaxed about criticisms of your work.

I tell Swayne about the work of Sharon Traweek, who has been investigating two groups of high-energy physicists, one at Stanford in California and the other in Tokyo, Japan. Traweek describes the extreme assertiveness and brashness of the Stanford group ('You have to be a sonofabitch to get anywhere in this game', is a fairly typical comment). A lot of their gossip consists of criticism and 'putting down' of other scientists in this field. Traweek contrasts this aggressive style of the Stanford physicists with the reticent and low-profile attitude of Tokyo scientists. 'Yes', says Swayne, 'that's the obvious kind of control that you'd need to set up if you were to get anywhere with Mitroff's stuff'. 'I take it', I say,'that you are not overly impressed with Mitroff's methodology?' Swayne replies: 'Let's just say that his controls are about as good as those of some biochemists I could name!'

Swayne has been shown Mitroff's Ideal Scientist Profile, and he has been asked to draw his own 'profile'. He is rather critical of the whole thing, complaining that it doesn't specify clearly what 'ideal' is supposed to mean. Does 'ideal' mean 'successful' (so that the successful Nobel Laureate mentioned before would be an ideal scientist)? Or does it mean the kind of qualities you would like a scientist in an ideal world to have, or the qualities you think a scientist should have in a given situation within a given discipline? In any case what would a study of how forty-two respondents reacted to the profile really prove? All that it would show is that a certain proportion of respondents thought that a scientist should be more 'impartial' than 'biased', more 'warm' than 'cold', more 'hard-driving' than 'easy-going', roughly fifty-fifty 'rational' and 'intuitive', and so on. But what is supposed to follow from this? It's a bit like Kinsey's report on the sexual behaviour of American males and females. Given that 55 per cent approve of such and such a kind of sexual behaviour, what follows? Bugger all, to put it politely!

I reply that Mitroff would say that his findings suggest that the 'operative logic' which scientists actually use is quite discrepant from the kind of logic or 'norms of rationality' which they are commonly supposed (by Merton and other philosophers of science) to obey. No doubt one can adopt a tough line and say that they should obey those prescriptive norms and that if they do not they are not doing 'authentic science'. But surely it's rather odd saying this when the majority of scientists don't in fact follow the so-called norms. Swayne clearly finds Mitroff's social science methodology so wildly at variance with his own scientific approach that he has great difficulty in taking Mitroff's findings seriously.

The Ideal Scientist Profile (from Ian I. Mitroff, *The Subjective Side of Science*, Elsevier, New York, 1974, p. 108)

The dark solid line represents the qualities that an Ideal Scientist should have, as judged by 45 practising scientists interviewed by Mitroff. The averages of the 45 scores for each of the sets of qualities are connected to form a profile.

The lighter dashed line forms a profile of the qualities that, according to what Mitroff calls the 'Storybook Image of Science', the scientist should ideally have. The discrepancy between the two profiles shows to what degree practising scientists question the stereotypical or mythical or 'storybook' view of the scientist.

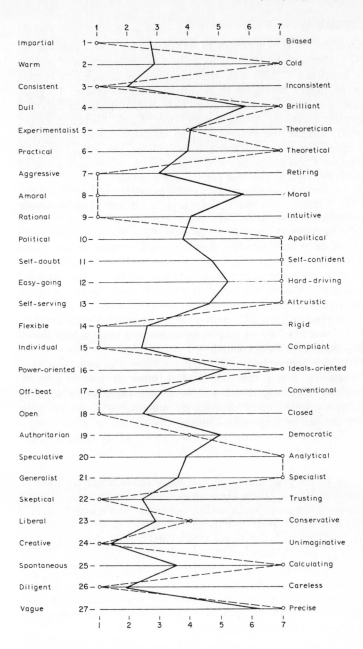

Creativity

In a contribution to *A Tribute to Sir Macfarlane Burnet* published in 1979, Melvin Cohn attempts to analyse the phenomenon of creativity in science.[29] 'Men with great creativity in science may or may not be highly intelligent or sensitive or knowlegeable. They are creative and that is another thing.' Cohn nominates as exemplars of scientific creativity Avery, Benzer, Bohr, Crick, Ehrlich, Einstein, Lwoff, Monod and Pasteur, and he includes Burnet among this creative élite. Using Burnet's investigations into lysogeny as an example, Cohn establishes a number of marks of genuine scientific creativity. Thus he says that greatness of creativity

(1) 'is driven by ambiguity (or paradox) to yield maximally general laws'. 'Creative individuals', Cohn says, 'are disturbed by (apparent) challenge to universality. They thrive on ambiguity...'

(2) is teleonomic in that it 'chooses the influences which will operate on it as a selective pressure, i.e. it chooses its ecological niche'. Thus, according to Cohn, 'Burnet in his papers on bacteriophage chooses carefully by what and by whom he will be influenced in setting his goals. He wends his way through the minds of his contemporaries like Marcel Marceau interpreting Bip';

(3) 'requires identification with other highly creative individuals';

(4) 'is nourished by (would starve without) a large substratum of individuals with lesser creativity';

(5) 'is demonstrated repeatedly in the lifetime of an individual'.[30]

Most scientists at the Hall Institute, however, tend to discount creativity. There are, of course, those who are capable of making big conceptual leaps and of 'thinking the unthinkable', but other qualities are just as important—general intelligence, a good apprenticeship, hard work at the bench, the ability to see what is before your eyes, a fund of experience, an array of techniques, and pure luck.

One of the principal sceptics at the Institute about creativity in science is Joseph Albers. He is an extremely intelligent man who is very confident about his capabilities and value as a research scientist and, despite his bluff 'no bloody nonsense' manner, he has an excellent sense of (sometimes cynical and 'black') humour. Albers divides scientists very strictly into 'thinkers' and 'doers' and he places himself firmly in the category of 'doers', i.e. scientists who work at the bench and who make their discoveries through their detailed and careful and arduous laboratory work. At the same time, although he is contemptuous of scientists who imagine you can do science by having bright ideas in an armchair with your feet up, and even of scientists who regularly read the scientific literature (i.e. who read *about* science instead of *doing* it), it is clear that he has reflected a great deal about the kind of science he is doing, what makes good and bad scientists, mythological views of science, and how science progresses. Albers adopts a pretty aristocratic view in that he clearly thinks that there is likely to be a relatively small group of 'good' scientists at any research institute at any one time and that the rest are likely to be 'bums'. The 'bums' are further sub-divided into those who are competent scientists but who will not progress after the age of thirty, and those who are quite useless and for whom one has to think and act and 'work one's butt off'. At the same time, while Albers's view of scientists is rather aristocratic, it is also an anti-romantic view in that you don't need to be a genius, having genius-like thoughts, to be a good scientist. You need to have had a good apprenticeship in scientific research, you need to be able to work very hard at the bench, you need to be lucky, and above all you need to be careful and attentive and 'sharp'. Most major scientific discoveries occur almost by accident and you need to be sharp to pick them up and capitalize on them. Albers dismisses apparent counter-examples such as Einstein and Crick who are supposed to have had Eureka-style creative insights. Biologists can't make breakthroughs simply by using pencil and brain. Biology requires the mastery of too many techniques and the creation of data-generation systems for creative brain-storming to be of much use. A good apprenticeship in scientific research is essential, he says, though this also often involves a good deal of luck. He himself had been lucky in that, after taking his first degree, he had had a year with a remarkable and eccentric scholar.

Apart from an adequate apprenticeship, Albers was inclined to think that one was either born a good research scientist or one was not. He once thought that you could by education and experience 'train a chimpanzee to be a scientist' or at least turn an indifferent scientist into a good one, but he was now almost inclined to think that 'it was in the genes'. His experience was that unless you had proved your worth by the age of thirty, you had had it. After thirty you were not likely to change drastically. In fact, he had never known it to happen. You can't make a silk purse out of a sow's ear and no accumulation of experience will change you from a scientific sow's ear into a scientific silk purse.

A lot of bright young scientists make one 'discovery' (usually by accident) but the number who make *two* 'discoveries' is very small indeed. They are the ones to watch for. Once again, Albers emphasizes that scientific work in his field depends on hard work at the bench, lucky accidents, 'sharpness' in being able to seize upon these accidents, to see their implications and to exploit them. He gives an example of one of his own experiments with leukemia cells. In the experiment what he had expected to happen didn't happen, but something surprising did occur—two layers of cells behaving quite differently from what he expected. Albers saw at once the possibilities in this surprising situation which was complex enough to be interesting—how in general it might be explained and what implications it might have. He knew at once that he had a life's work ahead of him.

I remark that Albers and the other scientists at the Institute seemed so busy that they must have very little time for reflection. Albers reacts very strongly to this since he understands 'reflection' to mean thinking about scientific problems in the abstract away from the bench. 'I spend eight hours a day looking down a microscope at colonies of cells', he says, and his thinking and 'reflection' emerge from this. He admits that he is pretty obsessive about his work, but he claims that most successful scientists are obsessives. He had once even dreamt that he was a leukaemic cell! When I ask if he meant that ignorance was bliss, i.e. that thinking *about* scientific problems in the abstract inhibits one's work, he claims that he thinks that this is so. He, for example, reads very little of the scientific literature in his field of research since he has found that if you read too much about a problem it muddles your own approach. (He admits though that he did incidentally read a good deal by virtue of the fact that he was called on to referee papers for scientific journals in his field.) In fact, he says that there is a correlation between reading the literature and mediocrity in scientific work, and not reading the literature and superiority in scientific work. He challenges me to set up a simple experiment in the Institute library by observing which scientists regularly read the literature—the implication being that regular readers were also mediocre scientists. He himself had at times duplicated his own work because he had forgotten that he had done that work before and he hadn't bothered to look up his own pub- lished papers! (He'd even read the same novel three times: after six weeks or so he'd forgotten the plot so he could reread the book and enjoy it!) The moral seemed to be that when scientists start reading about their own area it is a sign that they are losing touch and that they are attempting to escape from the hard work at the laboratory bench that is the one thing necessary.

Albers appears to think that this kind of doing-thinking which arises out of work at the laboratory bench is to some extent incommunicable. Scientists are very bad at communicating to other scientists what they are on about. He had attended a conference at Versailles which brought together sixty top scientists from various fields. ('Forty or fifty Nobel Prize winners and a couple of bums like the Director and me.') The idea was that each scientist would explain to his colleagues what he was doing and so provide a basis for an interdisciplinary approach to various intractable problems. It was supposed to be a kind of 'oral *Scientific American*'. However, not only were they incapable of communicating, they were also quite uninterested in listening to others. He had had to support one elderly Nobel Prize winner who went to sleep on his shoulder!

****

Later, reading Evelyn Fox Keller's book on Barbara McClintock, *A Feeling For the Organism*, I discover the following. McClintock is speaking of her minute and meticulous work on the genetics of maize:

> I found that the more I worked with them [the chromosomes] the bigger and bigger they got, and when I was really working with them I wasn't outside, I was down there with them, and everything got big. I was even able to see the internal parts of the chromosomes—actually everything was there. It surprised me because I actually felt as if I were right down there and these were my friends ... As you look at these things, they become part of you. And you forget yourself. The main thing about it is that your forget yourself.[31]

One might call this an attitude of 'passionate objectivity'.

Reflection

In an essay on Watson, ironically entitled 'Lucky Jim', Peter Medawar remarks that in his account of the DNA coup, Watson makes very little mention of his predecessors—Astbury, Avery, Griffith—even though without them Crick and Watson's success would not have been possible. To a non-scientist this may seem to betray a lack of generosity; however, Medawar defends Watson on the grounds that a scientist is quite properly uninterested in the history of his ideas.

It was not lack of generosity, I suggest, but stark insensibility. These matters belong to a scientific history and the history of science bores most scientists stiff. A great many highly creative scientists (I classify Jim Watson among them) take it quite for granted, though they are usually too polite or too ashamed to say so, that an interest in the history of science is a sign of failing or unawakened powers. It is not good enough to dismiss this as cultural barbarism, a coarse renunciation of one of the glories of humane learning. It points towards something distinctive about scientific learning, and instead of making faces about it we should try to find out why such an attitude is natural and understandable. A scientist's present thoughts and actions are shaped by what others have done and thought before him: they are the wave-front of a continuous secular process in which The Past does not have a dignified independent existence of its own. Scientific under-standing is the integral of a curve of learning; science therefore in some sense comprehends its history within itself. No Fred, no Jim: that's obvious, at least to scientists, and being obvious it is understood that it should be left unsaid.[32]

In fact there seems to have been a decided shift in scientists' attitudes to the history and philosophy of their ideas. Before 1945, scientists—or at least the great scientific figures like Poincaré, Einstein, Planck, Heisenberg, Jeans, Schrödinger, Bohr, Delbrück—had been ostentatiously concerned with epistemological and metho-dological questions. As Einstein put it: 'Science without epistemo-logy is—insofar as it is thinkable at all—primitive and muddled'.[33] But contemporary science largely eschews philosophical reflection and adopts a pragmatic approach. As it has been said: 'The implicit model for scientific progress is not solving a problem once and for all, but the evolving emergence of tolerable solutions from which better problems will become available for future work'.[34] The preferred method of contemporary science, writes the Harvard historian/philosopher of science Gerald Holton, is one best called 'improvisational heuristic'. 'If the older role models were the philo-sophically introspective Poincaré and Bohr, the newer ones are the apparently philosophy immune successors of the brash young experimentalist Rutherford'. Modern scientists, Holton goes on, see their 'chief duty to be not the production of a flawlessly carved block—one more in the construction of the final Temple of Science. Rather, it is more like participating in a building project that has no central planning authority, where no proposal is guaranteed to last very long before being modified or overtaken, and where one's best contribution may be one that furnishes a plausible base and useful material for the next stage of development.' What appears as philosophical naïvete in the scientist 'can in fact be a fruitful mode of operation at the bench', and it is what happens at the bench that is all important.[35]

When I put Holton's views to Richmond—science is 'like participating in a building project that has no central building authority' etc.—he says that this catches the approach in molecular biology perfectly, though in fact the whole scene is much more anarchic and pragmatic—more a matter of 'making do'—than perhaps Holton allows. Richmond says very emphatically ('saving your presence') that most of the stuff that historians of science and philosophers of science talk about apropos the emergence of molecular biology is pretty irrelevant to the practising scientist at the bench. Their views are almost always wide of the mark. He says that he has found only two books in the philosophy of science of any real interest to him: one is Thomas Kuhn's *The Structure of Scientific Revolutions* and the other is Broad and Wade's book on fraud in science (*Betrayers of the Truth*). Richmond says that he got a lot out of reading the latter book in that just as the study of oncogenes can show us a great deal about the normal cell, so also the study of scientific fraud can tell us a lot about good science.

****

I show a draft of this chapter to Anne Pascoe and we meet over afternoon tea to discuss her reactions. 'Most scientists', she says, would claim that the knowledge they gain is objective and impersonal, but they would also agree with you that the means of getting that knowledge is often very subjective and personal. In fact, I don't think I know a single scientist who really believes in the pure, objective view of science. 'It seems obvious to me', Pascoe goes on, 'that ways of doing science are as diverse as the personalities of scientists—that is, very diverse. So the anecdotal nature of what you have written is rather disturbing, since no one scientist's descriptions of how he or she does science is typical or representative. Each of the descriptions given would be hotly contested by other scientists.'

6

Professionalization, Gender, Ethics

A certain kind of anthropology can be written in such abstract terms as interaction, structure, culture, relation, function and so forth, after a manner in which only faint significations are allowed to come from the real world. But it can well be left to the very young, the very old and the very brilliant.

W. E. Stanner, *On the Study of Aboriginal Religion*[1]

Entering science

Scientists seem to drift into a scientific career without much deliberate planning or forethought. Chance and luck appear to play a large part, or so it seems later on. The French anthropologist Lévi-Strauss remarks somewhere that there is probably a reason why this anthropologist chooses such and such a tribe to study, and why that anthropologist chooses some other tribe as 'his' or 'hers'. However, none of the Institute scientists appear to think that they were predestined, either by temperament or innate talents, to take up the life sciences as against the physical sciences, or immunology as against other sections of the life sciences. Cuff, a young medico who is moving into scientific research via a Ph. D., says that in medical practice you get more or less 'immediate gratification' but that in pure science you have to learn to 'postpone gratification' since any rewards are usually a long way down the track. You need then to have that kind of predisposition for science, but that's about as far as it goes. The Director was led into immunology through the good fortune of studying with a charismatic professor at the University of Sydney and later paying a visit to the Institute when Macfarlane Burnet was director. When the Director joined the Institute in 1957, Joshua Lederberg, soon to become one of the US's leading biologists and scientific entrepreneur extraordinaire, happened to be visiting the Institute and the Director became a protégé of his. The Assistant Director, Metcalf, had also got into research science by good luck rather than good management. Most of his medical teachers at the University of Sydney were 'fossilized' and he had learnt nothing from them. His big break had come when he was offered the chance of doing a further year of research in order to gain a B. Med. Sci. During this year he had been strongly influenced by a remarkable lecturer. This teacher had been a prisoner of war of the Russians in the Baltic States and he could not bear to be in enclosed spaces, so he insisted on lecturing with all the doors open! Though he was quite eccentric, he was also an inspiring teacher and Metcalf caught his enthusiasm for pure science.

Scientists come to the Institute both from the medical side and the scientific side. A good deal of criticism is expressed about the inade-quacy of both medical and scientific training at the university level and only one or two Australian university departments in biology are thought to be of any value. Randall says he thinks that a good many potential research scientists are put off by the lousy teaching they get at university and by the old-fashioned 'disciplinary' ap-proach to biology that still prevails.

Could recruitment into research science be made less haphazard? Galway does not think so. Really, it's just like entry into any other profession—law, engineering, the church, or even entering into marriage. As a Ph. D. student you need to be lucky with your supervisor and with your topic; you can easily end in a cul-de-sac and find yourself, after several years' hard work, up the proverbial creek without a paddle. The same is true of training overseas: it's important to have a powerful patron and to be in a place where things are happening. Scientific staff at the Institute are recruited by a kind of grape-vine process. You know that so and so is a bright up-and-coming young scientist and you keep your eye on him or her and check him or her out through friends and colleagues in the network. Young scientists have to make their run between roughly twenty-five, when they finish their Ph. D., and thirty or thirty-two, by which time they will have had experience overseas, have pro-duced a couple of significant papers, and generally become known as 'promising'. The scientist's training is therefore an intense ten or twelve year process of formation: four or five years for a first degree (in science or medicine), two or three years for the Ph. D., then three or four years overseas or other experience. All that time you have to be proving yourself and making good and above all showing that you can attract funding.

Role models and 'heroes'

Role models and 'heroes' are of course important in the formation of scientists just as in the case of other professionals. In an interesting essay entitled 'How Scientists View Their Heroes: Some Remarks on the Mechanism of Myth Construction', Pnina Abir-Am reflects upon the social significance of the memorial volume *Origins of Molecular Biology: A Tribute to Jacques Monod*.[2] She says:

Scientists generally do not like to read what outsiders have to say about science ... When a suitable opportunity arises, scientists prefer to write about their science themselves. The compilation of anniversary or memorial volumes dedicated to publicizing the career of successful scientists offers just such an opportunity. It combines the official noble goal of paying tribute to either influential living colleagues or the notable dead with the less explicit interest of circulating a certified conception of science. The latter interest becomes especially acute when one school's conception of science, and its associated authority and intellectual property rights, is contested by competing schools.[3]

These memorial volumes are used, Abir-Am claims, to propagate certain mythical pictures about scientists and science which 'sustain both the social order within science and the position of science in society at large'.[4] Again, a picture is presented of the ambivalent egalitarian/feudal relationship between the male scientists on one hand and students and women scientists on the other, the latter two groups being among the 'most powerless "peers" in the supposedly egalitarian system of science'.[5] Further, these mythical accounts present the scientist-hero making his discoveries 'as a result of personal genius', while treating as trivial the role of social institutions (like the Pasteur Institute) in directing the creativity of the scientist-genius. Again, the rise of disciplines like molecular biology and of scientific heroes like Monod is presented as being totally independent of the socio-political context, as though the post Second World War science policies of Western societies had nothing to do with them. Finally, memorial volumes like that dedicated to Monod are implicitly attempts to legitimate a certain definition of the prestigious discipline of molecular biology as against other definitions and other contenders.[6]

It would not be difficult to analyse the various memorials to the work of Macfarlane Burnet in much the same way. The Director's Burnet Lecture at the Australian Academy of Science[7], and the special volume of the Institute's *Annual Review, A Tribute to Sir Macfarlane Burnet*, 1978–9[8] are full of these mythical messages.

The ghost of Burnet is still a powerful presence at the Institute in that his example reminds the Institute scientists that small can be beautiful, and successful. Similarly, a small scientific institute in a small country and with modest funding can still produce a major scientific breakthrough and a Nobel Laureate. (Burnet's devotion to simplicity of scientific means and 'small science' is emphasized by a number of his collaborators.)[9]

The present Director is not seen so much as a role model for the budding young scientist in the Institute since, although he has had a distinguished scientific career, he is now seen mainly as a very skilled administrator and entrepreneur. He keeps the various factions in the Institute in a state of relative equilibrium; he brings home the bacon in the form of government and other funding; he keeps the name of the Institute before the international scientific community; he is adept at discerning where the new waves in immunological research are likely to break. He takes the organization and administration of science very seriously and sees himself at the other extreme from what he calls the 'Darwinian' approach to the organization of research (collecting a bunch of bright, competitive individualists and letting them go to it).

On the other hand, the Assistant Director, Metcalf, functions very much as a scientific role model or hero (for some at least) in that he enacts a particular view of science, namely that science is working patiently at the bench and it cannot be done simply by theorizing with your feet up. He is also seen as someone who has resisted the seductions of administration and armchair science. He says, mock-plaintively, that at his age he should be a scientific entrepreneur like others of his contemporaries, but here he is still, experimenting and working at the bench. With a very powerful and no-nonsense personality, the Assistant Director has a great deal of presence. At the ritual displays provided by the Wednesday seminars, his presence can be almost tangibly felt. His own performances on these occasions are masterly, and aptly exemplify his whole approach to research with its strong emphasis upon minute and painstaking work at the bench and its downplaying of theorizing in the abstract. He seems to favour proceeding by a process of negation, 'getting hotter' through the cancelling out of various prima facie solutions. His manner is easy, almost jocular (he usually has a couple of good-humoured digs at colleagues) and he clearly knows all the ins and outs of his topic and manages all the questions put to him in the discussion time with great aplomb. All in all, he puts on a very impressive performance—a display by a tribal elder of his powers and capacities, and an enactment of his own view of science. The neophyte scientists at the Institute could not but be impressed.

Scientific motivation

Why do scientists do science? How do they get their 'kicks' and 'strokes'? Most give the conventional answers: out of pure curiosity, for the joy of discovery, the satisfaction of solving puzzles. Talking to Richmond, I mention the views of a mathematical physicist who says that penetrating the secrets of the universe is rather like solving a puzzle. Sometimes one fits together pieces on a small scale—like a jigsaw puzzle—while trying to imagine what the whole picture will look like when it's completed. Sometimes it's more like a crossword puzzle: you make a guess and build on it—knowing at the same time that you may have to go back and do it again. Richmond says that that's a good description of how he feels about the pleasures of scientific discovery. The metaphor of puzzle-solving on a grand scale, and the 'fun' of that, comes over very strongly in a popular book written by the Director, *Reshaping Life*.[10] The whole biosphere is presented as though it were a series of interlocking jigsaw puzzles set up expressly, so to speak, to challenge the scientist. Inkster speaks feelingly of the early days at the Institute when exciting breakthroughs seem to have occurred every other day. 'It just came away in your hands', he says. Barrow also comes alive when he speaks of the revolution in biology and the 'radical surprises' that are still possible in molecular bilology. Even the palmy days of physics in the 1920s and 1930s were not as revolutionary or as exhilarating. There's really nothing so exciting or rewarding, he says, as that moment in biological research when 'all the stuff is removed and the statue stands revealed'. Talking to Barrow, I refer to Vivian Gornick's book, *Women in Science: Portraits for a World in Transition*.[11] The book is based on interviews with women who have made it in US science. Most of Gornick's subjects have a rather romantic view of scientific discovery. 'I felt I was born for that moment ... Nothing else can touch such an experience for me', says one of her interviewees: 'Let me tell you, there's not an "I love you" in the world that can touch it. Nothing'. Another interviewee reports an experience of scientific revelation: 'It came to me on a Friday night in the shower ... I ran out of the shower dripping wet and immediately put my conclusions on paper ... It was a eureka moment ... It was one of those times you think, Jesus, I've put a tiny piece of the creation in place. I was *flying*'.[12] Barrow listens intently.

'Wow', he says.

Macfarlane Burnet often spoke of scientific research being animated by a spirit of intellectual play. Thus in his farewell speech in 1965 he said:

We can think of research essentially as intellectual play and equate it not with ethics or industry but with organised sport. Anyone who has ever made a significant discovery knows that experimental research is fun. There is the pleasure of skilful manipulation of material things, the pleasure of discussing strategy and tactics of experimental attack over the lunch table, and there is the elation of success ... Science to me is the finest sport in the world. There are aspects that remind one of chess, of billiards, of mountaineering.

Burnet even offers an evolutionistic explanation of the phenomenon of play:

Play is a means by which young animals are trained for the responsibilities and conflicts of adult life. The higher the animal the longer is the period of play and the more keenly it is enjoyed. There is something of Peter Pan in all of us and in good scientists more than most.[13]

There is clearly something in this 'ludic' view of scientific activity (science as motivated by the spirit of spontaneous play), though the thought of Burnet being a Peter Pan rather boggles the imagination!

Curiously, there is very little sceptical questioning of these romantic views of scientific motivation. It is as though a politician were to say that she entered politics solely to bring about the greatest happiness of the greatest number, or as though a lawyer were to say that he entered law so as to secure justice for all. No doubt, at the level of ideals, these declarations have a certain validity, but everyone knows that politicians enter politics and lawyers become lawyers for all kinds of reasons—the desire for power, oedipal grudges, narcissism, self-aggrandizement. We accept that motives are mixed in the other professions; but no one adverts much to the mixed motives of scientists (though, as I remarked before, some of the technicians see the motives of their scientific lords and ladies in a much more cynical light). Burnet's idea, that science is a game involving a certain amount of boyish competitiveness, serves to obscure the fact that science is very often concerned with power and struggles for power.

When I speak about these matters to Alan Becker, a younger Institute scientist, he reacts very strongly. He had entered science, so he says, simply because of avid curiosity about the natural world — a curiosity which had been in him when he was a child. Again, his main motivation derived from the high value he placed on the 'purity' or 'incorruptibility' of science, as compared with the often corrupt and morally suspect practice of such things as politics, law and finance. In science one was moving in a realm of pure dis- interested truth, although of course one's personal conduct in the practice of science might not always be all that pure.

The personal side

What effect does competitive science at an international level have upon the personal lives of scientists? Bella Black worked at the Institute for a couple of years but she left because, as she put it, you have to choose between being a research scientist and a mature human being. Black says that while she was doing her doctorate she became more and more convinced that the life of a research scientist (à la the Institute) was not for her. She had a large number of exter- nal, non-scientific, interests—politics, writing, feminism, etc. —and it wasn't possible to maintain those interests and to be a good scientist. She had the impression that she came to be regarded at the Institute as not being a fully committed scientist because of these wider personal concerns. Ann Collinge is also an ex-Institute Ph. D. student and she claims, with a good deal of passion, that the Institute scientists for the most part tend to be completely myopic, save for interests in music or activities at the hobby level. Most of them, she claims, have very simple-minded views about larger social and political and philosophical issues and their lives are dominated almost completely by their current scientific concerns. Unless their wives are prepared to totally subordinate their own interests to those of their scientist husbands, it is difficult for them to make their marriages work. Collinge gives a number of instances of marriage breakdown among research scientists. She says that I should try to interview the wives and consorts of some of the male scientists at the Institute. That, she says, would be very revealing.

Ann Fowler, another former Institute scientist, paints a rather grim picture of personal impoverishment and immaturity among the Institute scientists as though their scientific careers had inhibited normal personal growth. I ask whether scientists are really different from other professional groups—lawyers, medicos, engineers, aca- demics? She says firmly, yes, it is possible to be a lawyer or an academic and to live a full human life, but it is very difficult to be a top research scientist and to do the same. And it is even more dif- ficult to be a top scientist and a woman. (She refers sarcastically to the regular Friday afternoon gatherings of Institute people in the local pub as being oppressively male in atmosphere.) I read to Fowler part of a recent speech by the Director:

It is unfair to blame science and technology for ills in the human condition that are as old as mankind: for undue aggression, selfishness, greed and a chronic incapacity to live up to one's highest aspirations. It is as illogical to blame science and technology for not slaking our thirst for spirituality and transcendence as it would be to blame literature, art and music for not feeding, clothing and sheltering us. Science can only address part of the phenomenon of man. In my experience, few people realise this more fully than the scientists themselves, who, as a group, are better read and more concerned with humanistic values than many other technical and professional groups.[14]

Fowler makes a face: 'Very interesting', she says.

Although, perhaps, scientists are not, *pace* the Director, 'more concerned with humanistic values' than other professional groups, they are not notably less concerned. Again, the tensions that arise from the attempt to combine a demanding professional career and a personal life are common to most professions that require commitment.

Gender and science

There are half a dozen senior women scientists at the Institute, though not one is a Unit head. At the technician level of course they are almost all women, save for a couple of 'token males'. The glaring disproportion between women and men scientists is recognized and to a certain extent regretted, but it does not excite much comment. Not many are prepared to say that women simply are not up to doing science at international standard, and the difficulties in the way of women trying to break into research science are acknowledged. Given that a young scientist must make his or her run between the ages of twenty-five and thirty-five, there are formidable obstacles for women if they want to marry and have children. A woman must either have a sympathetic and compliant husband or delay having children until her mid-thirties, or both.

Banner, who has an American background, says that the US experience apropos women in science over the last few years has been very discouraging in that while there have been big changes in the teaching of women in science both at the school and college level, these changes haven't been reflected in what is happening at the higher levels. Large numbers of women now do biology at school and college in the US and they represent almost 50 per cent of undergraduate enrolments in biology. But then they drop out of sight at the postdoctoral level. There are, Banner says, obvious difficulties for women in science—the pressure to postpone having children until their thirties, and being unable to cope with the time commitment (at least sixteen hours a day) demanded by research science. He tells the story of a very good woman scientist who was left by herself to look after her child. She came to his Institute and did very good work, but then she met another man and had another child. That meant taking a year out. Theoretically she could return to the scientific fold after that, but it is difficult to move out of and then back into molecular biology since things are changing so fast in that area. Banner confesses that he doesn't know the real cause of women not making it in biology at the highest levels. At times he wonders whether there might be some kind of genetic reason, but of course it can't be that. Should the Institute have a policy of positive discrimination in favour of women so as to encourage them? He has always been against positive discrimination since in his view it is insulting to the recipient and in any case has a negative value in the long run. Certainly, something needs to be done. But what?

The women scientists at the Institute have (like Gornick's inter-viewees) in a sense all made it and to that extent it could be said that they have all accepted, and 'internalized', the prevailing situation of male domination. (Bella Black claims that to be 'successful', women scientists have to adopt 'male attitudes' in their work.) Whatever the reason, the women scientists at the Institute seem remarkably un-worried by the gender imbalance. Told of Evelyn Fox Keller's book depicting Barbara McClintock as an exemplar of 'female science', Mary Fennell expresses polite scepticism. Fennell had actually seen McClintock performing at a conference and had been very im-pressed; but she didn't see McClintock's style of doing science as being specifically 'feminine' — it was just science. Eva Lilley says that she hasn't found it especially difficult making her way as a woman scientist. She had not met any overt male prejudice and she thinks that if you are a good scientist you won't be penalized simply because you are a woman. On the other hand, mediocre scientists were sometimes kept on in research institutes just because they were males. A woman scientist couldn't afford to be mediocre: she wouldn't be tolerated in the same way that mediocre males were. (Lilley thinks that the Institute is in fact rather too tolerant of mediocre people and burnt out cases. In the US they would be sacked quite ruthlessly.) She says that women's attitudes to their career and promotion were perhaps likely to be different from those of men. There were severe pressures on men to climb the promotional ladder regardless of whether they wanted to or not. If she were faced with the opportunity of, say, becoming a director of a research institute, she would think twice about it since it would mean taking on administrative chores, so limiting her research, as well as interfering with her family life. Women, she thought, were more likely than men to make such a choice 'against this kind of ladder climbing': they were not pressured in the same way as men to go to the top regardless of the personal cost.

In the epilogue to her book *Reflections on Gender and Science*, Evelyn Fox Keller charts the development of feminist criticism of the natural sciences. Early criticism had focused on the absence of women in science and the need for political and other means to establish equal opportunity for women to enter scientific careers. The feminist critics then came to question masculine bias in science: since it was almost exclusively a male preserve, the problems that science concerned itself with, the modes of enquiry that were preferred, and the valuation of the 'tough' (physico-chemical) sciences and their methodological approach over the 'soft' (biological) sciences largely reflected male attitudes and pre-occupations. From this position other feminist scholars began to question 'the gender neutrality of the very criteria defining "scientific"', and 'objectivity itself came under suspicion as an androcentric goal'. As a consequence 'some authors concluded that perhaps, after all, science is a masculine project'.[15]

From that position certain feminist thinkers rejected science altogether as a male 'phallocratic' enterprise essentially inimical to female values. Others demanded that an alternative view of science be developed which would reflect genuinely female values. Fox Keller refuses both of these conclusions and argues for a transcendence of any gender bias (male or female) in science so that a higher, non-ideological objectivity becomes possible. It is only within the context of 'gender-free' science that attempts to use science for this or that 'political' purpose (i.e. where one class or gender uses science to exert power over another) can be seen for what they are. Fox Keller therefore sees science *as it is at present* as being 'socially constructed' by the dominant male interests, but she looks forward to a 'gender-free' situation (a little like the 'classless society' in Marxist theory) in which science will no longer be subject to (male-dominated) socio-cultural determination but will be able to flourish as pure science.

The ethical dimension

What part do the moral views of scientists play in their scientific practice—views at the most general level about the human and social value of science (should bio-scientists, for example, be concerned with alleviating Third-World diseases such as malaria?) and at the most particular level about the ethics of a certain kind of experimental approach (for example, the exploitation of recombinant DNA processes, or the use of foetal tissue in research)? Do these moral or ethical views, whether explicit or implicit, condition and shape the way scientists do science?

The traditional view was that pure science was a wholly autonomous realm: it might be *used* by others for good or bad purposes but in itself it is intrinsically valuable and worth pursuing for its own sake. This faith in the intrinsic value of science was coupled with the idea that there was in any case a kind of pre-established harmony between scientific progress in understanding the natural world and human happiness. Just as in Adam Smith's economic theory a 'hidden hand' nicely and conveniently arranges a harmonious coincidence between the individual capitalist's pursuit of gain and profit on one hand and the common good of all on the other hand ('What is good for General Motors is good for the world'), so also there is some kind of pre-established harmony between scientific discovery and the greatest happiness of the greatest number. It may, perhaps, *appear* from time to time that there are conflicts between the advance of science and human welfare, but all such cases, we may be sure, will turn out to be merely apparent and not real. It is therefore unthinkable that a scientist might be faced with a situation where a given piece of scientific research must be stopped on the grounds that it is likely to have anti-human or anti-social effects. Science, therefore, like the free-market economy, is self-regulating and must be left to its own devices without any interference from moralists or the guardians of the common good.

This comfortable faith suffered its first rude shock with the use of science to produce the atom bomb during the Second World War. The flower of Western European physicists, all committed to the ideals of pure science, participated in the Manhattan Project, knowing that the likely effect of their work was the bombing of Hiroshima and Nagasaki and the advent of weapons which could possibly bring about the destruction of the planet. It is of course possible to defend the scientists who produced the atom bomb by invoking the traditional rationale: the scientist's *discovery* of how to use atomic power in a bomb was one thing, the *use* of that discovery by President Harry Truman was another completely different thing for which the scientists of the Manhattan Project cannot be held responsible. Thus, for instance, Jacob Bronowski has argued that 'science has nothing to be ashamed of even in the ruins of Nagasaki. The shame is theirs who appeal to other values than the human imaginative values which science has evolved'.[16] But faced with the atomic physicists' involvement in the creation of the atom bomb and its nuclear progeny, the traditional distinction looks decidedly thin. In fact, as someone has unkindly said, it looks rather like the 'Eichmann defence'. Nuclear scientists cannot really disclaim complete responsibility for the way their scientific discoveries are used: they are human beings like the rest of us and willy nilly they have to make moral and social choices about their science. The practice of science inevitably involves ethics.

It might be argued that we can distinguish between three distinct levels; first, the development of nuclear physics; second, the application of the principles of nuclear physics to making nuclear weapons; and third, the use of those nuclear weapons in a particular situation. In much the same way, we can distinguish between the development of molecular genetics, the application of the principles of molecular genetics to gene manipulation in animals, and the use of gene manipulation in humans. Level one, it might be said, does not involve ethical choices, but the application and use of nuclear physics and molecular genetics clearly do involve such choices. However, as I have said, it is not really possible to make a neat distinction between science and its applications and uses and to completely absolve the scientist of any responsibility for the latter.

Recombinant DNA

In the biological sciences the moment of truth came (almost forty years after the atomic physicists' crisis of faith) with the discovery of the recombinant DNA technique which allowed the fabrication or engineering of new organisms never before found in nature. The possibility of hazards arising from 'genetic engineering' was recognized in the early 1970s: for example, what would happen if a new organism carrying genes from a cancer-causing virus were to escape from the laboratory and cause a cancer epidemic? Subsequently, in 1973 a committee of the US Academy of Science was set up, under the chairmanship of Paul Berg, to examine these potential hazards of genetic engineering. The Berg Committee called for a voluntary moratorium on potentially dangerous recombinant DNA experiments and for the setting up of a monitoring committee. In 1975, at the Asilomar Conference, these issues were debated by biologists from around the world, the result being a lifting of the voluntary moratorium and the establishment of a set of guidelines for experimentation in this field.

The Asilomar Conference is often presented by biologists as evidence of their willingness to face up to the ethical and social implications of their work and of their general sense of responsibility. However, while it may   be acknowledged that the 1974 voluntary moratorium and the Asilomar debate were notable events (all the more notable for being so rare in science), the ethical and social issues were not really faced at the time. As Charles Weiner has put it:

From the start, throughout the February 1975 Asilomar Conference, and during subsequent efforts to develop guidelines the issue was defined by the scientists as a limited problem that the scientific community could solve by technical means. Possible abuse or misuse of the research was mentioned occasionally, but it was excluded from major consideration, as were its social implications. The discussions focussed on whether there was any danger in the research and, if so, how the danger could be avoided while the research continued.[17]

In 1976 the Cambridge (Massachusetts) City Council investigated the potential dangers for the local community of recombinant DNA research being done at Harvard University and MIT. After a spirited debate, the City Council imposed a three month moratorium on genetic engineering experiments and then established a local Review Board to monitor safety regulations in this area. Since that time, however, despite some spasmodic controversy in the US, England and Australia, the concern over the effects of genetic engineering has largely died down. It is now taken for granted by most scientists in the field that the early fears about the dangers of recombinant DNA have proved groundless and that self-regulation has been effective. There has also been some criticism of those biologists who acted as 'whistle blowers' in the early history of genetic engineering, and some of those same biologists have now publicly recanted their earlier qualms of conscience.

The Hall Institute became involved in the recombinant DNA debate in 1978, some three years after the Asilomar Conference, through an enquiry set up by the University of Melbourne Assembly (an elected body of university staff, students, and others to oversee university issues). The Melbourne enquiry was inspired by the Cambridge City Council investigation and it looked closely at the University of Melbourne's scientific faculties and affiliated bodies like the Institute, which were engaged in recombinant DNA research. The enquiry recommended a moratorium on recombinant DNA research while a national body was set up to monitor and regulate research in this area. However, its findings were largely ignored both by the Australian scientific community and the governmental powers that be, though sometime later a national review body was set up to keep an eye on recombinant DNA research.

The Director of the Hall Institute has subsequently written a good deal about this whole debate and his views reflect the consensus of his scientists. Thus, he writes that

the experience of literally thousands of laboratories now engaged in recombinant DNA research has proved that the technology as such is entirely safe, and not a single health incident has been reported since the moratorium was lifted. Of course, the spectre of someone using the technology for evil purposes, such as germ warfare, cannot be discounted. All one can say is that no evidence of this type of research has surfaced. With the benefit of hindsight, it is now possible to state that none of the conjectural hazards have materialised, and that the initial guidelines were unnecessarily stringent.[18]

The Director believes optimistically that molecular biologists should be left free to regulate and control themselves:

Rather than legislation, I prefer the soft-edged, polyvalent methods of a free and decent society. I believe in a fundamental residue of idealism within the biomedical research community. I believe the threshold of consciousness of risks has been raised to the extent that most silly things will be stopped before they happen. I believe both scientists and the regulators have gained much from nearly a decade's intensive debate. I believe the fundamental challenge now is not to control but to promote recombinant DNA research.[19]

Within the Institute the issues of the 1970s are, then, as dead as a dodo. Allen speaks a little resentfully about his work on recombinant DNA being held up during the Assembly debate and he complains that the scientific community in Australia was unnecessarily conservative. The Institute had to install a laboratory with a much higher safety level than was really needed. This, he complains, was expensive and it took up valuable time and then it became a total white elephant. Allen estimates that his group was held up for almost nine months—a lot of time when you considered what some of their rivals did in that period. He clearly thinks that the whole recombinant DNA debate was much ado about nothing. Broadmoor, who was in the US during the Asilomar debate, was exercised by the challenge to his 'liberal values'. He had thought at the time that scientists should be socially responsible (he had been very critical of those scientists who had 'sold their souls' to the government during the Vietnam War). But at the same time he didn't see how you could possibly stop the development of areas of scientific enquiry like recombinant DNA research. All that you could do was to try and foresee as well as you could what the consequences of a given line of research might be and then attempt to make the public aware of those consequences and to promote public discussion about them. But you can't really stop scientific enquiry like recombinant DNA research: to do that was just Luddism motivated by irrational fears about the future.

Crotty, a Ph. D. student in the Institute, says that he is completely ignorant of the whole genetic engineering controversy. It's just so much 'old history' to him, and he says that the scientist has to live in the present. Crotty considers the regulations applying to the containment laboratories to be rather like the instructions pinned up near photocopiers. He works in these areas of the Institute regularly, but he has not really bothered to read the regulations and he hasn't even been told about them by anyone. In contrast, he has had to attend lectures on the safe use of isotopes in experiments.

While, then, the controversies of the 1970s provoked the Institute scientists to think momentarily about the moral and social implications of what they were doing, that time of painful soul-searching has now passed and the scientists have largely returned with relief to the traditional view that science as such need not concern itself with moral and social issues. The focus of attention has moved for the moment to the implications of reproductive technology. Perhaps when genetic manipulation of humans becomes possible on a large scale in the future, further moral questions will then arise—but for the moment, God is in his heaven and all is well with the world of biological science.

Immunology for the Third World

The Institute treads (or claims to tread) a middle way between a commitment to pure science and, on the other hand, a commitment to medically useful science. Thus, while in many respects the Institute scientists are devoted to pure scientific research without much thought being given to medically useful results, there is a good deal of talk about the Institute's concern with diseases such as cancer, diabetes, and malaria.

At the opening of the new building of the Institute, the Director promised the politicians present that the Institute would come up with answers to cancer, diabetes and malaria, as though the *raison d'être* of the Institute were a utilitarian or 'applied' one. But in fact the Institute's primary concern is really with pure science: if some medical benefit (a malaria vaccine, for example) should come out of its research, then that is a bonus. On the other hand, the Director himself has had a long-standing interest in 'immunology for the Third World'. In the 1970s he was associated with the Great Neglected Diseases program (sponsored by the Rockefeller Foundation), which was devoted 'to bringing the power of the finest scientific institutions of the world to the development of new and better tools (vaccines, drugs) and methods of control ... for the vast scourges of mankind such as malaria, schistosomiasis and diarrheal diseases'.[20]

In fact, the founding of the immunoparasitology laboratory at the Institute and the beginnings of the quest for a malaria vaccine resulted from a happy conjunction between the Director's sympathy with the Third-World interests of WHO and the Rockefeller Foundation, and the return to the Institute of one of its brightest young stars, Graham Mitchell. Within the immunoparasitology group itself, however, motives of pure science predominate and one hears little about alleviating 'the vast scourges of mankind'. White, who is a member of the malaria group, says: 'For me personally, seeing people suffering from malaria in the field is a very powerful motivation, but for most scientists this isn't a major thing at all. They are primarily interested in mechanisms and isolates: how parasites change coats *in vitro*. That's what hooks molecular biologists'. Although the group has satellite stations in Papua New Guinea and the Philippines, and visits are paid from time to time to these stations, not much notice is taken of the social conditions of the people among whom the scientists work. On schistosomiasis, after a seminar given by Marvell about a field trip to an area of the Philippines where schisto is rife, Allen says cynically to me that the disease could be wiped out by putting in concrete drains and channels in the village: 'but it's a very interesting immuno-parasitological problem and that's why they keep working at it'.

Foetal tissue

One issue which has raised ethical questions is the use of foetal tissue in diabetes research conducted by Tom Mandel. Diabetes is a major disease (there are some 10 000 sufferers in Melbourne) and it has, despite the advent of insulin, drastic human effects. Many people have come to believe that the discovery of insulin has meant that diabetes can be 'cured' and they are therefore upset when they find that there are major complications such as renal failure and blindness. (The latter is especially devastating since it means that diabetics can no longer effectively carry out tests, injections etc., for themselves.) Diabetics fall into three groups: a majority who cope successfully with the disease; a small proportion who become compulsive-obsessive about their disease and end up as psychological wrecks; and a few who give up completely. Apart from the human suffering and psychological damage done by diabetes, it costs the community a fearful amount in lost human resources, medical care, and provision.

Mandel's work involves the transplantation of insulin-producing tissue obtained from foetuses, the idea being that this may provide a means of treatment, and perhaps cure, of diabetes. The use of human foetal tissue has provoked criticism from a number of quarters, including the local Right to Life group and some Catholics. Some have even said, rather offensively, that it is reminiscent of the experiments done on human subjects by Nazi scientists like Mengele. Mandel says that there is absolutely no question of using tissue from living foetuses. Given that abortion is legal, it seems to him that the use of aborted foetuses, under certain strictly defined conditions, must also be legal. With spontaneously aborted foetuses the issue is even clearer, since they are really in the same position as cadavers, and since experimentation upon cadavers is licit, so also with spontaneously aborted foetuses.

What of the fears of some people that the IVF technique may be used in the future to produce foetuses for tissue transplants—a 'foetal tissue bank'. Mandel reacts strongly to this, saying that these fears are completely unrealistic since it is not possible by IVF techniques to produce foetuses of over eight weeks—the time when the pancreas begins its development. I remark that a well-known IVF researcher sees no difficulty in principle in extending the period of *in vitro* development. Mandel replies: 'Many clinicians who talk about "foetus farming" really have no idea of the complexity in getting growth, *in vitro,* of tissue beyond a certain small stage. No one has been able to get even a mouse foetus to the stage of development where a pancreas could be identified.' Further, he says, it would be illegal (as the law is at present) to use IVF foetuses (if it were possible to produce them) for transplants. He says that the medical scientist must operate within the bounds of community standards as expressed in the law. But, I say, isn't 'the community' a fiction? It doesn't 'set moral standards': standards are set by the government reacting to pressures from various groups including groups of medical scientists (like the IVF group) and their clients. In any case, 'community standards' as expressed in the law are a pretty fragile basis for ethics since it's easy to think of the community through its laws tolerating all kinds of things which are unethical. Mandel agrees that it is not enough to say, as some medical scientists sometimes do say, 'I will do anything in my research that is allowed by the law'. He says that his own personal ethical principles would not allow him to do certain things and he cites two dramatic cases. One refers to a woman in New York who is a severe diabetic and who had recently become pregnant. She intended to have an abortion. She had heard of his transplantation work and asked him whether he would be prepared to transplant tissue from her aborted foetus into her. (She knew that the chances of success would be markedly increased if tissue were taken from her own foetus.) Mandel refused the woman's request on personal ethical grounds: 'I told her it just wasn't on'.

The second case concerned a woman who had a diabetic child and who asked whether if she conceived another child and then aborted it, Mandel would use the foetal tissue to help the diabetic child. Once again, he refused on personal ethical grounds: 'I just draw the line at anything like that', he said. Mandel says that he can to some extent sympathize with the Right to Lifers and the Catholic Church authorities in fearing that the use of foetal tissue could doubtless be abused. But anything can be abused and we cannot absolutely condemn a certain line of medical research as the Right to Life group and the local Catholic Archbishop want to. Mandel is clearly exercised by the ethical implications of his research, but he justifies his work in terms of (a) its possible practical effects in alleviating a major disease; (b) certain intuitive moral principles (some things are 'just not on'); and (c) 'community standards' as expressed in the laws of society.

In a paper proposing guidelines for the use of foetal tissue Mandel has this to say:

Firstly, there is much evidence that foetal tissue has a place in medical research and possibly in medical treatment. Secondly, strict guidelines have to be laid down to prevent the potential abuses of the use of foetal tissue. Thirdly, the mere quest for knowledge is not sufficient grounds for the use of foetal tissue, and any researcher using foetal tissue must be able to justify the validity of his research to an independent Ethics Committee and must have done sufficient work in other systems to demonstrate unequivocally that foetal tissue is necessary. Fourthly, there must be a total separation between the user of foetal tissue and the practitioners who may have to make a decision regarding termination of a pregnancy. There must be an absolute separation of responsibility so that a conflict of interest does not arise. If foetal tissue is available, and the fate of that tissue would otherwise be its disposal, then it should continue to be made available for valid research and potential therapy.[21]

Fraud in science

In a recent book, *Betrayers of the Truth*, by William Broad and Nicholas Wade[22] the authors say that the conventional view is that

science is a strictly logical process, objectivity is the essence of the scientist's attitude to his work, and scientific claims are rigorously checked by peer scrutiny and the replication of experiments. From this self-verifying system error of all sorts is speedily and inexorably cast out.[23]

Broad and Wade, however, were struck by the number of cases of scientific fraud that have come to light.

At first we examined these episodes of scientific fraud in terms of individual psychology: how could a researcher, committed to discovering the truth, betray the central principle of his profession by publishing false data? We were influenced by the spokesmen for the conventional ideology of science, who invariably stressed the individual nature of the crime. The falsification of data was the product of a deranged mind, they would say: it had been discovered, as was inevitable, by the self-policing mechanisms of science, and there was nothing to worry about.[24]

In actual fact, Broad and Wade argue, fraud is much more widespread and much more structurally based than the conventional view allows.

The Institute scientists mostly adopt the conventional view of scientific fraud, namely that it is rare and pathological. Inkster, for example, says that top research scientists are fiercely competitive and high-achieving people with well-developed egos. In fact it is this, he argues surprisingly, that keeps them honest and prevents them from engaging in fraudulent science. Moore thinks that scientific fraud is bound to be uncovered sooner or later and that you would have to be either mad or stupid to go in for it. On the other hand a lot of erroneous results are published as a result of inadvertence or carelessness. Moore had once been taught a salutary lesson. He had published an article in *Nature* without being able to do all the checks necessary to really clinch the results. Another scientist had subsequently done the checks and shown that he, Moore, was wrong. He now rarely published without checks and double checks. This means that he is slow in publishing his results, but it is better to be sure than sorry. Eves says that there are lots of results that are published that are not exactly fraudulent, they are just rubbish, so much junk. And one sometimes has to spend a good deal of time on this stuff just in case there is something in it.

Richmond, who has read *Betrayers of the Truth*, says that he got a lot out of it, but he thinks that it takes a too moralistic approach to the subject of scientific fraud. Scientists themselves, he says, do not take a high moral line about fraud—though it is a nuisance and can of course have unfortunate political effects. There is a spectrum or continuum where legitimate exaggeration (e.g. drawing a curve on a graph) shades into deliberate exaggeration (everyone knows the scientists who like their results to look good), which shades into more or less tolerated fudging, which in turn shades into fraud proper. You couldn't employ someone guilty of scientific fraud properly so called because you simply wouldn't be able to rely on his results, and because he wouldn't get funds—not because of his moral faults.

Conclusion

What has been called 'the subjective side of science' is a tissue of conditions ranging from temperament to motivation, to socialization and professional identity to gender, to ethical sensitivities, to attitudes to scientific honesty and fraud. These subjective or personal conditions of scientific practice are usually left out of account in discussions of science because of the prevailing myth that science is 'objective' and 'impersonal'. But quite obviously these subjective or personal factors must influence the way in which a scientist does science, though they are no doubt to some extent idiosyncratic and it is difficult to make generalizations about them. (Thus, in my view, one cannot really say, for example, that there is a distinct scientific temperament, nor that there are discernibly 'male' and 'female' ways of doing science.)

Science is, after all, done by flesh and blood human beings and not by bloodless and impersonal instruments, and awareness of the personal side of science must surely be helpful, even if it merely reminds scientists of the fact that they are human beings. And yet, strangely, most scientists at the Institute tend to view the subjective side of science as being of trivial importance—'a lot of gossip' as one of them puts it, or *'Time* magazine human-interest stories' according to another.

****

I have to remember to apply to myself the same kinds of questions I am addressing to the scientists—to catch myself in the anthropological act, so to speak. The anthropologist is not just a participant observer but also an observer of herself participantly observing. What part have 'subjective' factors had in shaping my outlook; what roles have my socio-economic and educational background and my gender had in directing my social scientific interests; in what way have I been socialized by my professional formation? If science cannot be understood outside the complex network of social and other relationships and conditions that constitute its context, the same is true of my attempt here to construct an anthropological account of a group of scientists engaged in constructing an area of scientific knowledge.

****

I have the opportunity of spending some time at the Science, Technology and Society Program at MIT in Cambridge, Massachusetts, which is a large and prestigious science-observing institution. While I am there I am able to meet a number of the sociologists and anthropologists of science whose work I have been reading and I find myself observing the observers. Pnina Abir-Am is visiting Harvard nearby and I spend some time talking to her. She seems to oscillate between Israel, the US, Canada and England and she knows everyone who is anyone in the sociology of science field. She has written a great deal on how the new discipline of molecular biology managed to legitimate itself and she has a rather cynical view of the surreptitious 'politics' of science and scientists. She is not impressed by much of the writing on 'laboratory studies' and hopes that I can do better with my project. We travel out by train (the Boston T) to Boston University to see Robert Cohen, one of the main entrepreneurs in the history and philosophy of science area. Cohen receives us courteously but it is clear that he is not much interested in the sociology of science and that he thinks it rather marginal. Later I meet Sharon Traweek at MIT. Traweek has been studying her high-energy physicists for over ten years in an effort to understand their values and 'common sense' view of the world, and how that perspective shapes their everyday practices.

A young English scholar, Andrew Pickering, is also at MIT and I have several long conversations with him. He has written a good deal on the problems of 'big science', particularly with respect to high-energy physics. In the 1960s it was possible for small groups of physicists to engage in high-energy research. In 1983 two groups totalling 200 physicists were required to discover the electroweak intermediate vector bosons. In the 1960s an experiment could be mounted and data analysed within a period of months: today, experiments can span more than a decade. Relative costs of high-energy physics equipment (accelerators, detectors etc.) show the same tendency towards gigantism.

Pickering has been concerned to look at the sociological problems introduced by what is called 'Berkeleitis' (since big science began at Berkeley after the Second World War) particularly with respect to (i) the frustration of individual initiative and creativity within large collaborative enterprises, and (ii) the consequent tendency to conservatism and orthodoxy in communal practice (due to centralization of research resources and the proliferation of committees to control access to experimental beams and to funds). The experimenter who does not propose to tackle an established problem with established techniques is likely to find his proposal rejected. As the Nobel Laureate Luis Alvarez has put it: 'Our present scheduling procedures almost guarantee that nothing unexpected can be found'.

Freeman Dyson has argued that opportunities should be made available for 'heterodox' research both at the theoretical and practical levels. He argues that funding agencies should allot 10-25 per cent of their resources to such research. In this way, he suggests, the slide into the evils of gigantism may be checked even though big science or Berkeleitis is intrinsic to the technical and institutional structure of experimental high-energy physics. Pickering suggests that his findings regarding high-energy physics might serve as a valuable contrast with what is happening in the biological sciences (where, for example, you don't have Berkeleitis to the same degree and where there is not the same sharp division between theorists and experimentalists).

The great Thomas S. Kuhn is a professor at MIT and I arrange to meet him. He is a very charming man and he takes me to lunch. Although his work was one of the sources of the sociology of science movement he himself seems to have little interest in the latter and he does not appear to have read much of the recent work in the field. I am a little disappointed but we have an excellent lunch and a vigorous discussion and, after all, it is not every day that one is able to meet with and talk to such a scholarly monument!

Though I get an enormous amount of stimulation from my time at MIT, my general impressions are, in a sense, rather negative. I find, for example, that the general laboratory studies/sociology of science movement in the US is a much less coherent and well-established 'movement' than I had imagined. As someone said to me: 'The movement is not just in a state of anarchy, it comprises several states of anarchy'. Sociology/anthropology of science is still regarded as being pretty peripheral by the mainstream history and philosophy of science people as well as by mainstream sociologists and orthodox anthropologists. There is also a good deal of confusion about the appropriate theoretical framework for laboratory studies.

On my way back to Australia I go through Paris, and I arrange a meeting with Bruno Latour, the co-author of *Laboratory Life*. I meet Latour at the Ecole des Mines which is close to the Luxembourg Gardens in the Boulevard St Michel, Paris. He has high praise for the Science, Technology and Society Program at MIT (he had been a visitor there in 1983) and says that there is nothing even remotely like it in France. In France, History and Philosophy of Science has never been a major enterprise (*pace* Bachelard and Canguilhem) and the sociology of scientific knowledge has been an even more marginal field of study. He says that, apart from Michel Callon (who works with him at the Ecole des Mines), there are very few sociologists, and even fewer anthropologists, interested in the social construction of scientific knowledge. He gives the impression that he is hoeing a solitary row and sees himself as peripheral to orthodox sociology/anthropology. He remarks, rather ruefully, that his last book, *Les Microbes* (on Pasteur's scientific 'politics' or what Latour calls 'the Pasteurisation of science'), had not sold very well in France and had received very few notices. (I can vouch for this in that when I went to a bookseller in Paris to buy the book, they seemed not to know of it and had to send out hurriedly for a copy.)

He also remarks upon the vogueishness of much recent work in the sociology of science, and upon the fearsome amounts of time needed to do even the simplest 'laboratory study'. It had taken him some two years to do his slim study (*Laboratory Life*) on the Salk Institute, and Knorr-Cetina's study had also taken two years, while Gilbert and Mulkay had taken three years just to collect their 'data' for *Opening Pandora's Box*. So much labour for (relatively) so slight (and sometimes trite) a result.

Latour says that in France the science lobby is very powerful and has lots of influence on the government through the 'Grandes Ecoles' old boys network. Several members of the government came from this background, and the 'modernization' program of the government also favours science and technology. Because the French scientific establishment was so powerful, it was very unsympathetic to and uninterested in any kind of critical overview. Latour says that he thinks it might be better if French scientists had to beg a little for their funding from the government. For example, in England scientists are kept in their proper place. Perhaps that is why there is in England so much critical thinking, at all levels, about science!

Latour gives me a copy of a recent paper of his entitled 'Visualisation and Cognition: Thinking with Eyes and Hands'.[25] It is interesting as background to *Laboratory Life* in that it attempts to provide a justification for the idea of 'inscription devices' which played such a large role in the earlier work. Latour said that a number of his colleagues and students had found the idea of 'inscription devices' hard to grasp and he had set out to try to convince them that this was the key to understanding what science was all about.

We should begin, he suggests, by looking at quite mundane, apparently trivial, facts about the way 'in which groups of people argue with one another using paper, signs, prints and diagrams'. During his 'field-work' at the Salk Laboratory, Latour says,

I was struck ... by the way in which many aspects of laboratory practice could be ordered by looking not at the scientists' brains (I was forbidden access!), at the cognitive structures (nothing special), at the paradigms (the same for thirty years), but at the transformation of rats and chemicals into paper. The literature, and the way in which anything and everything was transformed into inscriptions was not my bias, as I first thought, but was what the laboratory was made for ... All these inscriptions, as I called them, were combinable, superimposable and could, with only minimum cleaning up, be integrated as figures in the text of the articles people were writing.[26]

Latour says that it is obvious that we need an anthropological study of science and scientists; however, the older 'sociology of science' has, unfortunately, given a bad name to the enterprise. First, American 'sociology of science', derived from Merton's *The Sociol-*

ogy of Science (1973), ignored the *content* of scientific knowledge and concentrated upon the social context of science and scientists with particular reference to rewards, citations, competition, and budgets; second, the English Marxists did consider the content of scientific knowledge but were interested only in large-scale contents and large-scale social factors (classes, the military-industrial complex etc.), neglecting the detail of scientific activity and of scientific discoveries which alone enable us to see at first-hand how scientific 'facts' are fabricated.

We have, he says, to leave aside these earlier approaches and look instead at the fine detail of scientific research and discovery. This kind of enquiry is quite properly called 'anthropology', although many anthropologists resist the idea. They are so fixated on strange and exotic forms of life and their knowledge systems that they do not see how strange and exotic *our own* forms of knowledge (including science) are.

Although, in a sense, Latour confirms the marginal status of the discipline I am professing (we have been much less successful in legitimating and respectabilizing ourselves than the molecular biologists!) his enthusiasm and vision give me new heart.

I return to Australia, and the Institute, slightly sadder and wiser, but also with revitalized spirit and hope.

PART THREE

THE MODE OF SCIENTIFIC PRODUCTION

7

Generating Data

Every anthropologist is confronted by this difference between us and them; it is omnipresent in his practice. Let us suppose he has become familiar with the culture he studies. Then his problem will be, as Evans-Pritchard used to say, 'translating' that culture into the language of our culture and of anthropology which is a part of it. I might add that the operation is even more complex than translation ... Among other things, our most general rubrics, such as ethics, politics, economics, are not easily applied to other societies: they can be resorted to only warily and temporarily. In the last analysis, in order to truly understand we must be able on occasion to ignore this partitioning and to search, in the whole field, for what corresponds on their side to what we acknowledge, and for what corresponds on our side to what they acknowledge. In other words, we must strive to construct on both sides comparable facts.

Louis Dumont, *Essays on Individualism: Modern Ideology in Anthropological Perspective*[1]

Data and data-generation

What impresses me more and more about a good deal of science at the Institute is the concentration on 'getting data'. Everything seems to be subordinated to the production or generation of data—putting the appropriate experimental apparatus in place and ensuring that it 'works'; coping with the raw materials (mice, rats, gels, blood sera); having people on hand with the right skills and techniques; establishing social networks among the scientists. Of course theories have their role, but it is mostly a secondary role. One of the young overseas Ph.D. students finds this obsession with data generation difficult to cope with. He had been used to a deliberately planned approach to a research problem—reading himself into the literature and thinking at some length about it before settling down to care-

The physiological laboratory in the first building of the Hall Institute in the 1920s

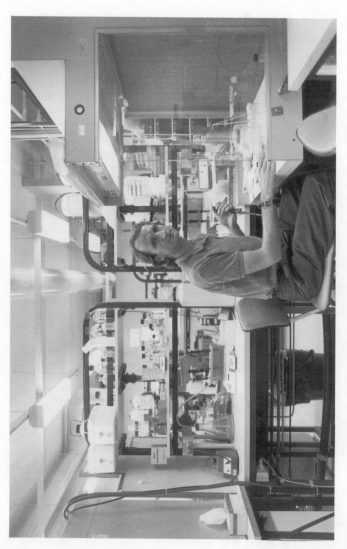

Dr Roland Scollay in his laboratory in the new Hall Institute, 1989

fully thought-out experimental work at the laboratory bench. But when he arrived at the Institute, Marvell insisted that he plunge in straight away to get some data by doing experiments. 'I relate best to data', Marvell says, 'Nothing speaks like data', although of course he admits that you have to analyse and think about the data.

The Assistant Director puts the same kind of emphasis on the generation of data. For him science is basically doing ('looking down a microscope eight hours a day'), and thinking and reflection come after doing. He points to one of his experiments on leukaemic cells. The results of the experiment were not at all what he had expected and this started him off on a completely new track. In hindsight it wasn't a 'failed experiment' but an experiment which 'opened up all sorts of new possibilities waiting to be grasped'. Very few scientists at the Institute spend long hours in the library reading. Visits are brief, to read or photocopy an article or to check through the most recent journals. Bound backruns of periodicals occupy most of the space. There are very few general scientific books, and most of these are for use by the trainee technicians. The only long-term inhabitants of the library are the Ph.D. students writing up their theses.

I call this complex set of interactive factors—apparatus and instruments, raw materials, skills, techniques, theories and social networks—a 'data-generation system', and in my view it is the setting up and maintenance of such systems that is the primary task of the experimental scientist.[2] I suppose a Marxist would say that the idea of a data-generation system focuses upon the 'material conditions' of science and the 'labour' involved in its production.[3] But, however you describe it, this idea of data generation seems to me to be a crucial feature of science and one that is often overlooked. On this view, the laboratory is the place where data are generated and science is 'produced' or 'manufactured'. It is also the place where, as Bruno Latour points out, phenomena are turned into 'inscriptions' on paper in the form of tables, graphs, formulae etc.

The small and invisible are made large, the large and unencompassable are made small. The fast are made slow and the slow are speeded up. Everything from the largest galaxy to the smallest particle is processed in the laboratory so that it can be captured on paper. Unlike the scientific phenomena themselves, the paper representations or 'inscriptions' can be 'read', superimposed, synthesised, integrated and transmitted. Above all they can be *manipulated*.[4]

Latour claims that any laboratory observer will be struck by the extraordinary obsession of scientists with papers, prints, diagrams, archives, abstracts and curves on graph paper. No matter what they talk about, they start talking with some degree of confidence and being believed by colleagues, only once they point at simple geometrised two-dimensional shapes ... Bleeding and screaming rats are quickly dispatched. What is extracted from them is a tiny set of figures ... Nothing can be said about the rats, but lots can be said about the figures.[5]

This, of course, goes counter to a favoured view by philosophers of science that scientific research is theory-driven in the sense that the theory dictates which experiments should be done and helps to interpret the data that are discovered by experiment. But, while the great general theories—the theory of evolution, genetic explanations of heredity—are taken for granted, the scientists at the Institute see theory as playing a secondary role. Bullock, for example, says that immunology is a 'soft' and 'very forgiving' branch of science. By that he means that the generally accepted high-level or macro-scopic theoretical framework—Macfarlane Burnett's clonal selection theory—does not impose very rigorous constraints on day-to-day low-level or micro-theorizing about T cells or how the malaria parasite tricks the human immune system. Or, put in another way, the clonal selection theory does not of itself help in formulating experimental strategies. Kline says:

You see, it's mainly because the systems themselves are so messy, and the data are open to so many interpretations, that people's belief that there is a true state of affairs—about the invasion of the red blood cells by the malaria parasite, for example—is so waffly that it is not very helpful. You simply can't use them for experimental strategies ... Theory has been surprisingly small in the role it has played. In fact molecular biology turned our project a bit on its head. We had a very rational strategy when we first started. We started off with getting the biology going, and then the immuno-chemistry, so that we could identify some antigens which would be important and then clone them. Then RESA got plucked out of the blue—a clone picked at random because it just happened to make a large fused polypeptide which would be easy to work with. It was an antigen that has never been previously described and that we weren't expecting to find. Something on the surface of an [immature] ring stage [of the malaria parasite] that had never been noticed before, turns out to be a very useful vaccine candidate. So in fact theory all followed behind.

Thus it seems that the immunoparasitologists could, with some degree of rational expectation, set out to produce a vaccine for malaria, without any fully articulated theory to guide them. On one hand there is sufficient high-level or macro-theory about recombinant DNA and protein structure to enable the isolation of given molecules, and sufficient low-level or micro-theory about antibody response to specify the broad class of potentially significant proteins. However, both the macro- and the micro- theories have unresolved difficulties and there is only the most tenuous of links between them. Nevertheless what I have called the data-generation system at work here provides for the production of useable data, the RESA molecule. The so-called RESA molecule also underlines another important point. Allen, a member of the malaria team, describes the presentation of results about the same molecule by their Swedish rivals in 1983.

What was presented at the Kyoto International Immunology meeting in 1983 by the Stockholm group was fluorescence on ring stages, the identification of an antigen on ring stages. They were looking for ways of making infected red cells the targets of antibody-dependent cytotoxicity. Then they were throwing in human sera and monitoring the system by doing immunofluorescence. They found, when they glutoaldahyde fixed, that they got this fluorescence on ring stages. No one had previously identified or even thought that there was an antigen in the membrane of cells infected with ring stages ... Meanwhile we'd cloned them and found the same thing.

What makes this interesting is that neither group had any reason to expect a RESA type antigen to exist and they came across it 'by accident' using different techniques. There is, of course, much rivalry between the teams as to who discovered it first and what it should be called, but what is important is that it was produced by two independent research groups, with roughly similar data-generation systems. The occurrence of the RESA molecule within two at least partially independent research networks can be seen as a consequence of the material character of its production.

Technique-driven research

The dominant role of instrumentation, technique and materials, in contrast with theory, in the work of the malaria group is brought out by Craddock who describes malaria research as 'hand to mouth' science:

If you think about, say, the pulse field work ... it was really a matter of 'here's a new machine, now let's play around with it and see what it does'. There has been a lot of tinkering and playing, and out of it has come some useful results. But the grand overarching theory, even as far as the rational planning of experiments for malariology goes, just hasn't been helpful in the work we've done. For example, we'd very much like to clone the cytoadherence molecule. So you start out with a rational set of strategies to maximize the chance of finding a clone pattern for the molecule, but since we don't know half the things we really need for that, like ready access to parasites growing in monkeys, we just attempt by trial and error to find them. So even when you have got the plan and theory and strategy, you may not be able to put it into place. There's been a very simple sort of reasoning going on. We have just simply done experiments, something has popped out and then it's been very obvious what the next step has been. There haven't been any great subtle insights or much of that sort going on.

Thus much of the data produced by the malaria research group at the Institute is dependent on the instrumentation they happen to have. Though a great deal of the apparatus used in the Institute is commercially available, significant items are either produced in-house or are given a local modification. The automatic protein sequencer temporarily installed in Melbourne University as a joint facility for the Institute and the Melbourne branch of the Ludwig Cancer Institute is a case in point. Its availability has dramatically altered the range of research that can be undertaken by the Fluorescence Activated Cell Sorter; the machine as supplied by the manufacturer has been altered to suit the evolving needs of those who use it.

Such equipment basically analyses by separating and labelling constituent components. Thus, for the experimenter, constitutive and structural questions are brought to the forefront of the agenda, along with the traditional issue of biological function. For a very long time the basic tools of analysis were the microscope and the balance. This restricted the analysis to a certain scale of event. Then, with the development of cell counters, a different and larger range of questions became possible. But these, too, are restricted by local and contingent factors, some deliberate and some accidental. Thus, in another laboratory there is a cell counter to which a microcomputer has been attached, automating the process. But it has been unused for more than a year for the lack of someone who knows how to operate the computer!

A good example of how instrumentation, or the lack of it, governs the style of research is provided by Danby, who planned to spend eight months of 1985 on sabbatical leave at the Basel Institute. Naturally, before leaving, he had given thought to the research he would do there. Much of Danby's work depends on the Fluorescence Activated Cell Sorter (FACS) which sorts individual cells on the basis of the way they scatter laser light. Because, like the Hall Institute, the Basel Institute specializes in immunology, it too had an elaborate FACS. And this was one reason why Danby chose the

Basel Institute for his sabbatical.

So he arrived at Basel with a plan of experiments which required the FACS—only to discover that a major fire had just taken place there and the FACS had been burned out. The generosity of the Basel Institute's patron, the giant Swiss pharmaceutical multi-national Hoffman-La Roche, meant that all the damage would event-ually be rectified. But for all of his sabbatical Danby was deprived of an instrument crucial to the pursuit of his main interests. Never-theless, he set to on another research project.

Not being able to do what I'd planned, I just followed my curiosity, as it was at that particular time, to answer a particular question about migration of cells into the thymus. Several other laboratories' work had re-stimulated my interest in an area where I had been doing experiments on and off for five years. At the time, there were several questions that I really wanted to know the answer to. So, despite the fact that I could probably have done the experiments better at the Hall Institute, I went ahead and did them in Basel.

One of the biggest innovations in the area of technique, since the development of *in vitro* culture, has been the use of monoclonal antibodies and radioactive markers. Until recently these were the exclusive skills of molecular biologists, but now they are becoming more common in the Hall Institute. The tool kit of the molecular biologist can be put to use on a wide range of immunological ques-tions. In fact so readily can this be done that molecular biology provides a very powerful data-generation system in itself. As a con-sequence the research agenda of immunology has become ever more technique-driven.[6]

The raw materials of science

An essential (but frequently overlooked by philosophers of science) component of data-generation systems are the basic raw materials. In the case of the malaria work they are principally parasites, human blood sera and monkeys. Research on malaria was heavily circum-scribed until it was possible to culture the parasite in the laboratory. This was not achieved until 1976 when Trager and Jensen cultured *Plasmodium falciparum*, and it has still not been done for other species of malaria parasite.[7] The serum comes from Papua New Guinean malaria patients and gives the Institute a considerable ad-vantage over groups that have to rely on synthetic techniques instead of being able to work on the 'real' thing. Similarly, since there are few suitable animal models, they are heavily dependent on monkeys for testing. However, monkeys are in very short supply and can only be used on a limited basis in the US.

The research agenda of the rest of the Institute is very heavily structured by one specific raw material—mice: some 125 000 of them are sacrificed each year. They are of course very special mice, disease-free and of genetically pure strains. Some pure-bred lines are laboratory artefacts lacking any immune system and have to be produced in an isolated, germ-free facility. The Hall Institute mice contrast with the animals of the Howard Florey Institute, just across the street, which uses sheep and other large domestic species for experiments. The research agendas of these two Institutes are structured so markedly by their reliance on different animals that, despite their common concern with human diseases, there is little interaction between them. Though some experimenters alternate betwixt sheep and mice, the world seems literally to be divided into the sheep and the mice, or sheep-dependent and mice-dependent science.

****

The simple but profound insight that is at the heart of the sociological/anthropological perspective on science is that scientific knowledge does not follow as a matter of necessity from some special conjunction of method, experiment and theory but *could have been other than it is*. Since the whole shape of scientific knowledge in any particular field could have been other than it is, then the fact that it is as it is must be due to other—'subjective' and social or 'cultural'—factors. If 'nature' signifies what is given and what constrains or necessitates, and 'culture' signifies what is humanly made or invented or constructed within the constraints and necessities of 'nature', then science is at least as much 'cultural' as it is 'natural'.

****

Research management

Just as an effective data-generation system is dependent on the local availability of specially tailored raw materials, so too it depends on co-ordinated team research carrying out a multiplicity of experiments. Orthodox accounts of science tend to portray experiments as specific isolatable events, but the complexity of life in a research team at the Institute belies this. In order to develop a malaria vaccine, the Immunoparasitology Unit has had to establish co-ordinated research linking several laboratories. The work of each laboratory, each group within the laboratory, and each individual within a group, is related to the other both deliberately and accidentally. Thus the success, failure or delay in one sub-project advances or retards progress in another. In addition serendipitous results from one group can re-orient both its own and other groups' work.

Such highly co-ordinated large-scale research is still rather uncommon in immunology. In most laboratories, the concurrent projects are not closely related. This co-ordination poses its own problems because projects sometimes pull at cross purposes and the laboratory head must constantly choose which to give priority to. Clear beginnings and ends to research are uncommon. Experimental results are not neatly co-extensive with either the publishing of papers or the ending of grants. Areas of interest normally develop and subside gradually. Over weeks and months, some ideas will peter out or be put on the back burner, some projects will suddenly burst into life with an unexpected advance. Experiments, and stages within them, range dramatically in size, from an hour or two, conception to completion, up to days or weeks. Some can be more easily interrupted and resumed than others.

Especially for the senior scientist who must co-ordinate and consult with technicians, students and postdoctoral fellows, no day is likely to pass with work focused on one project only. And there are always a host of other, non-research commitments which have to be fitted in—writing papers and grant applications; preparing reports on other scientists' papers and grant applications; looking after visiting guests; attending meetings, seminars and major conferences; handling personnel and management issues; and a myriad of other competing demands.

Bigger laboratories often appoint a laboratory manager to co-ordinate the technical support. However, the further scientists advance beyond the postdoctoral level, the more their work consists in doing paper work of one kind or another and managing the various activities of the laboratory. Very little time is actually spent at the bench. The more senior a scientist at the Institute, the more likely that technicians and students in the laboratory will execute the experiments.

I have been emphasizing the concern of scientists with getting the system working, and with getting reliable results. This means that they must be produced in a way in which artefacts can be distinguished from data, and such that the data are persuasive. Their persuasiveness partly lies in the manner of their presentation, in their readability and their transportability—that is, in their ease of assimilation into other texts. But in immunology, where theory has a comparatively weak role, reliability and persuasiveness depend heavily on the judgements of *other scientists* about the care and skill that have been employed.

Ambrose illustrates the importance of personal judgements in adjudicating the 'reliability' of data. He and Bradley had accumulated a large amount of data on a particular topic and decided to propose a model to account for it. As Ambrose admits with some chagrin, 'It must have been my shortest-lived hypothesis, since it lasted all of a week and a half'. He took it to the Basel Institute where close colleagues—and rivals—immediately produced some additional data that effectively demolished his model. Ambrose accepted their data without hesitation even though it made such a mess of his model, because he believed that these particular Basel workers produced reliable results. What makes the story interesting is that the Basel results had already been published by an American group but Ambrose 'simply hadn't believed them'. Some of the Americans' earlier work had turned out to be wrong, so he was inclined to believe the rumours about their unreliability. Indeed, so strong was this belief that he maintained that 'even though they got this one right I still wouldn't accept anything they say'.

Using the image of the laboratory as a place where data are generated or manufactured, it is illuminating to think of a laboratory as consisting of blue-collar workers—technicians (mostly women)—and white collar workers—students, postdoctorals and senior scientists. Students and postdoctorals can be thought of as managerial trainees. Especially in American laboratories, it is they who do the bulk of the routine bench work. At the Hall Institute it is mostly the technicians. Benchwork of course comes in many shapes and forms. There are aspects of benchwork that are now done by sophisticated machines, and here the technicians have virtually no role to play since the scientists themselves feed data into the machines and interpret the results that spill out. Much benchwork involves using standard procedures of a less sophisticated nature, but nevertheless requiring detailed interpretation, some of it subjective. Here the technicians may perform the bulk of the routine tasks while the bench scientist does all the interpreting, the planning of the next day's work, and overall supervision. In general it is the scientists who manage the production of knowledge.

Still, to focus too closely on technical expertise is to miss the forest for the trees. The main skill of the working scientists is not in bench manipulation, but in experimental design, in research strategy and tactics. Again, this must not be seen as a linear skill. Successful scientists are like jugglers who must keep their eyes on all the Indian clubs at once. While strategic decisions involve what kinds of experiment to conduct, tactical decisions turn on who should do what next.

Having a set of data-generation systems in place enables a number of experiments to go on concurrently. These interactive pieces of research require further tactical decisions about which particular elements should be isolated and designated with the title 'experiment' for the purposes of presentation in a journal article. This rhetorical device, 'the experiment', conceals the complex set of interactions between instruments, skills, techniques, raw materials, theory and social networks which together provide for the possibility of experimental data generation.

The products of data-generation systems are then not simply constructs, but are the combined effects of human labour applied to materials through the use of tools and techniques. As we have seen, the kind of science you do is heavily influenced by what equipment you have, what instruments give reliable results, what 'recipes' are in use, what models have been deployed, what materials and reagents are available at a given time, what they cost, what kind of skills and training the available personnel have. The data produced by this labour process are as a consequence materially constrained by reality in the sense that they reflect the conditions of their production.

Do the data reveal truths about reality? All we can say is that given certain kinds of instruments, raw materials and skills, techniques, ways of opportunistic tinkering to get things to work, and social relations between scientists—this is what comes out of the system. In other words, given the data-generation system, this is the kind of data produced. The laboratory is a kind of data factory and the data that are manufactured in the factory bear the mark of the labour process. In my view, this is something that sociologists of 'the laboratory' do not sufficiently emphasize.

Once you see scientific activity in this way, then all kinds of things which are assumed to be unimportant suddenly become important and worthy of notice. Thus, for example, technicians have a notebook with techniques written in at one end, as they are learned, and, starting from the other end, recipes for reagents. They, and scientists, also have notebooks for recording the day's experiments. This is where the experimental protocol—the way in which the experiment is to be done—is recorded. These protocols circulate widely and informally—though they are sometimes typed up as a service. The effect is to turn what is typically an elaborate and complicated set of procedures into a *routine* composed of comprehensible elements. These routines are a necessary part of the tacit knowledge essential to the effective running of the experimental system.

When an experimental system becomes routine, it is possible for the system to be employed for specific purposes rather than simply in the somewhat undirected way of seeing what happens when you deploy it. Thus at one extreme of scientific research a great deal of time may be spent making new methods, techniques or reagents work; at the other extreme the goals are more recognizably those of research—say, to identify the important antigens on the malaria parasite.

Facts and artefacts

The way in which data or 'facts' are distinguished from artefacts is usually glossed over in accounts of scientific work. Trump trained as a physician and then came to the Hall Institute to do a Ph. D. He began work in a laboratory, within the Clinical Research Unit, which studies disorders of the auto-immune system—where the body perversely turns its defences against itself. One example is lupus erythematosus, a chronic inflammatory disease of connective tissue, affecting the skin and various internal organs. Patients frequently have a red rash on the cheeks, long ago likened to the complexion of a wolf (*lupus* is Latin for 'wolf'). A more serious symptom of lupus is arthritis, and there can also be progressive damage from scarring to the kidneys, even the heart, lungs and brain. Treatment involves the use of the steroid drugs, which can have dangerous side-effects.

People who have lupus erythematosus have antibodies to one of their own proteins called Ro circulating in their bloodstream. Trump was faced with his first research problem when he was asked to try and identify the gene which codes for Ro. It was a classical example of a problem susceptible to some basic recombinant DNA (rDNA) techniques which Trump, who had no background in molecular biology, had to learn as he went. There were no molecular biologists in the Clinical Research Unit to teach him, and he had to venture onto other floors and into other Units in search of advice.

Trump began with a human DNA 'library' derived from liver

cells. The 'volumes' in this library consisted of thousands of colonies of bacteria kept frozen in suspended animation. To make the library, a single-stranded DNA copy of the code contained in the chromosomes of the liver cells was constructed. The DNA in chromosomes is double-stranded, and contains a lot of 'rubbish' which does not code for any protein. Only coding sequences are turned into RNA (ribonucleic), so by making cDNA from RNA, only 'useful' coding sequences are looked at.

This compacted genetic code, called complementary DNA (cDNA), had then been broken up and randomly inserted into bacteria in such a way that it was reasonably certain that all the genes that had been expressed in the original liver tissue would now be in several bacteria. These genes would be faithfully reproduced by the bacteria in which they were lodged when they divided. Moreover, the proteins they coded for in the liver cells would now be made (expressed) in the bacterial colonies.

In order to identify the Ro gene Trump had first to search among the bacterial colonies making up the library, looking for a colony which was expressing the Ro protein. To conduct the search, circular filters made of nitro-cellulose had anti-Ro antibodies of the sort found in lupus patients bound to them. They were then laid on top of the colonies growing on dishes in culture medium. The hope was that the anti-Ro antibodies would bind to any Ro protein that was being made by the bacteria.

If any had done so, they would take a photograph of themselves—an autoradiograph. For this to happen, the anti-Ro antibodies had a protein made by the notorious golden Staph. bacteria attached to them which, in turn, had Iodine I^{125} attached to it. Iodine I^{125} is radioactive.

After being carefully lifted off the bacterial colonies, the filters, with the radioactively labelled antibodies to which—perhaps—Ro protein had bound, were then exposed to X-ray film in lead cases kept at $-70°C$ overnight, and then developed.

Any colony expressing Ro protein should then be radioactive, taking a photograph of itself in the form of a black spot on the X-ray film corresponding to its position on the culture dish. All Trump had to do was to systematically screen his DNA library until he found Ro 'lit up' as a dark patch on one of his autoradiographs. Ideally, the conclusive result would simply be a single positive on an otherwise clear file, like that shown in Figure 1A. But this perfect, clear positive is an exhibit drawn from a thesis. Everyday results normally resemble Figure 2, a jumble of dozens, hundreds, even thousands of

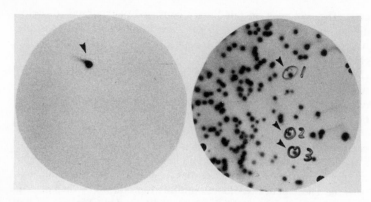

Figure 1A   **Figure 1B**

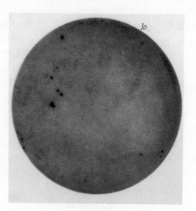

Figure 2

overlapping blotches of various intensities. And they are not all positives—indeed none of them may be a positive.

Trump asked the advice of Varley, an experienced molecular biologist, in interpreting his autoradiographs. From his long experience, Varley was able to swiftly divide the blotches into positives, false positives, and a few doubtful cases. He told Trump to test the colonies he had identified as positive, or possibly positive, by 'lifting' bacteria from them and growing up multiple copies to see if the darkening of the X-ray film could be reproduced (Figure 1B). Life would not be long enough to check every colony which showed some darkening, and all those Varley thought were false positives Trump was to ignore. (Indeed, even lifting only the possible positives was to prove a frustrating experience, none being repeatable.)

Up to a point, Trump could see how Varley made these discriminations. For example, Varley pointed out that dark spots which also exhibited a tail something like a comet's tail were always positives (see Figure 1A). However, focusing on the degrees of darkness, by itself, could be misleading. All experimental techniques sometimes produce data which appear to correspond to a biological event or fact, but which are actually a result of the experimental process itself. These are called artefacts. In the case of autoradiographs, experience had taught Varley that artefactual blotches were typically darker than genuine positives. They might, for example, be caused by spilt Iodine I^{125}. However, the *cause* of artefacts is more often than not very obscure and one could waste a great deal of time trying to eliminate them. Simpler by far to learn what they usually look like, and ignore them.

So much for the simpler examples. But Trump often found Varley's explanations of his judgements hard to follow or to apply himself. He had, in the end, to learn by doing. As Waller says:

With autoradiographs or anything like them, when you first look at them, they all look the same. Later, your eye comes to see small differences. It might make the process quicker to be told what to look for in the data, but I think there comes a point after a lot of experience when it becomes entirely intuitive the way you read the data. You can have it all explained to you in detail, but you cannot actually get into it unless you have a concept of it which is beyond words.

Waller gives a nice pastoral illustration:

When you get to know a flock of sheep well, they all look totally different. And you will have learned just from seeing them regularly. Your eye gradually comes to notice that some of them have ears that are longer than others, and that others have longer noses. All without any formal teaching, just by looking at the same group of sheep every day, you start realizing that there are differences. People can say 'Have you noticed that one's ears are bigger?', and that will distinguish it for you. But, until something in your head experiences that, you don't really see the difference. Exactly the same thing applies to integrating data—any kind of data. Say, a string of numbers coming out of a gamma counter. When you see them first, you have to look very carefully to even figure out which experiment is which. But people who look at them every day can take a sheet of numbers, glance down at them for a second, and know the result of the experiment.

FACS data of the kind used by Andrews are presented as a series of numbers, as a scatter diagram, and as a histogram. Figure 3 is typical. Andrews describes what he sees:

To understand this figure [two colour, two dimensional, immunofluorescence analysis, dot plot], you have to bear in mind three parameters simultaneously. On the left-hand axis, you have two antigens expressed together—but I know that they're expressed differently. So, from other experiments, I know how to interpret these two. On the other axis, you have another antigen—but then I also know from other experiments that each of these are different by yet a third antigen. And I can see all that as a kind of three dimensional picture. In the figure, there are four main groups of cells, including a little one at top/left which you might not even see as distinct. The main thing you'll see is this big blob at the right top/centre and a few other bits and pieces.

In fact if you plot the data together another way [Figure 4], as a contour plot rather than a dot plot, then the other groups—including the one at the top left—become much more obvious. Contour plots are a standard kind of plot that you can get from this sort of data. But I drew it up to emphasize that particular cell population, which you could easily ignore if you hadn't seen, as I have, a lot of similar data.

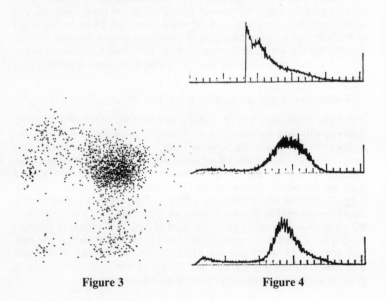

Figure 3   Figure 4

When Andrews has some cell samples for FACS analysis, he is himself present, standing before the glowing green cathode ray tube on which the scatter pattern develops. The crucial interpretive judgements are made there, on the basis of intuitive feel founded on experience. He scorns the crunching of numbers through a formula, saying:

There's no simple formula I can use. If I gave the data to a computer operator to run through a machine, the results wouldn't reflect the true answer. There are many situations where the numbers look straightforward, but are in fact misleading.

Experimental results in biology frequently lack the precise numerical specification that some have thought is the hallmark of science, especially of the physical sciences. Compared with physics, biology is not an especially mathematized science. There was a time—not so very long in the past—when physicists had to train assistants to search photographs for traces of whichever particle they sought. Now the process is largely mechanized. Molecular techniques have been welcomed into biology for the rigour they bring. But though the interpretation of some molecular techniques— notably those involving electrophoresis, the so-called Northern, Southern and Western blots—is quite straightforward and unequivocal, the appraisal of screening autoradiographs is, as we have seen, a hard-won art. And it is not particularly exact. Cell electrophoresis determining the size and position of a gene as a blurry radioactive band, for example, is certainly not 100 per cent accurate.

The scientific paper

Eventually there are enough data 'results', and they answer a sufficiently important question. The time has come to publish a paper in a specialist journal saying so. (You are, as it were, 'marketing' the product manufactured in your laboratory.) Sometimes this is anything but a leisurely decision. During 1982 Jerry Adams and Suzanne Cory became interested in the possibility that human and mouse cancers of the white blood cells were caused by the inappropriate expression of a gene translocated to an abnormal position on a different chromosome during cell division. But it was also a question that interested others, and by the middle of the following year, 1983, the molecular biologists at the Institute knew they were in a race with several other groups. It became urgent to prove experimentally as quickly as possible that a translocation was taking place, establish between which chromosomes genes were being exchanged, and identify which particular gene was responsible for causing the B-cell malignancies.

But finding the answers to these questions was only half the battle. The knowledge claims must be staked out and they must be staked out first. Almost all of the credit goes to the scientist who publishes first. As a result, very fine distinctions of priority are made. At the leading edge of science, races like the one which Cory and Adams were in are not uncommon. And, as a result of this kind of intensely competitive work, everyone is likely to arrive at an answer at about the same time. Consequently weeks, even days, can be crucial.

During December 1982, no fewer than five papers appeared staking out a claim to have discovered two cancers, one in humans and one in mice, both caused by a translocation of the same gene. Unfortunately, none of them were by Adams and Cory. Three groups beat the group at the Institute to the post, linking translocation of a gene called cellular *myc* (c-*myc*) with the human cancer Burkitt's lymphoma. One of those three, together with a fourth group, also established a link between c-*myc* translocation and plasmacytomas in mice. Though most of these groups knew the others were in the race, the group which first published both linkages—and so received most of the credit—was very much a dark horse.

Adams and Cory were desperately unlucky, for before any of these five papers appeared in print, they submitted a paper reporting the role of c-*myc* translocation in both Burkitt's lymphoma and murine plasmacytomas to the prestigious *Proceedings of the National Academy of Sciences* (USA). However, the margins of their typescript were too narrow to meet the requirements of the journal, and publication was delayed until April 1983!

Fortunately, perhaps, writing up and publishing experimental results does not always take place in such fevered circumstances. Barlow's experience is probably more typical:

In general in this lab. we're simply following an intellectual train of thought until we've got enough data. Usually it goes in spurts: you go for six or eight months and then you think, 'I must write some of this up'. So you write two or three papers. Or you reach a point where there's a quantum change in the information, and you write that up. The papers come as the work progresses in the general stream. The work is not divided into paper-sized sections. In addition to this mainstream, which is simply incremental development along several established lines, quite often one comes across tangential or peripheral questions. You say to yourself: 'We must do that experiment some day, and see what the result is'. It'll be either a relatively sharply defined experiment—or one you don't want to develop into a continuing interest. So you might do such an experiment—not consciously to write a paper, but it is a sort of paper-sized experiment. If the results are satisfactory, then you write them up.

The quantity and quality of the data are not the only considerations to be borne in mind either. There are different kinds of scientific papers, suited to different purposes. It might be just one or two paragraphs announcing an isolated but interesting finding or novel twist to an established technique. Another use for shorter papers is claim-staking of important new work where there is a risk of being pipped at the post; so-called 'letters' to the journal *Nature* are often used this way. Even if a standard paper is being prepared, consideration has to be given to which journal to send it to. Here questions of comparative prestige are important, but so is the kind of audience likely to read the journal. Scientific publishing is a highly specialized business, and even the most narrowly technical paper can have several potential destinations.

Some of the considerations involved are illustrated by Bamber. When I asked him why he was writing up a particular piece of work, he replied:

That's work in an area that I've been dabbling in for five years now as a continuing side-stream. It was getting to the point where I thought to myself 'Well, you know, probably you should write some of this up, else there'll be too much to make sense of or I'll get left behind the field'. And there were a number of other developments from other labs which impinged on what I was doing. Suddenly, several groups developed a similar interest and started doing similar experiments. When I began five years ago there was a lull in interest in that area. So there were two factors influencing me. One was that I didn't want my work to get left behind—since there were now many more people doing it and so advancing the field more rapidly. And so I had to publish before someone else did. Secondly, anyway, it was getting too close to being ready to publish. The place it was being aimed at was decided by the fact that we had an invitation from *Immunological Reviews* to do a piece. Those three things came together really.

Review articles are not usually the place to publish new results. They are generally accounts of recent developments in related fields for scientific readers who would not normally keep up with the literature as it is first published. Why then had he chosen *Immunological Reviews*?

Immunological Reviews is a very special journal. It is sort of half way between a review journal and a data paper journal. They want you to review your data, and not give a broad review. The papers can be a bit longer than a normal paper, you have more data—they're not so rigid in their definition of what you do and don't cover. You can be a little more speculative at the beginning or end. The structure is somewhat looser, and can include a large amount of recent data. From my point of view, it is a good place to publish because I have a lot of data over a long time with a lot of intellectual ramifications which would be difficult to squeeze in otherwise. In fact, I had a paper three-quarters written for *Journal of Immunology*, and then this invitation came. And I decided that *Immunological Reviews* would be a better place.

Scientists mostly say that they dislike writing. Betty Fellows says she finds it anticlimatic. Like most of her colleagues, she thinks the interesting work is over by the time of writing up. However, unpleasant chore though it is seen to be, writing up and publishing research is a quite essential skill. Scientists are not usually thought of as writers, but they are—and are frequently very prolific. In the course of a career, a successful and senior scientist will publish a great many papers. The Director had accumulated more than 300 publications by 1984, of which only six were books. The Assistant Director had a comparable corpus of writings. Mitchell's curriculum vitae lists his 'primary research papers' separately, and at the end of 1983, when he was forty-two, there were 138.

The paper is the predominant form in which new scientific knowledge reaches print. In modern science the monograph is almost never the mode in which research is first published. Of course, scientists do write books—but they are usually popular works or textbooks for students at one level or another. The Director has published popular works on medical research and its goals, the immune system, genetic engineering, and vaccine research. He has also written a textbook. Mitchell's lumping together in his curriculum vitae of 'conference proceedings, chapters and reviews', and their careful segregation from 'research papers' shows that, whilst it is successful scientists who are asked to write textbooks and literature reviews, their achievements are not measured in terms of those books and reviews.

As scientists are judged by the quantity and quality of their short, original research papers, so too are their institutions. Each year the number of papers published is one of the statistics considered sufficiently important to be included in the 'Year in Brief' section of the Institute's *Annual Review*. In the twelve months ended June 1984, that number was 170. There were three books and fifty-eight review articles, the remaining 109 (64 per cent) being original research papers.

A typical scientific article is from five to fifteen pages long. Even the most important and famous scientific articles are often very short. For example, Watson and Crick's announcement of their Nobel Prize winning double helical structure for DNA was a 'letter' to *Nature* barely a page long. Yet it is one of the seminal scientific documents of the twentieth century.

Part of the reason for this brevity lies in the fact that scientific articles normally include substantial amounts of compact, non-verbal material—mathematical formulae, tables, charts, autoradiographs, and so on. The scientist usually writes for 'the moderate specialist'—as one journal advises, with considerable understatement. In fact, a great deal is assumed. Consequently, a reader must be familiar with current technical literature in the area. Moreover, research that an academic trained in a non-scientific field would publish as a single article, scientists would more likely break into several. Finally, many scientific journals levy on authors a substantial charge per page published.

A further contrast between scientific and non-scientific writing lies in the typical number of authors per paper. Most articles in the humanities have only a single author, but most papers reporting the results of biomedical research have multiple authorship. A single paper may list as many as half a dozen, or even more, co-authors. For example, in the five years prior to the 1984 Quinquennial Review, Brack had thirty-four publications. Two of them had seven co-authors; he was sole author of only one. The average was four co-authors per paper.

The term 'co-author' should not be taken to imply having a hand in the writing—that is usually done by only one or, at most, two of the co-authors—though most of the others will have seen and commented upon the drafts. Scientists learn to write as they learn to do scientific research—in the course of an apprenticeship in the laboratory as postgraduate students, and as journeymen postdoctoral fellows. Early in this period, novice scientists first participate in the research for and writing-up of an article. To begin with, the papers will be written by more senior co-authors. But the apprentice will gradually play a more active part in the process, eventually writing up the papers which form the core of a Ph. D. dissertation.

The contributions of the co-authors of a paper range from the substantial to the negligible—a scientist may be listed as a co-author simply for providing material or performing a routine assay. Whenever the order of the names of the co-authors at the head of a paper is not alphabetical, it signifies a particular ordering of their relative contributions. A non-scientific reader would probably simply read from left to right, from most to least significant contribution—perhaps the original convention. Scientists, however, expect other scientists to attribute the labour to the first-named co-author, super-intended by the last-named co-author, and with the assistance of those between, in order of left to right. Further, they expect the principal credit for the ideas to be given to an eminent last-named co-author, otherwise shared in some degree with the first-named.

So, somewhat paradoxically, it is frequently the last-named and not the first-named co-author who is the real 'senior' co-author. Of Brack's thirty-four publications between 1979 and 1983, he is first-named co-author of fifteen and last-named co-author of seventeen. Any colleague, knowing him to be a senior worker, would discount as insignificant the last-named co-authors of his first-named co-authored papers. On only two of his papers does he occupy an un-equivocally minor position.

Co-author order is decided in light of, but not necessarily in accord with, these conventional expectations. Thus, some senior scientists at the Institute say that they tended not to attach their names to papers to which they had contributed only in a minor way, so that their reputation would not overshadow their junior colleagues and prevent them from obtaining credit.

Scientists are touchy about their position on the author list. On one occasion the Head of a Unit at the Institute decided to promote one of his colleagues to a first-authorship as a reward for long months of necessary groundwork for the results being reported. But the bright young Ph. D. who had actually done the experiments was outraged. Another ruckus broke out when it was proposed to give a first-authorship to a technician. The question was taken to a Unit Heads' meeting, which decided that technicians could be co-authors, but not first-named co-authors.

The scientific paper is not the main form of scientific communi-cation. In science, information flows down the informal channels of 'invisible colleges'—as Crane calls them. Pre-prints of papers sub-mitted to, but not yet accepted by, journals are distributed by their authors to all those they know who are working in the same field. Maybe more important still are direct personal contacts made at conferences, during visits to other laboratories, by letter or telephone or the 'grapevine'. Postgraduate students and postdoctoral fellows are often sent off to other labs specifically to learn new methods and techniques. More-senior scientists use their sabbatical leave for the same purpose.

In an important sense, a scientific paper is not designed to be *read*. It is designed to be *published*. If a paper is published, then it will be because the editor of the journal concerned has been advised of its acceptability by at least two specialists. The identity of these referees generally remains unknown to the authors of the paper— though they usually see the written comments made on their paper, especially if changes are demanded, as they often are.

So the scientists setting out to write up their results are really writing for these anonymous referees. This is all the more true in the light of an astonishing statistic. Assuming that one may measure how widely a paper is read by how often it is cited in later work, it has been found that the great majority of papers receive only one or even no such citation.

It is the function of referees to certify the validity of the knowledge claims being made. Thus, it is an important scientific skill to present data in a way which will satisfy the referees. And this comes with experience. Yet, the position of the scientist is not entirely without strength. As Asken points out:

The referee doesn't know more about it than the person who did the experiment. Often, what the referee sees is a claim that says these samples were analysed on the FACS, and this percentage was positive. He never sees the raw data, he never sees the plots. So the referee is not in a position to judge, he just has to assume that the author knows how to use the machine. There's nothing more you can do. You can't write back and say 'Show me the detailed FACS plots. Did you watch every sample go through the machine? What's the name of your operator? Which company made your machine?' I'm quite sure that a large proportion—as I say, around 10 per cent—of the results based on FACS analysis that exists in the literature is completely wrong. Maybe, though, for the general conclusion, it doesn't matter whether the cells are 20 per cent or 60 per cent positive. So some errors of interpretation don't matter too much.

****

When one focuses on the material conditions of data generation (and of scientific knowledge), all kinds of things that were taken for granted and never explicitly spoken about in traditional accounts of science, suddenly become important. Marx, of course, showed once and for all that what he called the means of production (the raw materials available, the instruments and technology at hand, ways of working, skills etc.) and the modes of production (the way a production system is organized—for example, in a feudal way or a capitalist way), powerfully condition and shape a society or culture. In the same way, the means and modes of the production of scientific knowledge condition and shape the data and results that are produced.

Marx saw his task as combatting 'Utopianism' (the refusal to admit the role of material factors in human history) and bringing people 'back to earth', and I suppose that what I am trying to do is to counter a 'Utopian' or idealized view of science and to bring it back to earth.

8

The Triumph of Technique: From
Molecular Biology to Biotechnology

*Linear precision ... the sheer clarity of line is a major concern of
Yoruba carvers, as it is of those who assess the carvers' work, and the
vocabulary of linear qualities, which the Yoruba use colloquially and
across a range of concerns far broader than sculpture, is nuanced and
extensive. It is not just their statues, pots and so on that Yoruba incise
with lines: they do the same with their faces. Line, of varying depth,
direction and length, sliced into their cheeks and left to scar over,
serves as a means of lineage identification, personal allure, and status
expression. But there is more to it than this. The Yoruba associate line
with civilisation: 'This country has become civilised', literally means,
in Yoruba, 'This earth has lines upon its face'.*

Clifford Geertz, 'Art as a Cultural System'[1]

Just how much biology has become 'technique driven' and dependent on what Marx would call its 'mode of production', is brought out
very dramatically in the interaction between molecular biology and
the new recombinant DNA technology. At the Hall Institute, that
interaction has been played out in the chequered career of the
Molecular Biology Unit which has been largely created by Cory and
Adams.

I spend a good deal of time with Cory and Adams and, although
they are both rather reticent and, I suspect, a little suspicious of me, I
am able to get some idea of what they are doing and of the dialectical tensions operating in this area.

Molecular biology before biotechnology

The rise of biotechnology has been both recent and swift. The most
basic tools of genetic engineering are the chemical scalpels, restric-

tion endonucleases, which cut DNA at precise locations. The first of these was discovered in 1970 by Hamilton Smith, who received his Nobel Prize in 1978 for this discovery. But genetic engineering was developed well before then. The biotechnologist's tool kit was essentially complete by 1975. In 1970, molecular biology was a discipline not yet twenty years old, but it had achieved a great deal in understanding the molecular basis of inheritance, growth and reproduction. Nevertheless these achievements were theoretical, not practical. Molecular biology had made no contribution to speak of in medicine or agriculture. There were certainly high hopes, but not everyone shared them. As late as 1968 Macfarlane Burnet held that even with all the new knowledge of molecular biology, there was no way even in theory by which it might help to prevent or treat cancer. Yet by 1985 Metcalf and his co-workers in the Cancer Unit at the Institute were using biotechnology to manufacture biochemicals that, so they had established, could suppress leukaemia in mice, the hope being that human leukaemias could be treated in the same way.

The origins and early history of molecular biology at the Institute showed little promise of this rosy future. Only a little that would today be recognized as molecular biology was done in Macfarlane Burnet's Institute. As we have seen, Burnet himself was profoundly suspicious of the complicated and expensive experimental technology involved. Ada's work on the influenza virus was really the only molecular biology done at the Institute before Burnet's retirement in 1965, although Burnet's early studies on viruses paved the way for their molecular dissection later on.

Burnet was not only a scientist of the old school, he was also a physician. His theoretical studies of immunological tolerance and the clonal selection theory of immunology were obviously medical in their orientation, and his experimental work had the same orientation. Many biomedical researchers who have, like Burnet, a clinical background are concerned to find practical justifications for their work. But until well into the 1970s, molecular biology merely offered a distant prospect of this. Moreover, its successes in revealing the molecular structure of genes and the way they code for and direct the construction of the raw materials out of which cells are made, offered another threat to the kind of science that Burnet had done—the threat of reductionism.

Scientists with a reductionist bent argue that all phenomena studied by chemists can really be explained in the terms of physics. Of course, they say, actually to *do* the chemistry in terms of physics would be too complicated to be practical. But it could be done in principle, so the basis of chemistry is really physics. Naturally, this tends to make chemists feel as though they do second-class, not wholly fundamental science. It is clear that Burnet thought that molecular biology was making much the same kind of claim— namely that cellular, bacterial and viral biology could, in principle, be fully understood in physical molecular terms even if it were not yet feasible to do it in practice.

When he succeeded Burnet as Director, Nossal attempted to counter Burnet's pessimistic view of molecular biology, but he did not feel any urgent need to establish the discipline at the Institute. Before I look at how he came finally to do that, I should say something about the nature of the discipline of molecular biology at the end of the 1960s, and what it had achieved. The name 'molecular biology' was coined by Warren Weaver in 1938. Weaver conceived the new discipline as studying all aspects of the structure and function of living things at the molecular level. However, it was not until the 1950s that a distinct discipline emerged out of bio-chemistry, biophysics and genetics: it had a narrower scope than Weaver's grand vision, concentrating on the molecular basis of in-heritance and reproduction. Thereafter, it was hard to distinguish molecular genetics from molecular biology. Nevertheless molecular biology/genetics had a program of research, and an intellectual agenda in the classic mould of a 'pure' scientific discipline.

The achievements of molecular biology

The seminal event was Francis Crick and James Watson's Nobel-Prize-winning double helical model of the structure of DNA, proposed in 1953. Crick and Watson were strongly influenced by the novel methods Linus Pauling had just successfully used to establish the structure of the protein keratin, and by the helical character of the model he advanced. Unlike Pauling, however, they believed that the molecular basis of inheritance lay in nucleic acid, not protein. (Chromosomes were known to be about half protein, half nucleic acid, but most scientists at that time believed that nucleic acids were too simple to act as the genetic code.)[2]

Crick and Waton's model consisted of two helical strands, made of sugar phosphate and twisted together like a double corkscrew. Inside and attached to the helices at right angles were four flat, sheet-like acid bases—Adenine, Guanine, Thymine and Cytosine. The bases were bonded to each other in pairs, thus connecting the two helical strands together like steps in a crazy spiral staircase.

Adenine always paired-up opposite G, T opposite C.

The sequence of base pairs provided a way of storing genetic information. Moreover, the model suggested a molecular mechanism for the duplication of that information, necessary for growth and reproduction. The idea was that the two helices separate, each taking with it one member of each base pair. A new strand and base would be synthesized simultaneously, using the complementary single strand as a template so that, when replication was complete, there would be two identical double-stranded molecules, each having one of the original molecule's two strands.

The program of molecular biology launched in 1953 was the confirmation of Crick and Watson's model of replication. Steady progress was achieved. Although minor modifications of detail were necessary, the double helix model rapidly gained acceptance. As the 1950s wore on, evidence began to accumulate that genetic information was encoded in the order of the base pairs, and that replication was semi-conservative. But DNA needed to be able to do more than store information and pass on copies of it. The information needed to be used to order and regulate the manufacture of living tissue.

It had long ago been suggested that each of the enzymes involved in biochemical reactions (which are proteins) was produced by a single gene. This idea now re-emerged as the one gene, one protein hypothesis. The question was, how do genes make proteins of various kinds? Protein molecules were known to consist of long chains made up of twenty different kinds of amino acids, linked by peptide bonds (thus also known as polypeptides). In 1958 Crick proposed the 'Central Dogma' of molecular biology, which states that DNA codes for protein, and never the reverse. This asserted the modern theory of evolution by natural selection at the molecular level which states that changes to an organism resulting from interaction with its environment could not be inherited.

The period from the end of the 1950s to the middle of the 1960s saw the unravelling of both the genetic code and the problem of how genes make proteins. The other nucleic acid, RNA (ribonucleic acid) turned out to have two key roles. As the similarity in their names suggests, RNA is chemically similar to DNA. In particular it also has four bases. Three, G, C, and A are the same as for DNA, however Thymine is replaced by Uracil. The process of making proteins begins with transcription of a portion of the genetic blue-print contained in the DNA into an RNA copy. The DNA is 'read' by a molecule called RNA polymerase which unwinds the two DNA strands, one of which then serves as a template for the production of an RNA copy of the other strand.

All of this takes place in the nucleus of a cell, on whose chromosomes the genes made of DNA store the information necessary to manufacture whatever kinds of protein molecules any kind of cell might need. However the cell's factories, the ribosomes, are outside the nucleus in the surrounding cytoplasm. The RNA which results from transcription is a message which will be sent out to the ribosomes, and so is called 'messenger RNA' (mRNA). The arrival of the mRNA molecule at a ribosome signals the next phase, translation of the message. The translator is another kind of RNA which can recognize the code in the mRNA and transfer to the ribosome the amino acid for which it codes. Consequently this kind of RNA is called 'transfer RNA' (tRNA). There are twenty different sorts of tRNA, one for each of the twenty amino acids. Each tRNA has its amino acid attached, and is attracted to the growing polypeptide chain in the ribosome by the code for that amino acid on the mRNA.

At the same time as these processes of transcription and translation were being worked out, so was the genetic code itself. This turned out to be composed of the sixty four three-letter 'words' which can be made from the four bases A, T (U in RNA), G and C. These triplets are called codons. Sixty-four is obviously more codons than are needed to specify twenty amino acids. One, AUG, is the 'start' codon. Three, UGA, UAA and UAG, are 'stop' codons. In addition, some amino acids are specified by more than one codon. But each codon only specifies one amino acid.[3]

Molecular biology comes to the Institute

This was how things stood at the end of the 1960s. In June 1969 the Director gave a lecture at the World Health Organization (WHO) Laboratory in Lausanne, Switzerland. While there he was approached by two enterprising young molecular biologists, Jerry Adams and Suzanne Cory, who were nearing the end of their training. Adams, an American, had completed his doctorate at Harvard under James Watson and had then gone on to do his initial postdoctoral research at the MRC Laboratory of Molecular Biology in the University of Cambridge with Frederick Sanger, the winner of two Nobel Prizes in chemistry, whose work on the structure of RNA played an important role in deciphering the genetic code. While working in Cambridge, Adams met Suzanne Cory, an Australian Ph. D. student in Francis

Crick's Department. Both, obviously, had exemplary scientific pedigrees.

When Cory had finished her doctorate, she and Adams visited Australia and while there, they married. Wanting to have a common professional life, they reconnoitred Australian universities and institutes of medical research looking for a congenial place to work together. When they visited the Hall Institute they were particularly impressed by the scientific atmosphere. 'It had', they tell me, 'a good international reputation. But mainly the people were very keen about science. It had an intellectual atmosphere similar to places we had been in before, where people did really good science'.

Adams and Cory were somewhat disappointed by the Director's initial response to them. To appeal to his immunological interests, they had put up a proposal to study the messenger RNA (mRNA) of the protein molecule Ig (immunoglobulin) of which antibodies are made. Probably he was not persuaded that Adams and Cory's proposal would in fact help immunology. Undaunted, they sought a second meeting at which he was much more enthusiastic. In the interim, the Director had begun to suspect that contemporary approaches to the problem of the genetic basis of antibody formation—working out the varying sequence of amino acids of which each different antibody is made up—would ultimately prove sterile. Molecular biology seemed to offer the potential of a different line of attack, via mRNA. It is typical of the Director—indeed it is a conscious policy—to try and predict developments in biomedicine in this way. On this occasion, as on others, he backed his hunch, offering Adams and Cory positions at the Institute. They then set about finding the money to pay their own salaries—one of the new Queen Elizabeth II Fellowships for Cory, an Established Investigatorship of the American Heart Association for Adams. They also brought a prestigious US National Institutes of Health (NIH) grant with them when they arrived at the Institute, towards the end of 1971, to set up the Molecular Biology Laboratory within the Biochemistry and Biophysics Unit. Introducing a new discipline did not prove easy. Cory recalls that

we had spent twelve months writing letters back and forth to try and have everything ready. We knew there wouldn't be any equipment that we needed here, and we spent twelve months trying to organize it. We got here, and walked into our room. It had been a store room, and admittedly everything had been cleared, but there was nothing in it except a table in the middle. No benches. No water. No gas.

Indeed, so little biochemistry had been done in the Institute that it was actually difficult to find reagent bottles. Starting from scratch, with barely sufficient funding and an accumulation of demoralizing delays, they eventually established a functioning and adequately equipped laboratory.

Early struggles

Immunoglobulins each have a heavy and a light chain of amino acids (one is much longer than the other). One of Adams and Cory's main aims was to set up a facility to determine the nucleotide sequence in the mRNA for the immunoglobulin light chain of cells cultured from mice suffering a malignant cancer of their bone marrow called myeloma or plasmacytoma. This necessitated introducing P^{32}-phosphate into the cells to radioactively label the RNA. This proved difficult to achieve because the cell lines produced far less Ig than the literature had led Adams and Cory to expect. All in all, they had a pretty tough time achieving anything much for a couple of years. Eventually, they switched to tumours that made more immunoglobulin, and began, at last, to get a few results—though nothing very startling, As Adams observes in retrospect, 'The main thrust of what we wanted to do really only became feasible with the development of recombinant DNA technology'. They were struggling to do molecular biology with techniques which were not up to the task.

When the Molecular Biology Laboratory was established, molecular biology was not merely a discipline new to the Institute, but the laboratory was among the first in Australia—certainly within biomedical research. Lack of familiarity with the discipline meant that many Australian scientists, including those at the Institute, had doubts about the value of the Director's innovation from the outset. They found it difficult to appreciate either the logistical difficulties or the technical problems which confronted Adams and Cory—problems which meant that their results were, in the early years, meagre even by the standards of molecular biology. Again, it was not widely understood that the frequency of publication in molecular biology—especially before rDNA technology—was, in any event, much less than might be expected, say, in cell biology. Unfortunately, just at that time there was a great burst of productivity from some of the cellular biologists at the Institute. The effect of the high tide of productivity (measured in terms of published papers) was to place Adams and Cory under steadily increasing pressure to come up with the goods. Cory remembers that they always had to fight the attitude of 'why don't you publish ten papers a year'? And Adams recalls that 'it was a bit depressing to see other people who seemed to be churning out so much, when we had such a struggle'.

In the early 1970s, the value of molecular biology to immunology was still on trial, and things were not going well. Pressure began to be applied to the Director too; 'Senior colleagues were beginning to whisper to me that, you know, you've got to think about what you're doing with these resources'. Cory's postdoctoral fellowship expired in 1974, raising the question of continuity. It was only partly re-solved when she was refinanced with a Roche Fellowship—once again 'soft money'. The Director has the view that it is 'maybe the most important single aspect of my job ... to have instincts about people, and belief in people, and then transmit to the people that I do believe in them'. So he says that, 'over the rocky period I think that Jerry and Suzanne knew that I would give them the time to prove themselves'.

They eventually did prove themselves. New methods of radio-active labelling in mouse tumour cell lines enabled them to pursue a hint in the research literature that animal mRNA has an unusual structure. Cory recalls that

we became very interested in these and tried to track them down with our own P^{32} labelled messenger. That is how we discovered ... that mRNA of eukaryotes is methylated at its end with this strange structure, now called a cap, which involves a sort of back-to-front phospho-diester bond.

This discovery, published in 1975, made the crucial difference. Its significance was probably not fully appreciated at the Institute be-cause it was a contribution to mainstream molecular biology and did not have any particular biomedical significance. However, the world of molecular biology took note. When the Director ran across Adams's former Ph. D. supervisor, James Watson, in the US, he asked for his views. Watson said he regarded Adams as one of his best students, and that he had proved himself with the paper announcing the cap structure. He also said that if the Institute was going to be in the forefront of fundamental immunology it had to have a molecular biology division. The Director's judgement of talent and research policy was reinforced by Watson's comments, and he was determined to persist with Adams, Cory and molecular biology. Adams and Cory, however, had yet to show that their work was helpful to the immunologists.

The toolkit of the genetic engineer

By 1975 the tools for the recombinant revolution in molecular biology were largely in place, making obsolete the cumbersome technology with which Adams and Cory had struggled.[4] At bottom, rDNA work is a scissors and paste job. The 'paste', an enzyme called DNA ligase which joins DNA chains together, was discovered in 1967. Three years later, in 1970, the first of many sorts of highly specialized 'scissors' was discovered. These are also enzymes, called 'restriction endonucleases', which cut DNA at different specific sites along the chains. There are two kinds, those that cut cleanly through both chains leaving a 'flush stub end', and those that cut one chain at one point, and the other a certain distance further along, leaving what is known as a 'sticky end'. Restriction enzymes occur naturally in bacteria, preventing viruses from hijacking their genetic machinery by attacking the viral DNA. About 300 are known. Each recognizes its own distinctive sequence of bases determining the points at which the cuts are made.

Recombination occurs naturally in sexual reproduction, so that offspring get some of their characteristics from one parent, some from the other. Molecular biologists do this artificially when they stick together—recombine—DNA fragments produced by restriction enzymes with DNA ligase. This was first done in 1972. Natural recombination has long been controlled and exploited by plant and animal breeders. But theirs is a slow and a comparatively blunt tool. Moreover, cross breeding can only take place within a given species. The value of artificial recombination is its speed, precision and ability to mix genes of different species. But it is not enough to be able to cut and paste genes; you also have to be able to transfer the pieces from one organism to another. The means by which this transfer is achieved is called a 'vector'. In addition to their ordinary genes, which are usually circular DNA strands, bacteria have small organelles called 'plasmids' which contain smaller circular pieces of DNA. The DNA of the plasmids in the gut bacteria *Escherichia coli* was the first vector. Another early vector was the lamda-phage, a virus which attacks bacteria. Foreign DNA was inserted into plasmids, and they were reinserted into *E. coli* bacteria in 1973. The foreign genes involved worked in the *E. coli* just as they had in the original organism. In 1974, Stanley Cohen spliced a plasmid of the bacteria *Staphylococcus aureus* ('golden staph') carrying a gene which conferred resistance to penicillin onto an *E. coli* plasmid, and reinserted it. The *E. coli* expressed the *Staphylococcus aureus* gene—for they too were now resistant to penicillin.

As bacteria reproduce by asexual division, each new bacterium is thus an exact copy—or clone—of its parent. As bacteria reproduce, any foreign gene which has been inserted is, of course, reproduced along with the rest of the DNA, each clone expressing whatever the foreign DNA codes for. This process of producing many copies of a gene is called 'cloning'. But first you must find your gene. To do this a gene library must be created. All the DNA (the genome)—say, of a mouse—is cut up and the pieces spliced into vectors which are reinserted into bacteria. These bacteria, with their random inserts of mouse DNA are grown in flat dishes on the surface of nutrient jelly. They form lump-like colonies around the point where the parent droplet was placed. Alternatively, if the vector is a virus which attacks bacteria—a phage—holes called 'plaques' will appear in the bacteria lawn where the phage have killed bacteria. Somewhere in this library of colonies or plaques are all the mouse genes. The library must now be screened for the gene of interest. One way to do this is with radioactive RNA probes made from the protein produced by the gene. These bind to any bacteria which have the gene inserted into them. Another technique involves binding radio-active antibodies to the protein, thus identifying which colony is making it.

rDNA comes to the Institute

By the mid-1970s Adams and Cory realized that they would have to make a commitment to acquire the new genetic engineering technology, and they nerved themselves for what they guessed would be a formidable undertaking. Because of the much discussed hypothetical hazard of live (albeit very much weakened) recombinant organisms, it was necessary to install an expensive containment facility, the first in Australia. As Cory notes, a regulatory 'committee organization wasn't even functioning so that we knew we would be a test case for everything, and everything would be ten times as slow'. But the Director, encouraged by Cory and Adams's discovery of the cap structure, and by Watson's high opinion of it, was willing to fund the substantial cost of a high-level containment laboratory. Work began during 1976, and the facility came into use the following year.

The C3 biocontainment facility was the penultimate level of physical containment, featuring an air lock, negative pressure, filtered exhaust and an autoclave. The recombinant host organism used was the enfeebled *E. coli X 1776*, considered highly unlikely to survive non-laboratory conditions, especially human gut. There was, of course, the inevitable and anticipated delay caused by the construction, inspection and certification of the containment laboratory and the work which it was proposed to do there. Moreover, Adams and Cory had themselves to learn a battery of novel techniques from the published literature and teach them to their technicians. Nevertheless progress was made, and the Laboratory began to grow, its main interest in the structure and arrangement of Ig genes now focused on the number of genes coding for antibody, and the relation between the variable and the constant regions of the Ig heavy chain. This entailed construction of a repertoire of pure Ig sequences by cloning of complementary DNA synthesized on mRNA, and the development of a mouse genome DNA library.

Since their arrival, Adams and Cory's group had consisted of two technicians, a postdoctoral fellow, and a postgraduate student, who had forged an uncommonly close working partnership. At the beginning of 1978, a more senior appointment was made, and Adams and Cory were joined by D. J. Kemp, who was responsible for the development of the mouse DNA library. Kemp is an Australian who, after doctoral and postdoctoral work at the University of Adelaide, had spent two years at Stanford University's Department of Biochemistry. The Director, emphasizing the comparatively low publication rate of molecular biologists, noted that 'David Kemp came here with a small but emerging world reputation based on a total of, I think, eleven papers'. In 1979, another senior worker, Ora Bernard, was appointed and in 1980 the Molecular Biology Laboratory had, in addition, four postgraduate students under supervision. The senior scientists had the help of a Research Assistant and technicians.

The work on the Ig heavy chain genes was productive. Using the mouse DNA library, it was established that there were multiple variable genes, and their arrangement was explored. The gene sequence of the Ig heavy chain constant region and the nature of the joining region between it and the variable region were elucidated. All of this amounted to a significant contribution to the solution of two outstanding questions concerning the genetic basis of antibody formation—how many genes are concerned and how they generate antibodies. The importance of this work was recognized by the University of Melbourne in 1982 with the award to Adams and Cory of the David Syme Medal.

An enquiry into the safety of rDNA research

However, all was not plain sailing. The world over, as rDNA techniques were developed and deployed successfully, fear of its potential dangers, reminiscent of Macfarlane Burnet's concern of ten years before, began to emerge among scientists and non-scientists alike. As mentioned before, there were calls for voluntary bans on certain kinds of recombinant experiments, and the international conference in 1975 at Asilomar, California, urged the adoption of strict regulatory guidelines. One focus of debate in the USA was Cambridge, Massachusetts, where in 1976 the Molecular Biology Department at Harvard University proposed to build a containment laboratory.

About six months later, in the middle of 1977, a rather similar episode entangled the Institute. A staff/student consultative body at the University of Melbourne had raised questions about recombinant DNA research within the University and had recommended that there should be a moratorium on such research until it was shown to be safe.

In the event, the recommendations of the University Assembly's enquiry caused little more than a momentary stir. There was no moratorium and work continued at the Institute's containment laboratory free of any real threat. The enquiry was, however, the local manifestation of world-wide concern over the safety of genetic engineering. Some of the consequences of this did hinder research. In response to the pressure, scientific bodies imposed controls which many scientists then thought unjustified; a view which would later be widely accepted. Once developed, the Australian approach to regulating rDNA was at least as conservative as the English and American. Australia had been represented at the Asilomar Conference of 1975, which had urged regulation of rDNA research. The Director had chaired a WHO study group on microbiological safety with special regard to rDNA work which had reached similar conclusions. The Australian Academy of Science set up a Committee on Recombinant DNA Molecules which devised guidelines and took responsibility for inspection and certification of laboratories. The research projects at the Institute had to be cleared by the Australian Academy of Science's Committee, and the Institute's own Biohazards Committee.

One example of the impediments imposed by the early constraints was that the enfeebling of *E. coli X 1776* to make it a safe host also made it a poor experimental vehicle. Problems of this kind were of far more real concern to Adams, Cory and their co-workers than the nuisance posed by the Melbourne University Assembly enquiry and its recommendations (though they complain that the enquiry did delay their work). When the restrictions eventually began to be eased at the end of the 1970s, the Institute's molecular biologists were able to use more vigorous strains of *E. coli* in more accessible lower-level containment laboratories. The C3 laboratory became an expensive white elephant.

Cancer genetics and the discovery of the c-*myc* oncogene

With the Molecular Biology Unit making notable contributions to immunological questions, the Director recalls that 'it was remarkable to see the change of perception about these young scientists by their peer groups. Suddenly they were the ones that everyone was watching, wanting them to find out the answers, hoping they'd get a bit of the global action—which they did'.

However, after two years of concentrated work, as the Director put it, 'the cream had gone off the antibody gene structure and function problem'. It became clear that much of what remained to be done was essentially a mopping-up operation and it was time to change direction again. Adams and Cory found themselves attracted toward the study of the molecular basis of cancer—specifically to the possibility that the origin of some cancers was to be explained in terms of the inappropriate expression of genes translocated to an abnormal chromosomal position.

The first paper reporting the inadvertent activation of one of these so-called oncogenes, the cellular *myc* or c-*myc* oncogene, appeared in 1981, and was an important influence on Adams and Cory. They dropped the tidying-up experimental work on Ig genetics in favour of reading themselves into this new field to assess whether they should enter it. They also travelled to contact people doing significant work in the area. After consultation with the Director, they finally decided to take the plunge into what was to prove a highly competitive field. As Adams remarks, there were connections to their earlier work:

We wondered whether, by using immunoglobulin genes as a handle, it might be possible to identify a particular chromosome translocation and later on to try to determine whether it had a direct role in oncogenesis—as seemed quite likely. It had been known for a long time that the particular kind of lymphomas (plasmacytomas) that we had been using as an antibody factory nearly always displayed a characteristic chromosome translocation. Evidence was increasing that the region on one of the partners of the exchange was very close to an immunoglobulin gene locus. Of course, you have to realise that it could have been an enormous distance away in molecular terms, so we took that evidence as no more than a strong hint.

By mid-1982, Adams and Cory had indeed cloned from one plasmacytoma an immunoglobulin gene linked to an unknown gene; they showed that this recombinant event had almost all the plasmacytomas. Moreover, they later found and published that the two genes had been brought together by the chromosome translocation. But what was the gene that had been activated by its altered location? Adams and Cory learned at a scientific congress that an American group, led by K. B. Marcu, was in hot pursuit of their problem. So was Phillip Leder's group at Harvard, and another led by Michael Cole in St Louis, Missouri. This kind of competition is very common in first-class biomedicine. It is a pretty good test of how close a problem is to the leading edge of scientific research to ask how many other groups are actively studying it. But there is a cost which must be borne—the possibility of being pipped at the post. And it is quite a substantial cost because of the value scientists place on being first to make a discovery.

So the race was on to establish that there was a translocation taking place, between which chromosomes, and to identify the oncogene concerned. Adams and Cory had begun by supposing that the oncogene would be novel. Now they began to suspect that it might be a known oncogene, cellular *myc*. So it was to prove, as everyone involved discovered more or less simultaneously. During November and December 1982, a flurry of no less than five papers appeared. In a news item reporting this work, the Deputy Editor of *Nature* arbitrated, crediting Carlo Croce's group, Philip Leder's group, and William Hayward's group all with having linked c-*myc* translocation with the human disease Burkitt's lymphoma. Leder was given credit, together with a group led by Lee Hood and those working with Michael Cole, for establishing the link between c-*myc* and murine plasmacytomas. Adams, Cory and their co-workers' paper reporting the role of c-*myc* translocation in both Burkitt's lymphoma and murine plasmacytomas was received by the *Proceedings of the National Academy of Sciences* (USA) on 14 December. But, as I have already related, it was held up for the most prosaic of reasons: the margins of their typescript were too narrow to meet the requirements of this prestigious journal, and publication was delayed until

April 1983. Meanwhile the work of a number of others, including Marcu and Croce, had appeared in print.

The significance of Cory and Adams's work in the eyes of the scientific community was marked by the appearance in the March 1985 issue of *Scientific American* of a detailed account of events as seen by Carlo Croce and George Klein. There they say that

studies of the mechanism underlying Burkitt's lymphoma ... have implications beyond this one disease. The translocations in Burkitt's lymphoma seem to provide a model for the majority of human B-cell cancers (and perhaps for T-cell cancers as well). In addition, knowledge of the translocation mechanism will provide powerful experimental tools not only for the study of other cancers but also for the study of the mechanisms that control genetic expression during the normal development and function of the human immune system.[5]

Crocè and Klein credit Adams and Cory with having been among

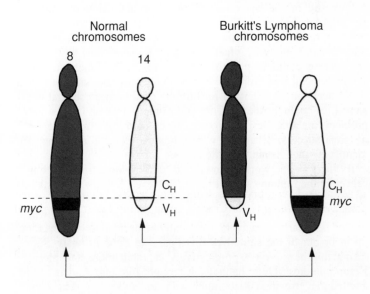

Burkitt's lymphoma is a tumour of the cells that make antibodies. It involves a translocation of chromosomes in which chromosome 8 and chromosome 14 exchange ends. Thus the normally dormant *myc* oncogene is changed to a position where antibody genes (V_H and C_H) are highly active. The activated *myc* gene then promotes uncontrolled growth of the cell, resulting in a cancerous tumour.

the first (after Cole and Leder) to elucidate the role of c-*myc* in mouse plasmacytomas. At the Institute, Adams and Cory's success greatly enhanced the reputation of the Molecular Biology Unit (the front of the *Annual Review* 1983–4 features an illustration of the Burkitt's lymphoma translocation). They have since gone on to do detailed studies of the translocation, and to demonstrate the cancer-inducing effects of the c-*myc* gene by inserting it into fertilized mouse eggs. Significantly, all the mice develop lymphomas. These remarkable 'transgenic' mice forged the definitive link in the chain of evidence that the translocation causes the tumour. They also provide, for the first time, the means to study the earliest steps in the disease.

rDNA technology in immunoparasitology and cancer research

As a result of the successes of the Molecular Biology Unit, the potential for the application of rDNA techniques to a wide range of Institute research problems began to be widely appreciated. The Immunoparasitology Unit had understood for some time how genetic engineering could help them. One of the senior scientists there, Robin Anders, was trained as a protein chemist and, knowing what rDNA technology might do for him, he tried hard on several occasions to encourage Adams, Cory and Kemp to take an interest in his problem, malaria. Despite vigorous discussion, his efforts met with no great success, because it was difficult to develop a strategy for identifying the relevant parasite genes.

By the time the work on the role of chromosome translocation in cancer of the immune system began, however, Kemp's interests had already shifted toward parasitic disease. A Ph. D. student of his initially began work on an immunoglobulin gene project which proved peculiarly intractable. Eventually he decided to give the topic up in favour of the cattle tick fever parasite *Babesia bovis*. Supervising this new project progressively captured more and more of Kemp's interest. Quite naturally it brought him into Anders's orbit and led to a growing collaboration with Anders's group, whose main interest was malaria. He remained on the staff of the Molecular Biology Unit, but increasingly in name only until, during 1983–4, he formally transferred to the Malaria Laboratory within the Immunoparasitology Unit. The malaria group now includes still another molecular biologist trained in Adams and Cory's Unit, as well as one trained within the Immunoparasitology Unit itself.

The main contrast between Immunoparasitology and the Molecular Biology Unit lies in their different research orientations. The Immunoparasitologists are strongly oriented towards an applied goal—a vaccine for malaria—whereas the Molecular Biology Unit has always been engaged in fundamental research. It is for this reason that the former group, rather than the latter, has established connections with semi-government and commercial biotechnology.

With the successes of the Molecular Biology and, later, the Immunoparasitology Units, came increasingly widespread awareness within the Institute of the potential value of rDNA techniques. The Cancer Research Unit engaged in close collaboration with molecular biologists at the Ludwig Institute for Cancer Research (Melbourne Branch). This culminated in successful cloning of the gene for the growth hormones granulocyte-macrophage colony stimulating factor (GM-CSF) and Multi-CSF, and determination of their structure. GM-CSF had been discovered in 1969 by the Cancer Research Unit's Head, Donald Metcalf, and it provided an on-going focus for the Unit's research. Metcalf is a scientist who sometimes reminds one of Burnet—for example, he has his microscope in his office. But he has shown himself willing and able to adopt the powerful rDNA techniques, which have rewarded him with results he confesses to being amazed by. In collaboration with the commercial firm Biogen (Geneva), GM-CSF and Multi-CSF of mice can be manufactured in quantity. Studies in the Cancer Research Unit indicated that CSF produced by rDNA techniques can be used to suppress mouse leukaemia, and Metcalf's group and its collaborators hope that human leukaemia can be treated likewise.

The Gene Technology Sub-Committee: discipline versus technique

By the time of the 1984 NH&MRC Quinquennial Review, the Thymus Biology and Cellular Immunology Units were actively seeking ways to obtain the services of professional genetic engineers. There, and elsewhere, younger scientists trained in other fields can be found attempting to pick up rDNA techniques.

One problem was that the desire to undertake projects requiring molecular biological expertise far outstripped any conceivable expansion in the short term. Another was how to attract new recruits of sufficiently high calibre in a world-wide seller's market. But the really difficult question was whether to expand the existing Molecular Biology Unit or establish 'molecular cores' within the cellular immunology Units.

Cory worried lest 'the rush to molecular biology jeopardize the further development of high quality biology within the Institute'. She pointed out that there were already 'people around who can do rDNA ... but they are not molecular biologists. One thing that is dangerous about that is that [in consequence] they are not necessarily going to have enough depth to realize when particular approaches are not feasible'.

Adams and Cory were trained as, and remain, molecular biologists and, if one can exaggerate a little, they tend to view aspects of immunology and oncology as sources of interesting problems within molecular biology which, as a 'pure' science discipline, has its own research program. In contrast, their colleagues in other Units tend to see rDNA technology as providing powerful ways to pursue the problems of immunology, auto-immunity, and so on, which are their disciplinary focus. It is to pursue these biomedical problems that they have been acquiring rDNA skills themselves and trying to hire specialists. Even those with formal training as molecular biologists since the rDNA revolution are inclined to take the viewpoint of the immunologists, parasitologists etc., for whom they work.

For Adams and Cory, the question of who was to decide which problems were tackled by molecular biologists was of great importance. From their point of view, if molecular biologists became mere itinerant technologists for hire, they would lose their own intellectual autonomy and disciplinary integrity. Thus the molecular biologists at the Institute favoured a model where new recruits were located within their Unit so that 'the cell biologists would be competing between themselves for access to these resources and the "best problem" should win'. Unstated, but far from unimportant, was the fact that this would allow molecular biologists to decide which were the best problems.

The Director set up a Gene Technology Sub-Committee chaired by Cory to advise on the deployment of biotechnological expertise within the Institute. The Sub-Committee recommended that the Molecular Biology Unit should get a new senior member. But it also counselled establishment of 'molecular colonies' consisting of a molecular biologist, a trained technician and a Ph. D. student within the cell biology laboratories. One was to serve the T-cell work, another immuno-regulation, and a third clinical projects. The 'molecular colonists' should be technically versatile and would be

expected to collaborate in areas of interest to the cellular immunologists. However, they should have enough independence and be
sufficiently experienced to decide whether proposed projects were
viable and of sufficient scope to warrant detailed molecular biological investigation.

Given the difficulty of recruiting first-class specialist molecular
biologists, the Sub-Committee suggested the appointment of what
they termed 'two-world' personnel, i.e. 'biologists who already have
minimal training in molecular biology or the capacity of absorbing it
well or fast. They would be interface people, capable of applying a
restricted number of molecular techniques, but who could also be
full members of a cell biology team'.[6]

These recommendations are hardly surprising, since they reflect
the view of all the Units, and the 'two-world' workers proposal reflects world-wide excess of demand over supply of molecular biologists. Not only were university and institutional jobs burgeoning, so
were commercial opportunities, as genetic engineering firms were
formed and expanded operations. In addition, more and more of
those at the Institute were discovering that you can learn and use
rDNA techniques without being a fully trained molecular biologist.
Indeed, what was even worse from the point of Adams and Cory
was that, at the Institute, the terms 'rDNA technology' and
'molecular biology' were rapidly becoming synonymous and inter-
changeable in use.

World-wide, as a greater and greater percentage of molecular
biologists work outside disciplinary divisions of molecular biology
in applied biomedical and especially commercial settings, the more
do they become itinerant technologists. It's a case of 'have restriction enzymes, will travel'. Anyone who is interested in any protein,
large or small, has only to ask, and the rDNA genetic technician will
locate the gene which codes for it (though this is often no easy task),
cut it out and insert in a bacterial host, and manufacture as much of
it as may be needed. It doesn't matter whether the protein is
antibody, insulin, human, animal or plant growth hormone. The new
molecular technicians can turn their hands as readily to finding a
vaccine for malaria as to improving control over the growth of
domestic pigs. All these various projects may well be justifiable, but
it is not molecular biology which decides which will be tackled, and
in what order. Even within 'pure' molecular biology laboratories,
what rDNA techniques can and cannot do increasingly determines
the scientific horizons. In a very real sense those techniques have
triumphed in that they have become so pervasive and dominant in

current molecular biology.

(Speaking to Adams about this whole episode, I get the impression that he thinks I give it far more prominence than it deserves. 'You set up the situation', he says, 'as a philosophical battle rather than what it really was—a pragmatic attempt to cope with the desire of the other Units to gain access to the new technology'. For him and Cory, he continues, the major issues were how to locate and hire sufficient molecular biologists of high calibre to satisfy each Unit's perceived need; how to protect young molecular biologists from supervisors who, though expert in their own fields, were too inexperienced in molecular biology to realize that certain projects they proposed were unrealistic; and how to ensure that the world-class biological expertise of these Units would not be neglected in the wake of their push to do rDNA work.)

The Director found the Gene Technology Sub-Committee's proposals workable and recommended them to the Institute Board, which adopted them. But, in endorsing the proposals, he warned that

the Committee and I feel it is very important to remember that recombinant DNA technology is, after all, only a technique. An intemperate rush to molecular biology, to the exclusion of the further development of high quality biology and clinical science within the Institute, could jeopardise the very traditions that have made the Institute famous.[7]

The Director alludes here to the technique versus discipline tension which has emerged at the Institute. Since the mid-1960s, research at the Institute has been dominated by cell biology, with its own powerful technology of cell lines, tissue culture and cell sorters. Without the armoury of rDNA technology, molecular biology posed no threat to cellular biology; indeed it was hardly able to contribute to immunological problems.

Equipped with the tools of the genetic engineer, however, the Molecular Biology Unit was able to reach towards the leading edge of research in molecular immunology and oncogenesis, so securing its reputation within the Institute. The same successes have led to rDNA techniques being welcomed by many other Units for their power, precision and rigour. Simultaneously, however, the arrival of molecular technique poses a challenge to cellular biology. For example, the new Whitehead Institute attached to MIT in Boston is entirely devoted to molecular biology. Many scientists think that molecular biology will replace cellular biology as the dominant scientific discipline in immunology. They also surmise that molecular biology will not merely contribute another powerful technique (recombinant DNA) to the service of medical research, but that that technique will become the be-all and end-all of molecular biology. The means of scientific production, as Marx might have put it, will then define the science of immunology itself.

****

I speak to Al Becker about these matters. Some molecular biologists, he says, simply become sequencers. They just sequence genes and become experts in all the allied techniques. In some cases genes are sequenced solely because they have been cloned. These people are really molecular technologists and, in Becker's view, they are engaged in an intellectually bankrupt enterprise. The best molecular work, he says, is where a biologist sets the agenda. In these instances the important biological questions (often poorly understood by the molecular biologists) can be intelligently approached. If a gene were to be sequenced it would be a gene selected for its importance in some wider biological context. In fact, in many cases molecular biologists need a biologist to tell them what the important problems (and genes) are. A good example of this, Becker says, is the Basel Institute where two very good cell biologists/ immunologists basically direct the research of some thirty molecular biologists, even though the latter regard themselves as independent scientists.

****

I give my friend Sam Wisden a draft of one of the chapters of this book. Wisden, who has a neo-Marxist outlook, thinks that any authentic understanding of a sub-culture is necessarily linked to discovering how that culture might be changed, and he is critical of my approach to the Institute because it doesn't indicate how it might be changed. 'You are mainly interested', he says, 'in "telling it like it is" and you, so to speak, leave the *status quo* in place. You protest against sociological positivism but really your own approach is deeply positivistic in that you religiously eschew making value judgements about the life-world, as you call it, of the Institute. Your method is as "value free" as that of any number-crunching American sociologist'.

I protest that most of my scientists accept the way science is, and the way the Institute is, just as they accept the universe. (One is reminded of the lady who said to Thomas Carlyle, 'I accept the

Universe'—to which the great man replied: 'By God ma'am, you'd better'!) No doubt the scientists want some things to change but, apart from a few of the technicians and a couple of woman Ph. D. students, no one really wants to question or challenge the whole system.

'But', Wisden replies, 'whatever *they* think, there are still value questions to be asked of the scientific culture of the Institute. Is this a good way of doing science? What are the human costs and benefits of this way of doing science? Is this a good way of organizing science or does it involve some people exploiting other people? Who benefits from the present set-up: do the wrong people benefit or do the people who should benefit miss out? From what you say, the technicians and women scientists obviously miss out, but the life-style of the scientists as a whole—one of 'Protestant Ethic' competitive individualism—seems also to be rather an alienated one. So there are plenty of things to change. No doubt, your anthropological account gives me some insight into the sub-culture of the Institute, but, as I have said, any understanding of the issues raised by the work and structure of the Institute is worthwhile only insofar as it gives us some idea of how we might *do* something about those issues'.

'You clearly think', I reply, 'like Marx, "our business is not merely to understand the world, but to change it"'.

'It's rather a matter', Wisden says, 'of understanding the world by seeing how one might change it'.

'Well', I say. 'I suppose that by showing that the scientist's world is "constructed" and might well have been other than it is—that it is not a necessity of nature that just has to be accepted without question—I am showing at the same time that it can be changed, can be reconstructed in a different way'.

'That was Foucault's reply', Wisden says, 'to the Parisian students in 1968 when they asked how much he was doing to help the revolution!'

'At least then I'm in good company', I answer.

I have to admit that as I get further into this project my approach to the Institute has become mainly concerned with understanding its life-world and not so much with standing in judgement on it nor with changing it. I suppose that I assume, like the classical anthropologists, that it is just intrinsically worthwhile trying to understand the point of any culture or form of life. I also assume that it is always valuable for the members of any sub-culture to become aware of and self-conscious about the hidden 'grammar' of their culture. I must say that I would be happy if this present study had that effect on my scientists. Whether it might cause them, or the Institute, to change for the better—whatever that might involve—is not mine to ensure. All the same, I have the uneasy feeling that this is suspiciously like the Eichmann defence!

PART FOUR

THE MALARIA VACCINE QUEST

9

The World of Immunoparasitology

If critics reproach me with not having carried out an exhaustive inventory of South American myths before analysing them, they are making a grave mistake about the nature and function of these documents. The total body of myth belonging to a given community is comparable to its speech. Unless the population dies out physically or morally, this totality is never complete. You might as well criticise a linguist for compiling the grammar of a language without having complete records of the words pronounced since the language came into being, and without knowing what will be said in it during the future part of its existence. Experience proves that a linguist can work out the grammar of a given language from a remarkably small number of sentences, compared to all those he might in theory have collected (not to mention those he cannot be acquainted with because they were uttered before he started on his task, or outside his presence, or will be uttered at some later date).

Claude Lévi-Strauss, *The Raw and the Cooked*[1]

Immunoparasitology

When I began this investigation, I thought that it might be possible to do a more or less complete survey of the life-world of the Institute scientists. That life-world or micro-culture looked to be small and enclosed and coherent and circumscribable enough for me to be able to do that. But even after a short time at the Institute I can see my study becoming alarmingly complex and opening up further and yet further vistas. I realize, in some panic, that I could well spend the rest of my scholarly life in the Institute, as a kind of friendly parasite, very much as some scholars spend their lives studying one poet or historical period. If I am to get anywhere I must concentrate my attention on some central and typical area and investigate that in detail. The difficulty, of course, is how to tell beforehand which areas are 'central' and 'typical'. I take some comfort from Lévi-Strauss's suggestion that it doesn't matter what part of a culture you select for examination since it ought to be possible to work out the 'grammar' of the culture from fragmentary samples of its 'language'.

I decide, for a number of reasons, to focus on the immunoparasitology group led by Graham Mitchell. A number of quite personal and subjective factors play a part in this decision, since Mitchell is such an outgoing and enthusiastic man and most of his group are also accessible and very ready to talk about what they are doing. In other words, the natives are friendly. Apart from that, the immunoparasitology unit is the largest and fastest growing section of the Institute. In 1975, Mitchell's laboratory consisted of himself, two other scientists and one laboratory assistant. By 1977 the laboratory had doubled in size and been renamed the Laboratory of Immunoparasitology. By 1981 the Laboratory had doubled in size again and was made into a separate Unit with Mitchell as Unit Head. The new Unit comprised two laboratories, the Laboratory of Immunoparasitology headed by Mitchell, and the Laboratory of Molecular Parasitology headed by Robin Anders. By 1985 the Unit had doubled in size yet again and now consisted of three laboratories—the Immunoparasitology Laboratory headed by Mitchell, the Malaria Laboratory headed by Anders, and the MacArthur Laboratory of Molecular Parasitology headed by David Kemp. In summary, in the ten years from 1975 to 1985 the Unit had increased from three scientists to twenty-eight and from one support staff to sixteen.

The Immunoparasitology Unit is now the largest Unit in the Institute. Its size and the comparative speed of its growth illustrate the extraordinary flexibility available to the Institute and its ability to respond and change quickly when the occasion (and resources) demands it. (When I compare this institutional adaptability with what happens in my own university and other universities I am quite astonished. A project initiated by one person could give rise to a small research centre in the university or even to a small department, but it is virtually impossible that it could happen so quickly because of the number of committees which would have to give approval, as well as other inertial forces, and it is almost inconceivable that any new organizational unit could make up such a large proportion of the university.This certainly looks like one interesting characteristic of the Institute which I should explore. Is this flexibility typical of scientific research institutes? Is it indicative of the way in which contemporary biomedical research is organized?)

Finally, the immunoparasitology group is engaged in the quest for a malaria vaccine and is a front runner in the international competition to find a vaccine for one of the main scourges of the poor world. At the moment, the malaria vaccine group is certainly the most glamorous section in the Institute.

I am not sure whether these are compelling reasons for focusing on the small world of the immunoparasitology scientists—though I suspect that they are no more accidental and idiosyncratic than the kinds of reasons that motivate any anthropologist or sociologist to study this group rather than that. But, in any case, I hope that by concentrating on the immunoparasitologists, I can get some idea about how the scientific life-world in general is built up and how the scientific agenda (what are the main problems to be tackled and how they are to be tackled) is set in a particular area.

The factors that have gone into the building up of the immuno-parasitology life-world and the setting of its agenda are of course many and various. However, it is easy to separate out the personal factors that derive from the two main actors—the Director and Mitchell—from what might be called structural factors deriving from the way scientific activity is organized in the immunoparasitology group, which itself depends on the organizational structure of international science in this field and projects such as the Great Neglected Diseases Program of the Rockefeller Foundation. Then there is the external 'political' dimension, since the malaria vaccine is meant for Third World countries such as Papua New Guinea and the Philippines, and again, the malaria group at the Institute depends on the collaboration of other scientists in Papua New Guinea and also upon Papua New Guinean native peoples for blood sera and field-work data. In the next three sections I look at each of these factors—the personal, the structural, the political—although in reality they are all mixed up together.

****

The Director's story

As I have indicated, the story about how the Institute got into the malaria business and caught up in the quest for a vaccine illustrates very clearly how the marking out of a new area or field of scientific research is the result of a complex blend of contingent events, personal factors, socio-economic-political pressures, pure luck, old fashioned idealism, and plenty of scientific 'chutzpah'. The Director was very willing to give me his account of the Institute's entry into the field of immunoparasitology and I had two long interviews with him. He is a marvellous raconteur with a strong sense of the dramatic, and I will reproduce his account more or less verbatim. If the account sounds a bit like one of Plato's later dialogues where Socrates/Plato holds the floor and the interlocuteurs are confined to remarks like 'You have spoken well Socrates: please go on'—then that's pretty much how my interview with the Director was! I began by asking how he came to be interested in Third World diseases like malaria.

'The saga of my involvement with Third World problems really goes back quite a long way. Since you were kind enough to ask me to give this some thought I've done so. I can pick the beginning point quite clearly, because in 1963 or 1964 there was a conference in Israel I was invited to where I met an American whom I'd known only by repute, called Howard Goodman. He was an unusual chap in that he was trained as a physician and also in clinical research at the NIH in Bethesda. And in what was looking like a very successful career he took the opportunity to drop it all and work for the World Health Organization. He was given the brief of building up the WHO's interest in immunology. He used that meeting in Israel as a time to familiarize himself with the immunological researchers of the world. I was very struck by his idealism. The thought of getting any immunological sophistication into Third World countries seemed to be drawing a very long bow. Goodman asked me to join an advisory committee on immunology which would meet and advise him on getting immunological research and training centres set up in the Third World. However, it turned out to be a pretty desultory exercise. Not much money was spent on it and, looking back, it wasn't very successful. The centres collapsed or half-collapsed when the expatriates withdrew and they weren't very successful in training local replacements.'

'This got me thinking about the Third World. The next stage had a dual origin, both of which were equally important in my mind. I was asked to give a talk at the First International Conference on Immunology—there were only four plenary session speakers at this very high-profile conference—in about 1971. I was given the topic "Immunology as an independent discipline—its scope and horizons". It was a big challenge to think about the immunology of the 1970s and 1980s. It was through pondering that title that I realized we had moved such a long way away from the field of vaccination. Now most of the immunologists were either theoreticians pure and simple, or they were people interested in newer applications of immunology such as organ transplantation, autoimmune diseases and cancer. That's where the drive was going. There was really very little drive going into new or improved vaccines, least of all Third World vaccines. So I wrote fairly extensively at the time about our need to increase our profile in that area.'

'Where did you go from there?' I asked the Director.

'I think that that 1972 talk and my friendship with Goodman were central, but in 1973 I joined WHO's Advisory Committee on Medical Research (ACMR): this is the global body which guides WHO in all its research endeavours. It is now known as the Advisory Committee for Health Research—ACHR. There were four or five of us on the committee who saw a really great opportunity. These included Jacques Monod, the great bacterial physiologist and Nobel Laureate who was then director of the Pasteur Institute in Paris, Josh Lederberg who was my former teacher and probably then still at Stanford (he was to move later to Rockefeller University) and who is one of the doyens of American science, and Christian de Duve, a Belgian who'd recently founded a large new medical research institute and who also was to get a Nobel Prize a few years later, and myself. I think they were the archplotters, together with Howard Goodman from WHO in the background, who said in effect that it was now time to do something serious. We were still thinking in fairly vague terms about the new biology, which was crystallizing around three disciplines—genetics, molecular biology, and immunology focusing on Third World diseases. But it became apparent that something as woolly as that wouldn't run. The idea gradually gelled in discussions that maybe parasitic diseases would be the field to which these disciplines could be applied. To be frank, I don't think anyone can tell who had the idea that it shouldn't be an expanded unit of immunology, cell biology, molecular biology and genetics—which was the first rubric under which we were working—but that it should be especially focused on parasitic diseases. It may even have been a decision from the WHO secretariat.

'Anyhow, the next year something went badly wrong, which is quite amusing. It was round about 1974. The ACMR had written a paper about this new initiative. The Deputy Director-General of the organization was a chap called Lambo, a very brilliant and very personable Nigerian. He used to be a psychiatrist and after that was Vice-Chancellor of the University of Ibadan. Anyhow, he was going on a State visit to Zambia and like many Nigerians he's rather impulsive. He's a man with a great sense of humour, a wide open ebullient personality. He was greeted by President Kenneth Kaunda of Zambia and taken to the second largest town called Ndola, one of the copper-belt towns way in the back blocks. There was a magnificent hospital there, as big as the Royal Melbourne Hospital, entirely empty. Kaunda said to Lambo, "What an ideal place for your Institute of tropical diseases". So the idea was born in Lambo's mind that a large institute in the middle of Zambia should be where all this research was to be done. I was asked to go and have a look at it the next year, 1975.'

'A delicate piece of scientific diplomacy', I observe.

'It soon became quite apparent that that idea could not possibly run. You might have a sporting chance of creating an institute in Nairobi, but putting it in a place where there were daily shortages of bread and paper—let alone test tubes and petri dishes—and where the communication linkages with the rest of the world were negligible, meant that it had no chance. However, on the visit there (to which a number of people went including Goodman, a Nigerian scientist called Lucas, myself and one or two others) we had to report back that it was no go. But we did see that you could use it as a centre for clinical studies, epidemiology and field trials if you could get the advances made elsewhere in the world. So we rescued something of the WHO Deputy Director-General's dignity and there is now a little clinical epidemiology unit there. I'm dwelling on this point because it's absolutely critical to the rest of the program—remember the name Lucas, public health professor from Ibadan, Nigeria.

'With the failure of the idea of the Zambian Institute came the idea of a paper institute, with its own scientific working groups, planning functions, grant-giving functions, and it was this idea that was proposed to the ACMR in 1975. The model was similar to that of a WHO scientist called Kessler who had started a small but quite effective human reproduction program with about US$10 million a year. This body gave grants to developed countries, created training centres in developing countries and tried to promote research on birth control.'

The Director continues. 'Now we come to my own part. I had planned to spend 1976 on sabbatical leave at the National Institutes of Health in the US and get back to the lab a bit more. I'd been offered one of these Fogarty International fellowships to live in splendour in the 'stone house' on the campus. Plans were not advanced (the Fogarty International Centre is in the NIH in Bethesda) but were being made. I was to have worked in the immunology section. When I was at a meeting of the ACMR, I ran into a very old friend called Rodney Shearman who's the Professor of Obstetrics at Sydney University and about three years older than I. When I found that he was taking his sabbatical leave in the WHO human reproduction program, I said to myself, "Gosh! mightn't it be better for me to spend my leave in Goodman's WHO immunology program rather than go to the Fogarty Centre—you know, really do something for someone?" Goodman also put the pressure on me. "Fogarty Shmogarty", he said, "you can go to the Centre any time; it's the same old names you meet at conferences. What do you need it for?"

'Goodman was a dreamer and somewhat impractical. He had basically good ideas of a wide-ranging sort about immunology for the Third World. But he found it impossible to make his ideas effective and when it became clear that he was now to run a special program in parasitology that would get big new funds—over US $25 million a year is what we aimed for—some of the WHO parasitologists started to gang up on him. This kind of backstabbing and backbiting can be done very subtly. I knew nothing of this at the time. I was literally on my way to spend my sabbatical leave working for Goodman in the WHO program. I spent Christmas with my brother in Washington and there got a telegram to say that they were looking forward to having me but that it wouldn't be Howard Goodman running the program. I thought, "What the hell is this?" But by that time it was Christmas and the kids were making snowballs and I said to myself, "I can't be bothered".

'When I got to WHO I found out that Goodman's head had rolled, and that Lucas, the Nigerian scientist, had been appointed Director of the WHO immunology program as a result of the excellent report he and I and others had written on the Ndola exercise. He would be starting on 1 May. This put Goodman in an incredibly difficult position. The whole program had developed over three or four years under Goodman but there'd been in effect a vote of no confidence in him. To do him justice, he worked very hard until the 1st of May, when Lucas came to head the program. They gave Goodman another job inside WHO but a couple of years later he left. So WHO treated Goodman shabbily. But they probably made the right decision in that he couldn't have done the job Lucas has done. Lucas is brilliant, and a worker. However, for Goodman it was a human tragedy in a way. The whole of his life had been leading up to something big and then at the last moment it was whisked away from him.

'So I found myself working for Lucas, and I spent nine months of that year essentially drafting out how the program should work. We decided there had to be quite a lot of training and strengthening exercises. Towards the end of 1976 or the beginning of 1977 the program was launched. I had to do much political work, particularly in places like the World Health Assembly where all the health ministers trot up and have their say, and in various other forums. Coming in as an outsider was a help. They knew I'd be gone soon and had no axe to grind; I had no power base within the organization. I was genuinely a consultant. So they told me all the things they thought were wrong with the program in a way they'd never have told the Director-General or his deputy. I went off to the World Bank and had to sell them the program. I also talked to the United Nations Development Program, and both contributed. It ended up as a joint program of WHO, UNDP and the World Bank. Many other aid agencies contributed when the hat was passed around.

'That's been a lengthy story but I thought it was important to show that things don't happen in a clearcut linear sequence. In this particular case my friendship with Goodman, the fact of being forced to think about Third World problems through that little talk in Washington, the Rodney Shearman exercise deepening my involvement over a full year—all contributed.'

The Director remained on the WHO Advisory Committee for Medical Research from 1973 to 1980. In 1976 WHO decided to have advisory committees on health research in the various regions too, and the idea of regional ACHRs reporting to Regional Directors was formed. Nossal became the Chairman of the Western Pacific Regional ACHR in 1977.

'All that's very interesting', I say, 'but how exactly did the Institute as such become involved in malaria research?'

'I must come back to Graham Mitchell. This is again a heartwarming and interesting story. I took over as Director of the Institute in September 1965. Somehow one's first students are among the most important students in one's life. It's wonderful to get some of these bright young minds focused on your problems, and then they become *their* problems, and then you've got to think of other problems that someone else takes over from you again ... and that's the way the system works. Late in 1965, in about November, an old gentleman called Professor Calne rang me. He was a professor of veterinary pathology. I knew him because I'd worked with his daughter in the 1950s. He said, "Look I want to send you the new

Bede Morris". (Bede Morris had been a Sydney veterinary graduate about ten years previously and had since had a brilliant career in immunology.) "His name is Mitchell. He's just completed his veterinary degree. I think he's just outstanding and I want him to do a Ph. D." This, however, wasn't so easy because Mitchell had started off studying agricultural science in a small college in South Australia. One of his teachers there, to his undying credit, spotted how bright Mitchell was and said, "You don't want to do agricultural science, do veterinary medicine instead at Sydney University", and he arranged a scholarship to see him through.

'Mitchell started at the Hall Institute in early 1966. I can remember it as if it were yesterday. It was a somewhat different era. The group was much smaller and one was closer to the new students. He had three to four years with us. He began in Jacques Miller's lab. and became an outstanding cellular immunologist. The Institute had a longstanding association with Stanford University, and Mitchell went off there for his postdoctoral where he did very well. In everybody's mind was the thought that he'd come back to join the cellular immunology group here. But one way or another his absence was longer than expected, because after Stanford he wanted to travel to the UK, and he and Jacques and I organized a fellowship for him at Mill Hill in London, the big national institute of medical research. At the end of that, a total of four years, Jacques Miller was going on sabbatical leave and thought it would be fun for Mitchell to come and work with him for a year at the Basel Institute for Immunology which had just got going and was vibrant and exciting. So he was away for five years, a good long time.'

Speaking to Mitchell later, he tells me that when he came back to the Hall Institute in 1973, he wanted to work on the immunology of reproduction—a still unsolved problem since we don't know why the mother's immune system tolerates the foetus, which is immunologically foreign (half of it comes from the father). Mitchell began work in a tentative way. But after talking to Nossal and consulting his own experience, he changed his scientific interests.

As the Director puts it: 'Within about six or nine months of his starting back with us, not through any kind of executive fiat but through much more dynamic and diffuse processes which really are the decision-making process here (discussion, sharing thoughts, thinking out loud), it finally became clear to us that there'd be absolutely no use in him becoming just one more cellular immunologist, because there wasn't much uniqueness in that. Jacques Miller and I were completely established in our careers by now. Ken

Shortman, though younger, had decided he would help us by becoming an expert in cell separation technology. That meant there were three pretty established cellular immunologists in the place.

'So that was the first definitive decision we reached—that Mitchell should do something different, and use his veterinary background to do something more applied. We shilly shallied between parasites and human reproduction (I'd come back and talk about the WHO reproduction program and the possibility of a birth control vaccine), and Mitchell even went back to the WHO group a couple of times to give them advice on the immunology of reproduction. But by 1974 he had decided to work on parasites. And here I must say something to Mitchell's very great credit. I'm always pressuring for verticality and a very focused approach. I think that the sort of scientists who get there in the end are those who have tunnel vision, so that they'll do the one thing always incrementally better and better. So I was saying to Mitchell that he should decide whether he was going to do malaria, schisto or whatever. But he in effect said he had to do it his way, and use his skills in mouse experimentation to examine a variety of parasites. He had at one stage a dozen different parasite systems, so as to get the feel of the field and an idea of the influence of genetics—strain variation in particular—and of the different kinds of antibodies the body can make, to see which is most important.

'For three years the program was almost entirely a veterinary parasitology program. All the time I was nagging him to focus on an important human disease. But gradually, as Mitchell became secure in the knowledge that he could make a contribution, he moved himself into malaria, leishmaniasis, schisto and filariasis. I'd like you to think of all this as a very dynamic and interactive process that has finally got us into the present position. It would be easy for me to relate it as if it was all a direct consequence of my great moment of truth talking about the future of immunology in Washington. That wouldn't be untrue entirely, but it wouldn't be completely true either. The realities are that in a place where you have a lot of people of high calibre, the question of directing them at all becomes something that can only be viewed in dynamic terms, not in terms that are hierarchical or authoritarian or definitive. I think Mitchell and I have a rather similar outlook on things. I think we both are of the view that an open and friendly and people-related approach to science is good. He's had a lot of interaction with people from other institutions.'

I ask the Director about the appropriate mix of concentration, or 'verticality', as he calls it, and wide-ranging latitude, in science of this kind.

'I do think that for the vaccine to become a reality we also need the other kind of science (the tunnel-vision science where people are absolutely focused). Maybe we have such people in the malaria vaccine team. That, I think, is a very beautiful balance. Had I been running the Unit by now I'd be making it entirely malaria and I'd be saying, "There'll be time enough in three years to look closely at schisto". But Mitchell has already moved so far into a focused approach that it wouldn't be right for him, running his extraordinarily successful Unit his way, to move any further at this point.

'However, Mitchell did make what I consider to be a strategic error, though he made it with generosity and real good will. For a variety of reasons he's never been deeply in the malaria work himself. But that's minor. He's doing excellent work on leishmaniasis and he's got a lead into schistosomiasis with that lovely field station in the Philippines, which will give room for diagnostic technology and epidemiology. So though the program still is a little bit more diffuse than I'd wish, I'm not, to be frank, anxious to change anything. It's going so well and Mitchell has a totally secure international reputation in parasitic immunology. He really has got to do it his way—and I think his mind works best when it's working on several fronts at the same time. However, while I don't intend to impose my view on Mitchell, I do intend to ensure that all incremental dollars go to the malaria vaccine project. It's clear that the incremental money from the National Biotechnology Scheme is going to malaria. If we get incremental money from the MacArthur Foundation that'll go to malaria too.'

I ask if there is a danger of his putting all the Institute's eggs in the one (malaria) basket?

'That's a very interesting question. I'm of the view that those who dare greatly, win greatly or lose gloriously. A lot of people have criticized me, saying that I'm too far out on a limb with malaria. But, if you don't put all your resources in and dare greatly there's one thing sure—it won't happen. There will be no great victory for the Institute. We won't be the Salk Institute of the 1980s. But if you do dare greatly and fail, it's very clear that while you're doing the science well—while you're still worshipping at the shrine of high standards and of publishing good papers—the society we live in is very forgiving of failure. We had Koprowski (Director of the Wistar Institute in Philadelphia) here last week. He did not invent the polio vaccine, though he was in fact the first person to have the polio virus in tissue culture. He mounted a small trial in the Congo under ethical circumstances that would never be permitted today, but he failed to realize there were three strains involved. He simply had attenuated Type 1 which is the most important, and let's face it, he lost in the race to get a polio vaccine. There is no "Koprowski polio vaccine" though there is a Koprowski rabies vaccine. But no one thought the less of him for losing. He still has a stellar career; he's the Director of a big institute and so on. So our downside risk of the vaccine not working, or of us being beaten to the punch by another group, is not very great. I know there'll be superb science done building up the pieces of the lovely mosaic. If we don't come first in the vaccine race it won't hurt the Institute's reputation.'

I bring up the problem of antigenic variation, which seems to be the big obstacle to devising a malaria vaccine.

'Yes, that's an important point. The other important point is that the parasite has had many millions of years of evolution to learn how to trick the immune system. And whether we can up the ante is another point. Some scientists, for example, think it's unlikely that we'll be effective. Black thinks we're absolutely mad, and further that we know nothing about malaria. He may be right on both counts. On the other hand, the generation of people that attacked the problem by mosquito control and by chemotherapy also have not eradicated the problem. So it's time for a new generation to see what the new biology can do.'

I ask the Director, 'What in your view are the real prospects for a malaria vaccine?'

'If you ask me what I really think about a malaria vaccine, I think it's likely to be considerably less than 100 per cent effective. I don't think it'll be like the smallpox vaccine. But I think that if you can get it into the kids in the first year of life just after maternal antibodies have waned, you'll materially reduce childhood mortality. I further think that if you have a partially effective vaccine, you should lower the transmission rate by having a lower average burden of parasitism in the endemic areas, and thus make it easier for more routine control measures to be effective.'

'But what happens when the immunity wears off?' I ask.

'That's a very important question in relation to whether the state of the vaccinated child, when that immunity wanes, will be worse than the beginning state when it's entirely non-immune. If the vaccine were to prove 100 per cent effective, so that there was no reproduction at the stage when the very first merozoite sought to enter the very first red cell as the liver cycle is finished and the merozoites come out of the liver, you might find yourself in trouble. There would be no natural build up of those sorts of antibodies which clearly are amongst the things that protect the adult, who in the main lives in some reasonable compromise with the parasites. Now if the vaccine is 100 per cent effective, paradoxically you build up a greater need for booster shots. There's no doubt about that. But if the vaccine is as successful as that, I think the will for the booster shots will probably be found. If, on the other hand, the vaccine is *not* 100 per cent effective there is therefore, let's say, a 10 or 5 per-centile of dribble through of merozoite growth. This means that you're not getting these very acute attacks—not getting the cerebral malaria, not getting the blackwater fever, not getting the things that kill people or make them very sick—you're just getting a moderately mild disease. This means in turn that there'll be a constant booster to the immune system. The actual mini-attacks of malaria should be providing their own booster immunization and there may not be the need for repeated boosters. So in a sense there's an each way bet, isn't there?'

'But how', I ask, 'is this all going to be explained to people at the village level in Papua New Guinea and the Philippines?'

'I think you can sell it to the villagers on the basis of lowering child mortality. I'm not at all familiar with their health beliefs or practices but they must know how those attacks of fever often end up killing their kids. There can be up to 150 per 1000, depending on the area, who actually die of malaria. I think that if you were to say to them, "Look, you remember in this village last year six kids died of that big fever?" They've got three main killers (if you forget neonatal deaths in the first week of life)—acute pneumonias, diarrhoeal illnesses and malaria—and they must know their kids are dying of one or the other. So you say, "We think that if all the kids are vaccinated you might eliminate the deaths from fever altogether or get it down to one or two". My own belief is that they'd understand that. I don't think you'd necessarily have to say any more. I think it would be unwise to say that you'll eliminate mortality altogether.'

I raise the question of testing the vaccine, if and when it is shown to be feasible.

'I think we'll certainly do phase 1 and phase 2 of the testing together. Phase 1 we'll do on ourselves. I'll probably be the first person to get it. Mitchell will probably be the second. But that will simply mean that we've got rid of the nasties from the *E. coli*. Phase

2 will be, say, 100 kids who'll then be followed for a couple of years. That, I think, will almost certainly be done in Papua New Guinea. But whether then, if that's successful, we'll even be allowed to do phase 3 (the first few thousand) in Papua New Guinea, or whether it becomes a global program masterminded by WHO, I'll take advice on. I want to do whatever's sensible if we get to that lucky stage. But for phase 2 we may need advice from anthropologists or someone with similar skills. We don't know much about that kind of thing.'

****

Not everyone at the Institute, of course, shares the Director's optimistic views about the malaria vaccine project. The favour shown by him to the project and the large diversion of funds to it has inevitably produced some friction among the scientists in other projects. Annas, for example, complains to me that the Director had put it to him across a crowded table at afternoon tea that he should drop his work on a non-malaria parasite for a year or two to work on malaria. After all, the Director said cheerfully, you can always go back to your own project later!

Again, those working on the non-malaria parasites stress the scientific importance of diversification and the dangers of excessive concentration on the one parasite, malaria. 'It's better to stay diverse', Alexander says, 'until the situation becomes clearer'. Mitchell himself is quite firm about the scientific benefits of diversification, or what he calls 'polyvalence', in parasitic research. 'Because of all the problems with malaria we want to maintain polyvalence and not focus on malaria solely ... I want to take a comparative approach and establish models in other areas. We are, for example, working on five parasites at the moment—malaria, schistosomiasis, leishmaniasis, cysticercosis, and babesia'.

Further, there is a spectrum of views about the likelihood of success with the vaccine. The Director calls the vaccine effort 'The Manhattan Project', but Georges says this is a bad analogy since the physicists on the original Manhattan Project knew that it would work in theory and that it was simply a matter of ironing out the technical difficulties. But the great unknown about the malaria vaccine project is the ability of the organism to change. You could get a good vaccine and then a strain of malaria might appear that was quite resistant to it. It's still not clear then that there can be an effective and cheap vaccine that can be used in the Third World. Banner says much the same:

I don't see it as a foregone conclusion that we can do it. You can either say that it is untested hypothesis and that we are attempting to test it, or on the other hand you can say that it is theoretically possible and that all we have to do (à la the Manhattan Project) is to solve a few technical difficulties in bringing it to actuality. I think it's safer to put it the first way because it's on the cards that the so-called technical difficulties can't be overcome. People then won't feel that they've been promised something that hasn't been delivered. But of course that's not the way to impress the public and the funding bodies. The Manhattan Project rhetoric is necessary for that.

Finally, not everyone sees the malaria vaccine research in the same light as the Director; that is, as an altruistic contribution to Third World health. Some members of the team have seen at first hand the terrible effects of malaria in Papua New Guinea and Africa and they view their work almost in 'missionary' terms—First World science helping to alleviate Third World health problems. Others see the vaccine project as a piece of pure science with the subtle and complex mechanisms involved in the malaria parasite being their main interest. For them the molecular biology of the parasite is intrinsically fascinating and the production of a vaccine that would help people in Papua New Guinea, the Philippines and Africa is a secondary, though important, by-product. Others again see the vaccine as the Institute's best bet for scientific fame and fortune. As Petra Bayles says: 'A Nobel Prize to someone working on the vaccine would be a prize for the whole Institute and it would ensure grants for the next fifty years. People wouldn't talk openly about this, but it's there'.

After a good deal of questioning, I finally get a list of the other groups in the malaria vaccine field. There's a group led by Miller at the National Institutes of Health in the US, Perlmann in Stockholm, Beaudoin at the Naval Medical Research Institute, Bethesda, US, a group at the Walter Reed Army Institute for Research in the US, Victor and Ruth Nussenzweig in New York, Scarfe in Edinburgh, Holder at the Wellcome Laboratories in the UK, Pereira da Silva at the Pasteur Institute in Paris. The great drug firm Hoffman-La Roche in Switzerland is also in the business and Connor says it has been rumoured that they have a multi-million dollar program. This rather goes against what I had been told before about the reluctance of the drug companies to invest in something like the malaria vaccine— 'Valium yes, vaccines no!' as Bayles put it—since first, vaccines (unlike Valium) are not profitable, and second, they are mainly for use in underdeveloped countries.

****

Most of the scientists I talk to are quite aware in a way that scientific knowledge is a kind of artefact of their method. Yet almost all profess to be realists, as though science merely held a mirror up to nature and as though they were simply reading off directly what was 'out there'. (When I explain to Richmond what anti-realism means he seems appalled. 'If that were true', he says with some feeling, 'I'd give up science'.) By chance I come across a nice piece in an essay on poetry by Jorge Luis Borges. Borges argues that a realistic account of anything at all is impossible. A Uruguayan realist writer, Quiroga, had argued that if a cold wind blows from the bank of the river, one must write simply, 'a cold wind blows from the bank of the river. But that latter sentence, Borges says, is 'as complex as a poem by Gongora'. So-called 'realism', I suppose Borges is arguing, is as artefactual and as fictional as any other genre or convention of writing. I speak to Alexander about this at morning tea, but he looks rather mystified. 'Are you saying that science is just so much poetry?' he asks. 'It all depends how seriously you view poetry', I reply.

Mitchell's story

Graham Mitchell remembers beginning research in immunoparasitology at the Institute primarily as part of his attempt to establish his own distinctive niche at the Institute. As he puts it: 'I had to be something other than just the junior partner of Miller and Mitchell'. (He had received his early scientific education from the prestigious Miller who had done fundamental work on T-cell lymphocytes in the 1960s.) As related before, Mitchell had returned to Melbourne in late 1973, after five years postdoctoral experience in America, Britain and Europe, to a Research Fellowship in the Experimental Pathology Unit headed by his former Ph. D. supervisor and collaborator, Jacques Miller.

Mitchell's decision to return was influenced by his personal resources and background, the situation at the Institute, and what he knew about the state of play in immunology. He assumed, in a way that would have been impossible fifty years earlier and much less likely twenty years earlier, that he would be able to pursue a career

in biomedical research in Australia. He sought out areas in immunology which would be a greater challenge, rather than simply
continuing along the lines that had in the past gained him an
international reputation as well as a Ph. D. The immunology of
host/parasite relations and foetal/maternal relations both fulfilled
these criteria. Moreover, they both had an applied emphasis which
Mitchell felt the Director would see as an advantage in maintaining
the balance of research in the Institute.

The foetal/maternal project got away to a quicker start than the
host/parasite project because Mitchell gained a Nuffield Foundation
grant for the former. The general idea was to study why the anti-
genically 'foreign' foetus can develop in the mother without being
subject to the kind of rejection that attends kidney or heart
transplants.

The Nuffield Foundation grant provided some $A50 000 over the
years 1975–6 for Mitchell's foetal/maternal research. But, in the
event, despite its potential, it wasn't as fruitful as the parasitological
research. In Mitchell's words:

the maternal/foetal was a good idea, but we just didn't have the techniques,
just didn't have the way of approaching the question. It's something which a
lot of people have actually got into for a short time and then got out of—the
immunological aspects of nature's most successful foreign graft—how the
foetus actually survives inside the immunologically hostile mother. We
know she is responding to the antigens from the foetus. So we did a little bit
on that and then got a couple of publications. But that was a bad year. We
had the idea and we thought, wouldn't it be nice to have got some money
for it, and then we were under pressure to deliver on the money we got from
the Nuffield Foundation ... We weren't into the field enough and I must say
we didn't really get into the field because I got absolutely seduced by
host/parasite relationships.

Although this implies that unravelling the immunology of foetal/
maternal relationships was the more difficult area—on another
occasion Mitchell called it 'a bit of a dream'—it is also clear that
Mitchell's own backgroud, experience and contacts fitted him better
for research into the immunology of host/parasite relationships. He
had no special background in reproductive physiology and was unfamiliar with key techniques needed in the foetal/maternal studies—
as he put it, "we were not particularly good at tissue culture'. But he
was *au fait* with the basics of parasitology:

I didn't have the hangup, which a lot of students do have, of learning the list
of fifty parasites and remembering the life cycles and remembering what

host they parasitize and so on ... That was behind me as an undergraduate. A little bit of boning up and that's all I needed for that.

Again, he could use the range of techniques developed in his previous immunological work to begin investigating how the immune system of mice reacted to parasitic infection. Further, he had good connections with Australian veterinary scientists carrying out parasitological research and was able to initiate joint projects with them.

Putting immunoparasitology on the Institute research agenda was then a consequence of personal decisions made by Mitchell, who was to be responsible for that research, in consultation with the Director, who was responsible for the overall direction of research at the Institute, and Miller, who was head of the Unit in which the research would take place. As I have noted, Mitchell's own reasoning about the matter seems to have been most influenced by his own personal goal of establishing an independent niche and scientific identity in the institution where he had originally trained and gained a precocious international reputation. Although he needed to find a 'problem domain' with a potentially high profile to achieve this goal, his final choice was heavily influenced by his own personal history. Thus, his original training in veterinary science seems to have been particularly important in making this choice. The Director, on the other hand, appears, as we have seen, to have been influenced in his decision to give support to Mitchell's parasitological work, by what he knew was happening in international biomedical research, and particularly by what was happening in WHO's development of the Program for Research and Training in Tropical Diseases (TDR). There was then a happy conjunction between Mitchell's personal interests and motives and the Director's interests in international research and the TDR program—a nice coincidence, as Adam Smith might say, of private benefit and public weal.

Listening to the Director and Mitchell, one gets the impression that the research agenda in immunoparasitology was largely set through personal decisions on their part, together with some lucky breaks and fortunate conjunctions of skills and problems and people. But, while it is true that scientific research is much more haphazard and contingent, i.e. much more a business of making things up as you go along, than is commonly supposed, personal choices and individual decisions only have meaning and significance within the wider context of the organization of the biological sciences. Personal factors have to be balanced against structural factors.

The life and times of *Plasmodium*

The minute organism which is the object of so much scientific study and organization is *Plasmodium,* the malaria parasite. Parasite organisms come in several forms: viruses, bacteria, fungi, unicellular organisms (protozoa) like *Plasmodium,* and multicellular organisms like worms. (The term 'parasite' is usually confined to protozoa, worms and larger creatures such as ticks and lice.) Parasites present a special problem for immunology in that they are so cleverly adapted to their hosts that they are normally able to replicate at the latter's expense without completely destroying them, and they are also able to ingeniously evade the body's defence system. *Plasmodium* has four species: *P. falciparum, P. vivax, P. ovale,* and *P. malariae.* Of these *P. falciparum* and *P. vivax* are the most common and *P. falciparum* the most lethal. The malaria parasite has obviously developed an ingenious strategy of living off human red blood cells without being recognized easily and attacked effectively by the immune apparatus. People in malarial regions develop antibodies to the parasite in profusion, so that the parasite is clearly recognized by the human immune system as an interloper, but few develop full protective immunity. The thing then is try to see how *Plasmodium* evades the immune system and how its escape mechanism may be foiled. Mitchell once described smallpox as easy to combat because it was a relatively 'dumb bug', but *Plasmodium* is anything but dumb. In fact, the single cell parasite undergoes an astonishingly complex series of changes and transformations as it goes through its life cycle.

The lance-shaped sporozoite (the infective stage of the parasite) which lives in the salivary gland of the female anopheles mosquito is injected into the victim's bloodstream as the mosquito bites to get a meal of blood. Each sporozoite finds its way very quickly (in less than one hour) to a liver cell. The liver cell acts as a kind of factory which transforms the single sporozoite into thousands of small spherical merozoites. One sporozoite multiplies into 500 to 1000 merozoites which are then released into the bloodstream. Each merozoite then invades a red blood cell where it again multiplies asexually until the blood cell bursts and releases between ten and twenty new merozoites which then invade yet more red blood cells. The fevers and chills of malaria are caused by this bursting of blood cells and the release of further merozoites and toxic wastes into the body of the victim.

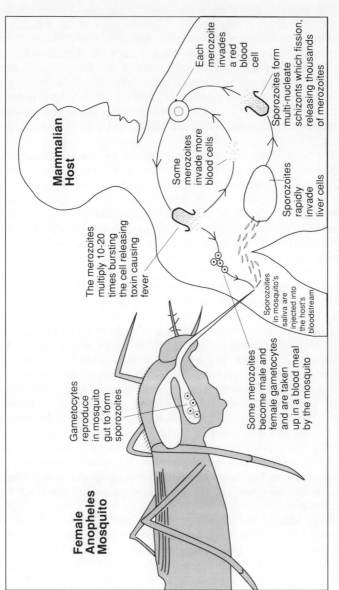

Mammalian Host

Each merozoite invades a red blood cell

Sporozoites form multi-nucleate schizonts which fission, releasing thousands of merozoites

Some merozoites invade more blood cells

Sporozoites rapidly invade liver cells

Sporozoites in mosquito's saliva are injected into the host's bloodstream

The merozoites multiply 10-20 times bursting the cell releasing toxin causing fever

Female Anopheles Mosquito

Gametocytes reproduce in mosquito gut to form sporozoites

Some merozoites become male and female gametocytes and are taken up in a blood meal by the mosquito

Life cycle of the malaria parasite *Plasmodium falciparum*

The process, however, is far from being over. Some of the merozoites develop into male and female gametocytes which initiate the sexual stage of the parasite's life cycle. These gametocytes are sucked in by the mosquito when it bites the human victim to get blood. They then mature in the gut of the mosquito and fuse to form a zygote—a new generation of the unicellular organism. This zygote undergoes another astonishing series of transformations and eventually a mature sporozoite appears in the salivary gland of the mosquito, ready and willing and able to begin a new cycle.

The bewildering biological complexity of the host-vector-parasite relationship, and the subtle adaptation of parasite to human host suggests that *Plasmodium's* evolution must have paralleled that of the primates. In other words, *Plasmodium* has been evolving and learning its tricks almost as long as we and our primate ancestors have been in business. But this story of biological complexity and ingenuity is even more complex and ingenious in that each developmental stage of *Plasmodium* has its own distinctive form. Although each stage is controlled by the same set of genes, in each particular stage a different part of that set is being expressed. In other words, a different sub-set of that set of genes is turned on and off in a programmed sequence.

These genetic programs are a kind of code or set of instructions specifying which proteins (the building blocks of life) are to be made at any one time. In the case of *Plasdmodium,* the proteins of the cell's outer coat are highly stage-specific; they are expressed in that particular form only at one specific stage and no other. They must therefore be subject to strict regulation by the genetic program which controls their making. Again, these proteins are on the surface of the cell and it is therefore likely that they play a major part in helping *Plasmodium* perform various functions including evasion of the host's immune response mechanisms. It is because of this that so much attention has been given to investigating the genes which encode and so control the major surface antigen/proteins of the sporozoite.[2]

Some idea of the extremely intricate work involved in investigating *Plasmodium* can be gauged from the paper published by the malaria group at the Institute in 1985. The group looked at strains of *Plasmodium* from different countries such as PNG, Thailand and Ghana, and while they found the same number of chromosomes in each strain, they also found that the size of the chromosomes varied quite dramatically. The finding is obviously very important since variations in the parasite are crucial to the success of any vaccine. If it were possible to say whether the different patterns of chromosomes correlate with different malarial areas and different types of the illness, then this would be a big step forward. At all events, the technique used by David Kemp and his group at the Institute involves separating the different molecules that compose the chromosomes of *Plasmodium falciparum* and is based on calculating their lengths. *Plasmodium* cells, it must be remembered, are many times smaller than the red blood cells in which they grow, and their chromosomes are difficult to recognize and count. In the malaria group's experiment, the molecules that compose the chromosomes of *Plasmodium* are placed within an electric field through a gel with cross-links that form a kind of net. Because the molecules are much longer than the holes in the gel's net, they must orient themselves end-on·to pass throught the net. Every 80 seconds an electric pulse forces the molecules to make a 90 degree turn, and the longer the molecule is the slower it will turn. The molecules are therefore separated out according to the time they take to pass through the gel. Those that take the longest time will be the longest in size.[3]

Research by Godson and other US immunologists in isolating the gene which encodes and controls the making of the protein of the major surface antigen of a sporozoite, has shown that this and similar proteins of the blood stages form structures which enable the parasite to evade the host's immune defences by 'focusing' the immune response and concentrating it on a few targets to the detriment of its ability to find and fix on other targets. In other words, the structure acts as a kind of decoy. As Godson puts it:

It seems clear that many of the major surface proteins of both sporozoites and merozoites are immune decoys and that the antibodies they induce are not protective ones: they do not incapacitate the parasite. That probably explains why natural infection rarely results in protective immunity. It also leads one to conclude that vaccines designed to stimulate antibodies against these major surface antigens are probably not the best candidates for inducing lasting immunity.[4]

****

The question of method again. A colleague who has read a draft of this book so far questions whether my approach is really an anthropological one. 'It's true', he says, 'that you have put in a good deal of field-work (of a kind) and that in a general sense you are trying to get to grips with and to understand the life-world of the community of scientists at the Institute. But, if I may be unkind, a good deal of your discussion looks very much like an exercise in history and philosophy of science with a few illustrations, and some gossip, taken from the Institute. You refer a good deal to literary texts from within and without the Institute, you make much of the history of the Institute and the history of biology, and you are clearly concerned to make large philosophical points about the nature of science. If it is anthropology, it is anthropology of a very attenuated kind'.

It is true that anthropologists usually study non-literate peoples, but I of course have been studying a highly literate sub-culture which produces large numbers of 'inscriptions' (to use Latour's term) both at the scientific and meta-scientific levels. It would be absurd for me to eschew, for the sake of some kind of anthropological purity, use of these writings (Burnet's reminiscences, the Director's speeches, the Annual Reviews of the Institute etc.), so I have fully exploited them for my own purposes here.

Again, it is true that anthropologists have for the most part concerned themselves with a-historical or 'synchronic' analyses of cultures and have tended to distinguish their point of view very sharply from the 'genetic' approach of the historians. The anthropologist is primarily concerned to show the structure of a culture as it exists and not by what process of development in the past it came to be as it is. However, this hard and fast distinction between the historical and anthropological points of view is not really sustainable, and contemporary anthropologists now concede that history has a significant place in anthropology. In the case of the Institute, while my present study is not an historical one, the historical dimension is clearly important for understanding why the Institute is as it is and has the shape and direction it has.

Finally, it is true that I have been concerned to interpret my data and to make general points about the nature of the scientific process. That, of course, can be dangerous, for what might be true of a small group of scientists at one institute working in the very circumscribed field of immunology may not be true of other scientists in other fields. But that is a methodological problem faced by every anthropologist. No anthropologist is ever really content with providing a purely descriptive account of a particular people or sub-culture: there is always a concern to show that some kind of general point or message emerges from the particular account. This ability to arrange and present the particular in such a way that it has general human significance is something that the good anthropologist has in common with the artist or novelist or dramatist. I can only hope that something of this kind might occur in this account of mine. Whether it is called 'anthropology' or by some other name is not really important.

10

The Malaria Vaccine Project

Dowayos baffled me at first by the way in which they used their categories prescriptively.
'Who organised this festival?' I would ask.
'The man with the porcupine quills in his hair.'
'I can't see anyone with porcupine quills in his hair.'
'No, he's not wearing them.'
Things were always described as they should be, not as they were.

Nigel Barley, *The Innocent Anthropologist*[1]

Organizing scientific research

The research agenda of the Immunoparasitology Unit was to a certain extent set by personal decisions of the Director and Mitchell. But those decisions were significant only within the organizational structures of the sciences in general and the biological sciences in particular.

Scientific research institutes are essentially an innovation of modern industrial society. A number were established in the 19th century but they have become much more common in the 20th. Our view of the nature of science is still coloured by a history that focuses on heroic individuals such as Galileo, Darwin or Newton, who worked for the most part by themselves. But, now that laboratories of large research institutions have become more important in science, we have to come to see that science is not produced by the lonely and individualistic scientific genius. Any adequate account of science has to recognize that most science is the result of the collective work of many people and is produced in research institutes and laboratories. Increasingly the scientist is an 'organization man or woman'. This is recognized by a number of recent studies which have made life in the laboratory their focus.

Richard Whitley, for example, tries to understand the organization of modern research laboratories through an historical analysis of the employment of scientific researchers. Scientific research became a distinct profession only in the late nineteenth century, but by 1900 this new profession had established its own niche, particularly in European and North American universities. Employment in scientific research, however, was still organized along the disciplinary lines that had emerged as the way in which the sciences were taught at universities. However, during the 20th century, and particularly since the Second World War, the range of employment possibilities for professional scientific researchers has greatly expanded through the development of military research, industrial research, and much goal-directed research financed mainly by governments but also by non-government agencies. Whitley argues that the proliferation of scientific research institutions has brought about a variety of organizational forms and research practices. As a consequence 'academic science' and its disciplinary traditions are no longer seen as the norm to which all other forms of scientific research should conform.[2]

Whitley distinguishes three types of scientific research practice: 'academic science', 'industrial science' and 'state science'. By 'academic science', he means the kind of science typified by the employment and organizational practices of early twentieth-century European and American universities. In academic science, scientists, though employees of their universities, have the freedom to choose their own research projects. Academic science has developed a collegial system of disciplinary associations which are largely responsible for overseeing the training and certification of new researchers in the discipline. They also provide the means for publishing research findings and making judgements about the quality of research or the reputation of individual scientists. The dominant form of social organization in academic science is based on the discipline, and there is a close identity between scientific disciplines and university departments.

Academic science, says Whitley, is characterized by a commitment to the production of the best possible knowledge as judged by scientific peers organized in international disciplinary associations.

Industrial science, on the other hand, is dominated by the goals and practices of *employers*. Scientists employed in industrial science are not paid to perform in accord with the ideals espoused by the disciplines in which they were trained, but rather to meet the specific needs of their employers. In this kind of science, research is unlikely to be organized along traditional disciplinary lines and scientists frequently find traditional ideals and practices irrelevant to their industrial context.

'State science' refers to scientific research carried out in purpose-built, state-funded research institutes where the goals of the employer body partly overlap with the traditional goals of academic science. However, the central goal of producing disciplinary scientific knowledge is carried out alongside, and often subordinate to, specific medical or social goals. According to Whitley:

The expansion of such 'goal-directed' research ... has had radical effects in many parts of the sciences with traditional boundaries and goals being broken down and transformed into highly fluid and changeable social and intellectual structures. ... These multiple, sometimes conflicting goals, result in skills being combined in novel ways for new intellectual goals so that results cannot easily be fitted into existing boundaries and reputational priorities ... The growth of employment opportunities in such 'hybrid' organisations has inevitably meant a weakening of traditional boundaries and of the control exerted over scientific research by traditional 'disciplinary' groups.[3]

The organization of science in a particular area will then be influenced both by the customary disciplinary practices upheld by scientific peers and international disciplinary associations, and by the more general social pressures coming from goal-directed research, the requirements of funding agencies etc.

The immunoparasitology program

The front page of the local newspaper carries a story about the Institute, headed 'Breakthrough on malaria vaccine', reporting that a vaccine developed by a research team at the Hall Institute has been successfully tested on monkeys at the US Centre for Disease Control at Atlanta, Georgia. Graham Brown, one of the leaders of the research team, is quoted as saying: 'For the first time, a genetically engineered vaccine has protected monkeys from potentially lethal doses of malaria. It's a major breakthrough. We're not there yet but we're well on the way ... Making sure the vaccine works on monkeys was a prerequisite to trying it on humans ...' The story also reports that the malaria vaccine project is being conducted by Saramane Pty Ltd, a joint venture company set up by the Walter and Eliza Hall Institute, Biotechnology Australia Pty Ltd, the Queensland Institute for Medical Research, the Commonwealth Serum Laboratories, and the Australian Industry Development Corporation.

The news about the malaria vaccine makes quite a splash in the papers, and on television and radio, though it is greeted with some polite scepticism in some other scientific research institutes. Plummer, for example, who works at a nearby laboratory, says rather acidly, 'They [the Institute] are always making breakthroughs that are not quite breakthroughs'. However, the general view is that the Institute is on to something important and that its group might win the vaccine race.

The Institute's immunoparasitology program and its quest for a malaria vaccine present a complex picture. Its subject matter is biomedical, but its method is a theoretical and technical mix of the new 'molecular' genetic engineering, the slightly older but already classical 'cellular' immunology, the much older and less glamorous 'organismic' parasitology, and the 'social' epidemiology of parasitic diseases. Funding for the research comes from Australian, American and international sources, with general funds for medical research and special purpose funds being granted by both government and non-government agencies. Goals associated with the research vary from the specific search for a malaria vaccine, to a more general search for improved tools in tackling tropical diseases, to improving the basic understanding of the immune system, to developing better techniques of genetic engineering. Employment and career patterns of Institute scientists are an amalgam of Whitley's 'academic' and 'state' science but with opportunities rapidly opening up in the new 'industrial' science of biotechnology. The link with the joint venture company, Saramane Pty Ltd, for the development and marketing of the malaria vaccine is something new for the Institute scientists.

The biomedical context

The biomedical sciences can be distinguished from a number of the basic scientific disciplines such as biology, chemistry, geology, and physics, because they are closely related with the practice of medicine.[4] Biomedical sciences are more concerned with both the 'pure' and the 'applied' in their teaching and research and they oscillate between the two poles. As a consequence the intellectual and social institutions of biomedical research—the organizational structures that make such research possible—can be expected to be quite different from those of other sciences.

In their book *The Cancer Mission: Social Contexts of Biomedical Research*, the American sociologists Studer and Chubin arrive at just such a conclusion in their study of cancer research.[5] According to them, biomedical research has come to be organized around 'problem domains', i.e. transitory areas of research at a 'sub-specialty, noninstitutional(ized) level' which rely on inputs in terms of personnel, techniques, theories etc., from various disciplines. In general, they do not see problem domains as giving rise to new institutional forms as such but rather giving way to further new problem domains as time passes. Studer and Chubin cite the view of the former Director of the US National Institutes of Health, Dr James A. Shannon, that 'biomedical science is a complex, inter-related, n-dimensional universe'.[6] In such a universe seemingly un-related areas of research can emerge as crucial factors of the solution to a set of problems encompassed by a 'problem domain'. This is of course close to the Hall Institute Director's research philosophy that I discussed before.

The biomedical context is also strongly influenced by the seem-ingly insatiable (though selective) desire of our society to control disease and prolong life. With the success of such goal-oriented, science-related projects as the building of the first atom bomb, going to the moon, and the eradication of smallpox, a conviction has developed that substantial medical goals might best be obtained through the proper management of society's resources. Such tech-nological enterprises often bring together scientific research and other components which, as Horwitch writes, may 'have quite different cultures, assumptions, priorities, and goals'.[7] In fact, the joint venture company set up by the Institute to manage the malaria vaccine project has some of the characteristics described by Horwitch in that it involves biomedical research institutions, a government corporation, a public sector pharmaceuticals producer, and a private biotechnology company.[8]

Contemporary biomedical research is then embedded in a series of overlapping contexts, whether it is approached from within science or from the wider society outside. In the case of immuno-parasitology and malaria research the microcosm that exists in the Institute depends on international networks of biomedical re-searchers, its high profile as a 'flagship' of Australian biomedical research, and the complicated web of political and economic relations between the First World and the Third.

Once again, I am confronted with an embarrassment of themes to pursue here. One could look at any one of the networks or contexts in which the Immunoparasitology Unit at the Institute is embedded. I decide for the moment to concentrate on one of the world-wide contexts—that of international tropical medical research—because I see the decisions made at the Institute linked directly to developments in the wider international sphere.

Parasitology and tropical medicine

The study of human parasitic diseases has generally been confined to tropical medicine, a specialty which emerged at the end of the nineteenth century to serve the needs of expanding Western empires.[9] The rapid break-up of these empires after the Second World War led to a decline in the funding of tropical medicine research, and Western medical scientists employed in parasitology or tropical medicine in the 1950s and 1960s found it a depressing period. There was, however, a revival of interest in the 1970s when immunology and parasitology were brought together.

One of the main advocates of the application of immunology (and other contemporary biomedical research techniques) to parasitology was the important scientific power-broker, Kenneth S. Warren, Director of Health Sciences for the Rockefeller Foundation and an authority on the parasitic disease, schistosomiasis. Warren took up his Rockefeller Foundation appointment in 1977 and in June of that year he attended a workshop on the Immunology of Parasitic Infections, sponsored by the US National Institute of Allergy and Infectious Diseases, one of the USA's National Institutes of Health. In his introductory remarks to the workshop, Warren produced the following table and commentary to explain why parasitology had not developed in the same way as microbiology.[10]

Warren said that

While the science of microbiology developed largely in Europe and North America, bacterial, viral and fungal diseases are prevalent throughout the world. The major constituency for parasitology, however, is the developing countries. The clinical counterparts for microbiology and parasitology are, respectively, infectious diseases and tropical medicine. While the former has become an integral part of the new divisional structure of many departments of medicine and is a rapidly growing subspecialty, tropical medicine has been in a steady decline since its heyday in World War II. Academically, microbiology has been securely localised in schools of medicine, while parasitology has had a spotty and often ephemeral existence in these institutions. The flowering of parasitology has been mainly in schools of public health, veterinary medicine, and, abroad, in schools and institutes of tropical medicine. With respect to the major advances of medicine in this century, microbiology and infectious diseases have been in the forefront with the development of molecular biology, immunology, antibiotics and vaccines. Major advances in parasitology and tropical medicine have largely been in the field of vector control via insecticides and molluscicides.'[11]

Comparison of the Disciplines of Microbiology and Parasitology

CHARACTERISTIC	DISCIPLINE	
	Microbiology	**Parasitology**
Component fields	Bacteria	Protozoa (single cell organisms, e.g. malaria parasite)
	Viruses	Helminths (worms, e.g. tape worms)
	Fungi	Arthropods (segmented invertebrates, e.g. lice)
Constituency	Developed countries	Developing countries
Clinical counterpart	Infectious diseases	Tropical medicine
Academic localization (schools of)	Medicine	Public health Veterinary medicine Tropical medicine
Major advances	Molecular biology Immunology Antibiotics Vaccines	Insecticides Molluscicides

The politics of medical research

Warren and other parasitologists like him engaged in a political battle to raise the status of tropical medicine. A key aspect of this battle within the medical and scientific communities was to gain access to resources in the form of funds or trained expertise. This political struggle continues on two fronts. First, there is a struggle by the parasitologists *within* the scientific community itself to achieve 'proper' status in comparison with other fields, and a 'fair share' of the resources available to the whole medical science community. Second, there is a battle between the biomedical community and other sectors of society such as defence, welfare, and education for as large a share of community resources as possible. Randall Albury sees these struggles in terms of the 'internal' and 'external' politics of science: any new development in science has to make its way against other competitors *within* science, and also against competitors *outside* the realm of science. Its supporters therefore have to play politics.[12]

In the internal politics of the biomedical sciences it was important for Warren and his colleagues in tropical medicine and the 'parasitological' disciplines to show how major advances of 'microbiological' and affluent Western medicine, such as molecular biology, immunology and vaccines, were relevant to the scientific and medical problems of their disciplines. The name, 'immunoparasitology' itself can be seen as part of the rhetoric necessary to raise the status of parasitology within biomedical circles. It implies that the techniques and knowledge associated with one of the fashionable new disciplines in biomedical science—immunology—can be fruitfully deployed in one of the old-fashioned and peripheral biomedical disciplines. The success of this strategy was exemplified by the 1977 gathering of immunologists and parasitologists for the workshop I mentioned above. It is also revealed in Warren's statement to the group:

Looking at the distinguished group of people gathered here I must, with scarcely concealed elation, begin to believe that the immunology of parasitic infections has entered into a renaissance of scientific endeavor. What is even more exciting is the potential consequences of these investigations, carried on largely in the scientific laboratories of the developed countries, 'for the well being of mankind throughout the world'.[13]

As far as the external politics of biomedical science is concerned, a number of things helped to raise tropical medicine out of its post-war and post-colonial torpor. First, there was the increased political activity of newly independent nations, particularly in international organizations such as the United Nations and the World Health Organization. Second, improvements in transport and communications enabled the rapid movement of people and goods round the globe. This has been associated with an increase in the occurrence of tropical diseases in affluent Western nations among travellers, whether tourists, soldiers, business people, or immigrant workers. Third, the experience of the American and Allied military-forces in the Vietnam War made them sharply aware of the human cost of tropical diseases. All of these factors helped the 'parasitological' disciplines to heighten their profile in the 'external' politics of bio-medicine. In particular, they formed the political background against which both the World Health Organization and the Rockefeller Foundation were able to establish substantial research programs in tropical medicine.

Funding for tropical medical research

In the 1970s, the World Health Organization developed a series of 'special programs' in an attempt to resolve the paradox that, despite US$10 billion being spent annually on medical research, health problems in developing countries were getting worse. The second of these programs came to be known as the Special Program for Research and Training in Tropical Diseases. It focused attention on six topical diseases which were particularly prevalent in Africa—malaria, filariasis, schistosomiasis, trypanosomiasis, leishmaniasis and leprosy.[14] WHO took the initial decisions to set up this program in 1974–5. It was described by Lambo, the Hall Institute Director's Nigerian friend, as 'a bold new attempt to harness scientific re-sources on a global scale to help the developing countries find solutions for their health problems'.[15]

The program began in 1977 and drew funds from the United Nations Development Program and the World Bank, as well as funds granted directly to WHO by national governments, and be-came known as the UNDP/World Bank/WHO Special Program for Research and Training in Tropical Diseases (or TDR for short!). The total amount of money available to this program was of the order of US$25 million per annum in the early 1980s.[16] Equally important, perhaps, was the funding for tropical disease research stimulated by the WHO initiative in national research programs and from private foundations especially in the USA.[17]

A major addition to the WHO initiative came from the Rockefeller Foundation, which in 1978 set up its Great Neglected Diseases (GND) Program under the leadership of Kenneth S. Warren. This program involves the funding of research in a world-wide network of laboratories including the Hall Institute. Other laboratories in the network are in the USA, England, Sweden, Israel, Egypt, Mexico, and Thailand. The GND program largely complements the TDR program in the diseases it targets[18], though TDR, being sponsored by the UN, is global in scope while the GND program is much smaller. Again while TDR funds a large number of investigators in many countries in an even-handed manner, GND targets what the Rockefeller Foundation sees as the very best groups.

Warren refers to this concerted attack on tropical diseases by the biomedical scientists of the developed world in almost evangelistic terms:

Malaria is a significant component of the Great Neglected Diseases Program of the Rockefeller Foundation, in which we have proselytized among outstanding scientists in order to engage them in research on the diseases of the developing world. Conversions have been surprisingly simple because of the humanitarian concerns of many of the scientists and their perception of a unique opportunity provided by systems of known etiology where relatively rapid breakthroughs could be accomplished.[19]

In the international biomedical networks concerned with research, the TDR and GND programs raised the profile of parasitological research and increased the funding available for such research (though in 1979 the total funding for tropical disease and parasitic research was less than 2 per cent of the US health research budget). As Warren points out, such research represented a response to humanitarian concerns, but it also promised to give reasonably quick medical and scientific payoffs. Parasitologists therefore had powerful ethical and political arguments, as well as good medical and scientific arguments, to persuade researchers to turn their attention to parasitic diseases. All of these elements played their part in immunoparasitology coming to be a major part of the Institute's research agenda.

I am not sure how many of the scientists in the Immunoparasitology Unit at the Hall Institute are aware of, or even interested in, the historical process which has brought them to where they are now. As prominent actors in that process the Director and Mitchell certainly are aware, but the younger members of the Unit seem to take it all for granted. For them the contingent and almost haphazard conjunction of scientific and extra-scientific factors that went into the making of immunoparasitology as a new research area is forgotten, and they tend to see their field of research as a necessity brought about by the inexorable logic of the development of science.

****

The question of style: It is clear to me now that I must 'write up' my study of the Institute scientists in a way that is accessible to them. The idea that my account should be written solely for my 'peers' in the sociology of science now seems more and more outlandish to me. This decision to write for my 'subjects' (and for anyone else who wants, so to speak, to listen in) means that I have to find a style that is appropriate for the task. Some idea of the difficulties with this comes out when I show Swayne a paper of mine on the sociology of science which includes terms like 'epistemology', 'methodology', 'constructivism' etc. Swayne clearly feels threatened and put off by these 'big philosophical words' as he calls them. Paula Martell at MIT in Boston once told me that she had struck a similar problem with the group of physicists she was studying. They reacted very strongly to her professional anthropological prose and said they felt that they were being 'got at'. She then asked her mother to read anything she wrote for her group and to circle any 'big words' in red ink! The offending words were then excised.

However, it's not only a matter of writing simply: it's also a matter of devising a stylistic vehicle which will enable me to capture the 'feel' of my scientists' world, while at the same time making it clear that this is a 'story'—one account out of a large number of possible accounts, neither purely 'objective' nor purely 'subjective'. I want also to catch myself in the act, so to speak, and to build myself into my account of the scientists' world. After criticizing the scientific myth of the 'impersonal observer', I cannot in all conscience pretend that I am an impartial observer! Theoretically, my account should appear as a mutual negotiation or transaction between my scientists and me, and I have to find a style that will carry a sense of this.

I remember reading Norman Mailer's book *The Siege of Chicago*, on the Democratic convention for the US Presidency (the year the Republicans selected Richard Nixon). Mailer refers to himself as 'the Reporter' and this device enables him both to report and ruminate on what is happening in the smoke-filled rooms in Chicago and at the same time to establish a critical distance for himself. I toy with the idea of following Mailer's example and calling myself 'the Investigator'—'the Investigator listened to Archer talking about the excitement of scientific discovery and couldn't help thinking how full of boyish enthusiasm and gee-whiz he sounded ...'—but it is clearly too arch. I also re-read June Goodfield's book on women in science (*An Imagined World: A Story of Scientific Discovery*) where the account is carried by a story about a Portuguese woman scientist. Evelyn Fox Keller has done something similar with her fine biography of the US geneticist and Nobel laureate Barbara McClintock in *A Feeling for the Organism*. But both are mainly biographical 'life histories' and they are not really suitable for my purpose, which is to convey a sense of the 'life-world' of a group of scientists and also to convey some idea of how that world is 'constructed'.

I find something of the ironic tone I want to achieve in Janet Malcolm's study of American psychoanalysis, *The Impossible Profession*. Malcolm's razor sharp reportage and her malicious analysis of the analysts is marvellously well done. But I don't want to 'put down' my group of scientists in the way in which Malcolm 'puts down' her analysts.

At the other extreme there are various journalistic accounts like Philip Hilts's *Scientific Temperaments* and Horace Judson's blockbuster *The Eighth Day of Creation*. However, these are romanticized approaches: if Malcolm's style is too critically sharp, these are too uncritically bland.

One book I like very much is Russell McCormach's very unusual *Night Thoughts of a Classical German Physicist*. McCormach attempts to give an account of German physics in the late 1920s and he presents a fictional story of an elderly German-Jewish professor, based firmly on contemporary records of, for example, the Prussian Academy of Science. This idea of fictionalizing on the basis of a solid collection of factual material appeals very much to me in that it gives the observer-author (me) a good deal of freedom, while at the same time being securely grounded in observable fact. McCormach's 'fiction' tells us more about the world of German physics in the late 1920s than any straight historical or biographical account.

****

The Institute and international medical research

In August 1973, the Director's 54th *Annual Review* to the Board of the Walter and Eliza Hall Institute of Medical Research began with a section headed 'Immunology and World Health'. The Director wrote:

A curious paradox has become apparent within the current immunology research explosion, now in its second decade. Despite the brilliant achievements both in basic science and in clinical fields such as organ transplantation and cancer research, the impact of the new immunology on the development of more and better vaccines has been slight. In fact, the emergence of effective immunisation against viruses such as poliomyelitis, measles or german measles has been due almost entirely to experts in the field of virology, a specialty by now well-demarcated from immunology. Furthermore, we remain without vaccines to combat the major public health problems of the third world. Diseases such as malaria, schistosomiasis and leprosy continue to take their devastating social and human toll.[20]

The Director went on to tell of his experience in June 1973, when he took up for the first time his membership of the Advisory Committee on Medical Research of the World Health Organization. He was surprised by 'the immense hope cherished by the representatives of the developing nations that immunology would soon provide major new weapons' and noted that, in fact, 'cancer immunotherapy is closer to realisation than malaria vaccines!' Having indicated that this state of affairs was due to the disproportionately low number of researchers in cellular immunology who were working on Third World problems, he asked, 'Have the academic leaders who set the tone of the new immunology been neglectful of their global responsibilities?' The Director's own answer to his rhetorical question makes it clear that he thought that medical researchers should take a lead in giving a much higher priority to the problems of the Third World.

'The issue', he wrote, 'is only part of the wider question of why affluent man is not doing more to aid the emerging nations. As medical advances are less politically charged than many other aspects of human progress, it seems appropriate that medical researchers should give a lead in devoting themselves to human health on a world, rather than a national, scale'.[21]

A year later he was proposing the creation of a malaria vaccine. Thus in the 1974–5 *Annual Review*, he spoke about the need 'to enlarge our understanding of how vaccine molecules work on white blood cells. Better understanding will pave the way for practical advances in fields as diverse as malaria and cancer'.[22]

As I have already related, the Director spent the whole of 1976 on sabbatical leave acting as a consultant for the World Health Organization. On his return to Melbourne he again drew attention to the goal of obtaining a malaria vaccine. This came well before scientists at the Institute began research on malaria in 1978.

The Director has always been especially concerned with the ethical motivation of medical research—the call to respond to public health needs and especially those needs in the Third World. But his commitment to a quest for a malaria vaccine, and more broadly to the establishment of research in immunoparasitology, also fits in with his general philosophy and strategy for the development of research at the Institute. In a sense, what is good for world health is also good for science at the Institute. Thus, he had always been determined that the Institute should maintain a high profile in international medical research.

The Director has attempted to meet these goals by anticipating major new trends in medical research and by encouraging international contact and collaboration between Institute scientists and those from other countries. In the case of parasitic diseases, he was confident that the new molecular biology would help immunologists to develop diagnostic tests and vaccines for those diseases as well as throwing light on fundamental processes of the immune system. The project also clearly provided plenty of opportunities for international contact and collaboration.

In the first few years of work in immunoparasitology at the Institute, there was a considerable gap between the Director's rhetoric about finding a vaccine for malaria and Mitchell's vigorous pursuit of what he calls 'the art of the possible'. There was, for example, a need to build up the appropriate expertise and resources to carry out competent laboratory research with parasitological material in an Institute which had no expertise in this area. Moreover, much of parasitology in Australia had always been concerned with veterinary and not human medicine. Even if Mitchell had wanted to start work immediately on human malaria, the problem was that none of the human malaria parasites had then been cultured (necessary if they were to become the subject of immunological investigation). In considering the 'art of the possible', Mitchell needed to set his short-term goals in relation to the resources and expertise available to him. These, for the time being, consisted largely of himself and his contacts.

So, Mitchell sought advice from his veterinary contacts about which parasitic systems could be used for laboratory research. He spent a lot of time reading the relevant literature, though his veterinary background meant that there was less time lag in beginning experimental work than otherwise might have been the case. In the circumstances, he decided that the best approach was to get first-hand experience in the laboratory with as many parasites as possible, before deciding what would become his principal focus. This decision led to criticism from some that he was trying to do too much on too many parasites. His first research in the area was in collaboration with Dr Stirling Hogarth-Scott of the Division of Animal Health of the Commonwealth Scientific and Industrial Research Organization. In late 1974 experiments began in order to see how mice would respond immunologically to the ingestion of *Ascaris suum*, a pig parasite artificially introduced into mice.

The research program expanded to deal with a variety of different parasites, some of which were chosen because they were involved in human or animal diseases and others because they could serve as useful models of host/parasite interactions.

This expansion was dependent on new sources of funding and strongly influenced by the goals of the major funding agencies, the WHO/UNDP/World Bank TDR program and the Rockefeller Foundation Great Neglected Diseases program. The funding attracted more research scientists to work on projects aligned with the goals of the TDR and GND programs.

Once again, it is worthwhile making the important, but often neglected, point, that new research programs arise from the conjunction of a number of interests. Thus, the evolution of scientific research in immunoparasitology resulted from a dynamic interaction between the originators of the program, the resources (both human and material) which became available to the program, the goals of the funding agencies, of the Institute, and of individual scientists, and the repertoire of knowledge and techniques which could be brought to bear on the research problems. This is clearly reflected in Mitchell's memory of these events:

So the veterinary connection was first. Then the Director went on sabbatical to Geneva which was the start of his involvement in the tropical diseases program. Then he came back and that was more or less the start also of our involvement in human parasitic diseases which came from a more political interest. First getting involved in that program as a source of money to study malaria. Our first grant in malaria was, in fact, to study mouse malaria, funded by the TDR program. With the advent of Graham Brown, Robin Anders, and others coming in, then it had Papua New Guinea connections. Then the PNG connections evolved much more rapidly, naturally. So that was the progression.

In the period from 1974 to 1985 Mitchell's group investigated twenty different species. By 1985 the unit was concentrating its attention on just five of these parasites. Three, *Plasmodium falciparum, Leishmania major,* and *Schistosoma japonicum,* are human parasites responsible for three of the diseases included in both the TDR and GND research programs. The other two, *Taenia taeniaeformis* and *Babesia bovis,* are continuations of the veterinary collaborations with which Mitchell began his immunoparasitological researches. In the case of *Taenia,* research continues because this mouse parasite system serves as a very good model for the work towards vaccines and immunodiagnostic agents involved in all the other continuing work. In the case of *Babesia,* there is the hope of developing a better vaccine than that currently in use against the cattle disease, babesiosis (tick fever), a disease of some significance in Australia.

Although Mitchell expressed his goals in general immunological terms when he began his research on parasites in 1974, by 1978 the goals were expressed in terms very similar to those used by the TDR and GND programs. In the 1974–75 *Annual Review* of the Institute we find the following:

Like cancer, parasitic infections represent an immunological puzzle. The parasite, like the cancer cell, possesses foreign molecules or 'antigens' which stimulate the immune system. Why, then, are so many parasitic diseases either long-lasting or frequently relapsing? Dr. Graham Mitchell is developing a new approach to this problem. In the Experimental Pathology Unit, great strides have been made in discovering the true functions of the three separate families of immune cells (B cells, T cells and macrophages). This knowledge, involving specialised techniques of cell separation and the use of certain genetic types of mice ('nude' mice) deficient in T cells, is being applied to various models of parasitism. Already it is clear that nude mice cannot handle certain parasites normally, thus showing an important role for the T cell system.[23]

However, three years later it was stated that 'the principal challenge facing the laboratory is to utilize the insights and technologies developed from analyses of model host-parasite relationships in highlighting strategies for the control of parasites in man and his domestic and companion animals'.[24] In the case of the immunoparasitology research unit, the 'problem domain' came more and more to be defined by the networks of the TDR and GND programs. By 1985 this trend was even clearer when, according to Mitchell, 'whilst there's no question that the quest for a vaccine is what we are daily focused on, there's also no question about the importance of diagnostic tests of high predictive value, high specificity, high sensitivity'. In other words, the major emphasis of the unit had changed from the production of knowledge about the immunology of host/parasite relations to the production of vaccines and immuno-diagnostic tools. Of course, the production of knowledge is still regarded as a crucial part of the process of producing vaccines and other practical medical techniques, but the change of focus has made the unit's research program more like part of a technological enterprise—'goal-directed science' rather than 'academic science'.

Getting resources

The rapid growth of the Immunoparasitology Unit required sub-stantial funds to pay the salaries of scientists and other staff as well as to obtain all the material resources needed to keep a modern bio-medical laboratory running. Big science depends on big funds. The immunoparasitological research first began to attract such funds in 1978. Thus the TDR program sponsored by WHO, UNDP, and the World Bank provided approximately $A50 000 per year from 1978 to 1984.[25] Since 1978, the Rockefeller Foundation has provided about $A185 000 per year through its GND program. In 1983 the unit received $A55 000 from the Australian Government through its Australian Development Assistance Bureau to assist in setting up a field station in the Philippines for the joint schistosomiasis research between Mitchell and his collaborators at the University of the Philippines.

In 1984 the Unit's activities became even more of a 'tech-nological enterprise' with the first of even larger grants. This took the shape of an Australian national biotechnology grant awarded by the Federal Department of Science and Technology to the Hall Institute and the Queensland Institute of Medical Research for their joint malaria project. From this the Institute received approximately $A185 000 in 1984. This was followed in 1985 by a much larger grant to the joint venture company established to develop a malaria vaccine. This grant from the Federal Government's Australian Industry Development Corporation is worth $A2.5 million per annum for three years. In the same year the Institute received a five-year grant worth $A2 million from the Chicago-based MacArthur Foundation. This money has been used to create the Laboratory of Molecular Parasitology within the Immunoparasitology Unit as part of 'a network of laboratories devoted to a fundamental study of parasites, with a long term view of the tools that may be required for control of the major tropical diseases'.[26] In addition to the sources mentioned, the Unit has also received funding from the US National

Institutes of Health, Biotechnology Australia, the Australian Wool Corporation, and from various Australian charitable organizations. This spectacular growth in funding is a good example of the 'Matthew effect'; in other words, that to them that hath, more shall be given. We are here far removed from the small and modest, even parsimonious, approach to scientific research of Macfarlane Burnet.

Employing scientists

Each of the major grants received for the Unit's work has been used to build up a team of scientists to achieve the principal aims of the TDR and GND programs; namely, to control the parasitic infections responsible for some of the major tropical diseases. The grants have also been used to build linkages with biomedical institutions in countries where the diseases under study are endemic, and to provide some of the infrastructure necessary for field studies and trials. Mitchell's research strategy has included two very strong organizational elements. The first of these follows from the scientific techniques chosen in the quest for vaccines and other useful immunodiagnostic reagents. The second follows from the necessity of working with samples of the actual parasites causing tropical diseases and being able to trial potential immunodiagnostic tools and vaccines in the field.

By the second half of the 1970s, it was clear that a consensus had emerged among biomedical scientists associated with the TDR program that the new biotechnologies of monoclonal antibodies and genetic engineering should be used in an attempt to make vaccines against the major parasitic diseases.[27] To move in this direction the Institute scientists required the knowledge and techniques to identify antigens which might become candidate vaccines against one or more of the targeted diseases. This meant that Mitchell had to add biochemical and molecular biology skills to his own immunological ones. Or, as he later put it to me, 'The program has matured from immunobiology to immunochemistry to molecular biology'.

The second set of organizational patterns depended on which of the diseases were to be researched, with a consequent setting up of linkages to a locality where the disease was endemic. Malaria was an obvious choice. It was possibly the most important of the diseases on the TDR and GND lists. It was certainly the one to which the Director had drawn attention. Further, it was a major public health problem of Australia's nearest tropical neighbour and ex-colony, Papua New Guinea.

Malaria was the subject of the first TDR grant to the Institute group when studies of the mouse malaria parasite, *Plasmodium berghei*, were undertaken in 1977 by Russell Howard, a post-doctoral fellow in the Unit. Soon after, Rockefeller money funded the appointment of two scientists with experience in Papua New Guinea. Robin Anders was a biochemist who had taught for a number of years in the University of PNG Medical School before undertaking full-time research in Norway and then in the Clinical Research Unit at the Institute. Anders helped provide immuno-chemical expertise as well as PNG contacts and experience. Graham Brown, a Melbourne medical graduate, had worked in PNG, and had been a Lecturer in Medicine at the University of Dar es Salaam in Tanzania before taking up an appointment in 1978 as a Senior Research Officer at the Hall Institute. Brown provided epidemio-logical expertise as well as experience in tropical countries and contacts in PNG. He was given the task of culturing the human malaria parasite, *Plasmodium falciparum*, a task that had only been accomplished for the first time in 1976 by Trager and Jensen.[28]

The other two human parasites still on the Institute's immuno-parasitological research agenda have less obvious connections to an Australian setting. The study of leishmaniasis was introduced to the immunoparasitology group by a visiting WHO postdoctoral fellow, Dr Emanuela Handman, whose doctoral thesis at the Hadassah Medical School, Hebrew University, Jerusalem, had been on the immunological processes in leishmaniasis. Handman's original short-term visit turned into a long-term appointment and work on leishmaniasis has continued at the Institute since 1977. In the case of this disease, international connections are maintained with Israel which is within one of the endemic areas for the disease.

Schistosomiasis was introduced as a topic for research follow-ing a trip by Mitchell to a WHO-sponsored conference in the Philippines in 1979. There he met Dr E. G. Garcia and visited his laboratory at the Institute of Public Health in the University of the Philippines. As Mitchell put it to me:

I saw in Garcia's laboratory a whole terrarium full of snails which is the intermediate host of *Schistosoma japonicum*. So I thought: here's a guy who has a genuine interest in trying to do something in respect of schistoso-miasis, but also at the same time, more importantly for us, actually has the parasite material ... So I thought: good, this is our link; we will start with schistosomiasis.

Mitchell set up such a link using a provision of the Rockefeller

GND program which provided for 20 per cent of their grants to be spent on establishing effective collaboration between institutions in the First and Third Worlds. He has maintained a strong interest in schistosomiasis research in collaboration with Garcia and his colleagues. This has led to exchange of personnel and material and to the enrolment of a doctoral student from the Philippines.

By 1981, when immunoparasitology was established as a separate Unit, Mitchell and his colleagues had put together most of the elements needed to pursue their goal of creating vaccines against parasitic diseases. A crucial element was the molecular biology expertise needed to use 'genetic engineering' techniques in the identification and production of antigens which might become the basis of vaccines. In the first instance, the immunoparasitologists relied on the collaboration of members of the Molecular Biology Laboratory (later Unit). This led eventually to the transfer of two scientists from the Molecular Biology Unit to the Immunoparasitology Unit. It also led to the direct recruitment into the Immunoparasitology Unit of scientists with molecular biology expertise.

The quest for a malaria vaccine

Although the Immunoparasitology Unit has the goal of working towards vaccines against the five parasites on its research program, it has gained much more substantial funding to support the quest for a malaria vaccine than for the others. That quest for a malaria vaccine serves as a good background against which to ask questions about how biomedical research is influenced when it becomes involved in a technological enterprise designed to provide solutions to Third World health problems. Concentrating on the malaria vaccine quest is a good way of locating the work of the Immunoparasitology Unit in its socio-political and medico-scientific contexts beyond the laboratory. This is especially the case when the quest is viewed from Papua New Guinea and from the perspective of the Institute's collaborating partner, the Papua New Guinea Institute of Medical Research.

Why is there such a concerted effort to develop a malaria vaccine? What are the alternatives? Will it actually help malaria sufferers in the endemic regions? These sorts of questions should of course always be raised about any scientific or technological development, but they are particularly important when the development in question is one carried out in the First World for the benefit of the Third World. Some of these First World technological advances are notorious, like the 'green revolution', for working to the disadvantage of the poor of the Third World. In the case of medicine and the WHO, the most striking negative example is the failure of the malaria eradication program largely based on the use of DDT. On the other hand, the total eradication of smallpox is an outstanding counter-example.

Successful vaccines are among the most cost-effective medical treatments so far devised. At one extreme is the example of small-pox. The eradication of smallpox, for instance, has saved enormous sums of money previously used to provide the full range of public health measures designed to prevent an outbreak of the disease. In the United States, for example, such measures cost more than US$150 million per annum before the eradication of smallpox. Any effective vaccine, such as the triple antigen given in infancy and those against polio and measles, save huge bills for doctor and hospital visits, drugs, terminal care for the dying and lifetime care for those permanently damaged.

However, the most effective public health programs based on vaccines depend on effective delivery of the vaccines to a large proportion of a given population. It's not much use developing vaccines if they cannot be made available to those who need them. Vaccines in the Third World are problematic because of the difficulties associated with delivery. (Currently in PNG it is difficult to achieve more than a 50 per cent delivery rate.) Vaccines may also be hard to store in a useable condition, especially in the tropics. Thus the measles vaccine in Africa, which is unstable in hot conditions, has only a 5 per cent delivery rate in contrast to the smallpox vaccine which is stable in hot conditions.

In the case of parasite vaccines very little is known about the details of the functioning of the immune system. The ways in which different aspects of the immune system interact are unknown, so that the effects of vaccinating people who already have various degrees of immunity are also unknown. In the case of malaria little is known about its epidemiology, except that it varies considerably from region to region and over time. Recently it has been found that in PNG there is even variation at the village level, thus requiring micro-epidemiological analysis.

Again, as I mentioned before, the complicated life-cycles of parasites, together with sophisticated mechanisms of 'immune evasion' that they seem to have developed in the course of their evolution, make the task of finding effective vaccines for them very difficult.

The complex organizational underpinnings of the scientific process are often neglected in the usual mythical accounts, but the study of organizational structures involved in the Institute's malaria vaccine project shows just how important they are. If the immunoparasitology group win the race and produce a vaccine, the three or four leaders of the group will probably get the Nobel Prize and it will appear that it was all their own work—three or four scientific geniuses making a revolutionary breakthrough. The intricate and elaborate organizational framework—ranging from the Great Neglected Diseases Program to the staffing of the malaria vaccine group at the Institute—certainly won't be mentioned in the citations. And yet, of course, without that framework nothing would be possible.

11

The Politics of Malaria

Let us consider first the contents of a certain medicine chest. It contained within it spider's web, ants, eggs, snake's skin, extract of wood lice, extract of foxglove, beetle's blood and, in pride of place, an elixir with seventy-nine different ingredients. This was not, as would be reasonable to suppose, the first aid kit of a local witch left behind and found after her arrest; it was part of the pharmacopoeia of the University of Glasgow found by William Cullen on taking up an appointment as Professor of Medicine in 1751.

Christine Larmer, *Witchcraft and Religion*[1]

I decide to visit Papua New Guinea so as to get a view of the malaria vaccine quest from the other end. James Thurber once claimed that he wrote his thesis at Harvard on 'The New England Fisheries from the Point of View of the Fish', and what I want to find out is how the malaria vaccine looks from the point of view of the malaria sufferer and of the medical scientist in the field.

The Institute has a connection with the Papua New Guinea Institute of Medical Research which is funded by the PNG Government and WHO and located at Goroka and at Yagaum near Madang. Through this arrangement the malaria group at the Melbourne Institute are able to keep in touch with what is happening in the field and to gain samples of the malarial parasites and blood sera from the villagers. PNG will also probably be a main site for trials of the vaccine when it comes on stream. The relationship between the two Institutes is a rather sensitive one, with the smaller and more modest PNG Institute feeling rather overborne by the rich and powerful and glamorous Melbourne Institute. The PNG scientists, all white expatriates, and their technical staff, mostly Papua New Guinean, are anxious to assure me that their Institute is quite autonomous and independent and that their relationship with the Melbourne Institute is not an inferior/superior one.

****

Malaria in Papua New Guinea

I begin at Port Moresby and talk first to John Waiko, a Papua New Guinean professor of history at the University. He is a highly intelligent and very amusing man and talks at length about malaria and the hoped-for vaccine about which he has many reservations. Waiko comes from a swampy region where mosquitoes are bad and there's a lot of malaria. But the locals have learned to live with malaria and they don't link a number of deaths with the disease. There's also some evidence to suggest that people in this area have a higher degree of immunity than people in the highlands. Many of the villagers were very hostile to the DDT spraying program since the DDT often killed their animals and pet dogs and cats. It also involved invasion of the villages by the government spraying teams and interference with the local 'wantok' (a patronage and reciprocal exchange network) system. There are also, Waiko says, stories that DDT was used in vengeance killings. The DDT was put in the victim's tea! Waiko complains that the local villagers are often used as guinea pigs.

Various 'development' schemes are sold to us as being completely beneficial. That's okay for us in the social élite, but people in the villages are never warned about the possible bad consequences of these schemes. For example, logging in the forests is justified by talking about the advantages of having roads put through those areas. But the tree felling causes soil erosion, which in turn leads to conditions favourable to malaria, and then the roads are not maintained after the felling is finished.

Waiko clearly thinks that the introduction of the malaria vaccine ought to be seen within the context of 'development', and that we ought to be cautious about rushing in with First World panaceas to solve Third World problems. To a white scientist in Melbourne or New York it seems self-evident that the introduction of a vaccine to combat malaria must be unquestionably beneficial. But that same mentality has resulted in a number of 'development' disasters in the past. Later, in Madang, I am told that there are increasing difficulties in doing epidemiological work since the local people are no longer willing to co-operate. They have been subjected to so much research that they are no longer willing to engage in any medical program that is not of obvious and immediate benefit to them.

In Port Moresby I talk also to an official in the Department of

Health. After discussing the failure of the DDT spraying program and arguing that the vaccine should be seen as an adjunct to a general battery of treatments for malaria, the official makes some very interesting remarks about traditional medicines. This is the first I have heard of PNG traditional medicine and I prick up my ears. The official says that for example:

One of the problems, when you are trying to look at community attitudes to malaria, is that you've got several hundred different communities with different attitudes to various illnesses which makes it a bit difficult to get an overall view. We had the same problem with 'traditional medicine'. People had been saying that we should integrate traditional medicine with our Western medicine, but there are several hundred different types of traditional concepts of disease and medicines. In some regions people believe diseases are related to things they have done wrong in their traditional environment, ranging from their relationships to people, relationships to nature, this type of thing. If they transgress certain rules, then they get ill, and then this is rectified by work-defined relationships with other clansmen, or the people who have died. If you go across to the mainland, then you find sorcery. Sanguma men go around and stick pieces of bamboo under their skin because of illnesses. In other areas, such as around here in Moresby, they get pieces of your hair, or some of your excreta, this type of thing, and this makes you vomit. Up in East New Britain, people can travel like birds and go into houses, and make magic. I was in West New Britain just before I came here four years ago, and I did a survey of traditional medicine men, looking at basic concepts used in their diseases, and also people using herbs, using coconut shells to set bones, removing stones from people's stomachs. Each had its own concept of disease handed on from family to family. So it's impossible to have a *system* of traditional medicine. There are just lots of individuls who say they can do various things. Our attitude is that if the patient wants to use traditional medicine then he's very free to do so. So long as it doesn't interfere with the Western scientific treatment.

The official concludes by making the point that malaria control is linked to socio-economic factors.

If you have a good socio-economic system and a good health service you can get the mortality rate down to forty per thousand. We have actually reached that level in the North Solomons, but in other areas it's up around one hundred per thousand. So economic advancement would make a huge difference to disease control, including malaria, in this country. There's also the problem of getting people to set their priorities right: in other words, as they become more affluent, learning to spend their money on what we health people see as the best things to spend money on.

On the plane to Madang I strike up a conversation with a PNG lawyer. He is going to Wewak to visit his sick mother. He has had malaria and suffers recurrent bouts for which he gets two aspirin and shots. There is, he says with a fatalistic sigh, no point in getting cured of malaria since you can often get it again immediately. He says that he is not particularly worried, but it can be dangerous if you fall ill and don't have someone to take you to hospital. You get weak, you can't eat and you sometimes hallucinate. He had had a return bout of malaria while he was visiting Singapore not long ago. They had wanted to take blood tests but he had refused because (here he laughs uproariously) he thought that they might have found he had AIDS and they would have insisted on hospitalizing him until he was cured!

When I get to Madang, which is on the north coast, I go to the Institute at Yagaum, about 20 kilometres out of Madang. The Institute is located in a set of old fibro huts rather the worse for wear after nearly fifty years' exposure to the tropics. I am in luck in that a USAID team is visiting. The United States Agency for International Development is a government agency concerned with health matters in developing countries and this particular team's task is to visit half a dozen sites around the world and to select two that would be suitable for a stage three trial of a malaria vaccine developed by Ruth Nussenzweig's group at New York University's Centre for Vaccine Research. A stage three trial takes place after the potential vaccine has been tested for possible harmful effects and for its ability to produce antibody formation. Phase one and two trials have already taken place using animal models and human volunteers in the US. The stage three trial will be the first ever full-scale attempt to find out whether a malaria vaccine will work in a region where malaria is endemic, and that is why PNG is on the list.

I am introduced, facetiously, as a 'spy' from Melbourne. The dozen or so scientists at the PNG Institute—mostly Australian and English—are a little wary of me but basically welcoming and I manage to interview a number of them.

Any discussion of the vaccine program in PNG has to be seen against the failure of the DDT spraying program. Three major problems were encountered: the high cost and powerful bureaucratic structures required to sustain quality control; change in behaviour of the vector (the female Anopheles mosquito) from resting indoors where it is vulnerable to spraying to outdoor resting where it is invulnerable; and finally, lack of co-operation by the villagers. These problems show that malaria is as much a social problem as it is a technical one. Interestingly, DDT resistance, usually given as the ultimate reason for its failure, has not developed in PNG. This lack of resistance can be taken as an indicator that no effective pressure was applied to the mosquito vector.

Malaria at the village level

The villagers' perceptions and beliefs about the significance of malaria and the efficacy of the treatment are all important. They came to reject spraying for a variety of reasons. First, it involves strangers entering your house, always something fraught with anxiety in PNG's culture which focuses so strongly on rivalry, enemies and 'payback'. Then, by an odd twist of fate, it turned out that DDT is effective in killing the parasites of a larva caterpillar that eats thatch. The parasite is much more susceptible to DDT than the caterpillar, so you end up by killing the parasites of the caterpillar and the newly invigorated caterpillar literally eats you out of a house! The roof falls apart and instead of it lasting four or five years it will last only a year and a half. So you begin by using DDT to control malarial mosquitoes and end up with your roof collapsing! Someone tells me that some of the spraying teams have been killed when they went back to a village for re-spraying, but I am not able to verify this.

The principal method of dealing with malaria is chemotherapy, which, though extremely effective in the short term, has the drawback that resistance invariably develops. In addition the drugs all too frequently have significant side effects. There are, however, a variety of alternative approaches that have had some success. They include environmental modification, health education, biological control of vectors, and reduction of vector-person contact. These last two are worth considering since they illustrate aspects of the socio-political reality of malaria in PNG.

One form of biological control is the introduction of a species of fish (*Gambusiae*) which eat mosquito larvae, into streams and lakes. *Gambusiae* were first introduced in New Ireland in 1933 and are still being introduced today. The PNG Department of Health is optimistic about their success but the researchers at Yagaum are rather dismissive of such solutions. A more recent biological control is a bacillus, BT14. This microorganism destroys the mosquito larvae that consume the bacillus after it has been spread on pools and lakes. It is completely non-toxic to all other life forms and is extremely effective. In Africa it has been supplied to villagers in a form which they can prepare and spread cheaply and easily on water in the area as it becomes necessary—a very effective way of putting control into the hands of the locals at low cost and using low technology. In PNG the story looks different. An Australian company is in the process of signing a deal with the PNG Department of Health to supply BT14 in its fully prepared form with the recommendation that it be sprayed by specialist teams. This deal, someone complains, seems likely to go through without proper evaluation or reference to the African experience; consequently it will be under the control of the central bureaucracy rather than local communities. It also seems to involve some skilful playing of government agencies off against each other to secure Australian government aid. Thus it seems that it will be expensive, be under expert and not local control, and likely to cost the Australian taxpayer a lot of money.

Another way of tackling malaria is to reduce mosquito/human contact. One example of 'low tech' research at Yagaum has used insecticide-impregnated bed nets. The major carriers of gametocytes are infants. If they can be kept from being bitten by infecting mosquitoes, one of the more enthusiastic supporters of the scheme claims that the transmission cycle can be broken in three months. By providing households with bed nets and persuading mothers to sleep with their infants under the nets at night, children simply would not get bitten and hence the malaria parasite could be prevented from breeding in the mosquito. A splendidly simple and cost-effective solution! Obviously there would be problems about supplying and maintaining the nets, but if the Institute at Yagaum undertook the task of supplying the nets with a follow up to make sure they were being used properly, it could be integrated with, and increase the effectiveness of, the health services.

Another way of achieving the same effect, so the locals say, is to sleep with a dog or a pig! The mosquitoes are apparently attracted to the animals and so diverted from their human bed-mates. One might well wonder whether the prophylaxis is not worse than the disease!

As was pointed out in considering the failure of DDT spraying, one of the most significant factors that has to be taken into account is the perceptions and beliefs of the indigenous population about malaria. It is tempting to say that their beliefs are simply 'folk' beliefs and should be set in contrast with the 'reality' of malaria in PNG. This temptation should be resisted. The perceptions of the indigenous peoples are the reality and they vary from group to group. The lowlanders, having spent their lives in a hyperendemic region, have high degrees of parasitaemia, continuous reinfection, but also consequently a high level of 'natural immunity', as well as some genetic advantages. Their perception of malaria then is one of a permanent unshakeable condition. Indeed they find it hard to imagine life without malaria! They expect to get 'hot skin', i.e. fever, several times a year and seem to think of it much as we do a heavy cold or flu. In fact they describe it in pidgin as 'samting nating' (something nothing). Since they do not think of it as a serious disease like filariasis, they are likely to be less willing to comply with a vaccination program, especially if the results are ambivalent. On the other hand, the highlanders have no natural immunity or genetic advantage. Many of them go down to the lowlands to work on the plantations, become infected, and on their trips home are responsible for bringing malaria into their region for the first time. They suffer quite severely from malaria and it can be fatal in their children. The highlanders are thus more likely to be in favour of a vaccination program.

The perceptions of both highlanders and lowlanders about disease and how it can be treated have changed quite dramatically in the last generation. The disfiguring disease, yaws, for example, was virtually eliminated overnight with one injection of antibiotic for each person. More recently the opening up of the highlands highway and increasing traffic along it has brought an epidemic of venereal disease which is not so easily controlled.

From a medical perspective, the real incidence of malaria in PNG is hidden in the inadequacy of the data base. According to one of the doctors at Yagaum:

In the hospital at Port Moresby you might as well toss a coin as rely on malaria blood slides for case detection. There is no effective quality control and no blind controls. They are understaffed by people in need of retraining and support. The cause of death is often attributed to malaria just because of parasitaemia. In Port Moresby and Rabaul they have to read 100 slides per day. Verification work is supposedly done in the provinces. But basically since the quality is unknown the data is fundamentally unreliable.

Everyone I asked agreed that children often die of malaria and adults occasionally. Thus malaria must be considered a serious disease, but there is considerable difficulty in saying precisely how serious and to whom.

Though I did not get to meet any of the villagers, I did talk to Papua New Guineans working at PNGIMR, and in planes and hotels, about their experience of malaria. At each level the picture seemed to blur and then refocus, and it came home to me how much my questions were determining the answers I was getting. In other words, my story was dependent on the prior knowledge I brought to the facts. Simply observing and soaking up information was not enough. Only by having the right questions in mind would I learn anything. Equally clearly, I was part of the story. The participants began to treat me as conveyor and source of information about and to the other players. Even now, when I am back on relatively familiar territory, I still find that my informants, for whatever reason, have significant information that they do not convey to me unless I ask exactly the right question. The result is that my account of the 'reality' of malaria research is just as 'constructed' and just as partial as my subjects' views of the world. For the moment, then, all I can do is tell an interesting story in the hope that it will be illuminating. Method and theory talk are in a sense secondary to action and the criterion of a good story can only be practical interest, not final and absolute truth—though of course a good story can often be revelatory about 'the human condition'.

****

To an outsider what is striking, at least at first sight, in the malaria project as a whole is the lack of any very positive co-operation and ecumenical spirit among some of the scientists involved in it. There is some contact and exchange between the groups, but the immunoparasitology group at the Hall Institute and the PNGIMR group both emphasize their respective autonomy and do not seem to see the malaria venture as a really collaborative one. Then again, on the international scene the various contenders—the Australian Institute, the Nussenzweigs in New York, the group at the Walter Reed Institute etc.—keep in contact with each other but they apparently do not see any real merit in active collaboration by setting up a research consortium. The emphasis, so it seems to me at any rate, is very much on winning the race and getting first to the malaria vaccine.

The spirit of competitive individualism is so much at odds with the official rhetoric of science, which emphasizes intellectual co-operation and openness and self-effacing 'objectivity', that there must be some sociological reason for it. Some indications are given by the American historian/philosopher/sociologist of science Robert K. Merton in a brilliant series of essays, written some twenty-five years ago, on scientists' resistance to the idea of multiple and independent discoveries in science.[2] After showing how pointless it is, from an historian's point of view, to ask who discovered something first, Merton then goes on to ask why it is so important for scientists to emphasize so strongly the idea of absolutely original and independent discovery and to refuse to acknowledge the obvious fact that there are multiple discoveries of scientific ideas (a fact noted by Francis Bacon some 350 years ago).

It is no doubt because of this spirit of competition that prizes play such an important part and that scientific discoveries are named after individual scientists. However, the copious literature on the Nobel Prize for the most part neglects the sociological significance of the Nobel Prize as a kind of sacramental ratification of the primacy of competitive individualism in science. Thus, in her fine study of US Nobel Laureates, Zuckerman is primarily interested in the scientific élite as a sub-set of social élites. After noting criticisms by Chargaff, Lwoff and others that the Nobel Prize has contributed to doubtful competitive practices in science such as 'keeping one's ideas secret until they are ready to be unveiled', Zuckerman says that the prize 'is more nearly a symbolic expression of competitiveness in science rather than a prime source'. On whether the competitiveness symbolized by the Nobel Prize is 'good for science', Zuckerman professes agnosticism: 'Far less is known than we need to know in order to assess the actual effect of the prize on the advancement of scientific knowledge and on the quality of the scientific life'.[3] On the other hand, Elisabeth Crawford in her book *The Beginnings of the Nobel Institutions* sees the early Nobel Prize as a symbolic affirmation of the internationalism of science, particularly at a time when nationalism in science was very strong. 'Viewing the prizes as a "peaceful contest" among nations represented a ... smoothing over of political tensions between nationalist and internationalist values'.[4] However, Crawford does not explain how the competitiveness fostered by the Prize, and the 'winner takes all' mentality that goes with it—even if it is given international recognition—can be squared with the central values of scientific enquiry.

To get back to Merton; according to him, the social structure of science is organized around the idea of 'original discovery' and 'accredited innovation'. He also shows the costs of this kind of social organization which stresses individuality and originality and induces a kind of blindness or myopia which prevents scientists from recognizing what they know to be true (that scientific discovery is never truly 'original'). This kind of competitiveness means that there can be only one winner. The 'discovery' of DNA was of course a classic and florid case of this kind of competitive individualism with Rosalind Franklin and others involved in the DNA quest relegated to nonentity. And the recent unedifying quarrel between the American Gallo and the French Montagnier over who was first to 'discover' the AIDS virus—as though one or the other just had to be the winner—is another dramatic example. Again, competitive individualism encourages secrecy, completely at odds with the intellectual openness that is supposed to be of prime importance in science, and of course it leads to wasteful duplication of scientific effort. One can understand this kind of competition and 'Protestant' individualism in the international economic and political spheres, but it is so much at odds with the official rhetoric of science—co-operation, anti-individualism, the devotion to what Mach called 'egoless' objectivity, openness, universalism and internationalism—that it is difficult to comprehend.

I read somewhere a statement by the great Max Delbrück when he received the Nobel Prize: 'By some random selection procedure, you pick out a person and you make him an object of a personality cult. After all what does it amount to?'[5] Metcalf, the Assistant Director of the Hall Institute, makes a similar statement when he receives a prize in New York: it's his Unit, he says, which should be getting the prize and not him as an individual. But those kinds of anti-individualistic gestures are not, alas, the norm.

Later when I return to the Institute I discuss with the Director some of my observations on competitiveness in the malaria project and in science generally. He clearly thinks that I have got the whole thing wrong and he reacts with considerable passion in a note to me.

Wherever did you get the idea that the major groups have little to do with each other? There is in fact the most amazing amount of active collaboration, sharing of reagents, debate about strategies, collaboration on World Health Organization Task Forces, endless attendance at each other's meetings and lectures, and a very active and highly idealistic commitment to working together to achieve the final goal. This, of course, does not mean that there is no competitiveness; of course there is! But at the same time, the competitiveness is subjugated to a true active collaboration and sharing. We have the warmest of collegial feelings towards both the Nussenzweigs and the Miller group, and have in fact exchanged some of our very best students with the latter. I am in constant touch with Nyle Brady of the USAID, also but to a lesser extent with the two major commercial firms, both of whom have been out to Australia as our guests to talk about patterns of collaboration and to anticipate the future in which our different streams of activity might merge for the benefit of people in the Third World.

In general, I think you have got this business of 'winner take all' quite wrong! The reality is much more complex than what you paint. There is, of course, a fierce spirit of competitive individualism in science. In fact, if you care to look at the record, this does not conflict at all with the rhetoric—

I am on record in a number of places as stressing the positive value of this competitive element in moving science forward quickly, and contrast this with the pattern in centrally controlled economies, where usually fundamental science moves at snail's pace. One big point about competition and racing for the goal is that no investigator does the experiment exactly the same way as another one, and if four or five groups come up with rather parallel conclusions, this achieves two goals. First of all, it means that the work really is basically correct, the confirmation being absolutely crucial to the progress of science. Secondly, the fact that different teams with highly different nuances of the problem will speed the lateral extensions of the work and the posing and solving of downstream problems much more than if a particular area of work were the 'property' of one team.

Now the question is, does the winner really take all? Of course not! The peer group is not stupid. They recognise that frequently the important goals will be reached at more or less the same time. The second or third in the race may not win the Nobel Prize, but there are plenty of very strong and important subsidiary rewards that really will go to every participant. Organisers of congresses on AIDS do not really care whether Gallo or Montagnier got there first; they are desperate to hear the progress that each has made. Adams and Cory themselves are an excellent example. You say that they lost the race for the description of the c-myc translocation, but ask about the status of Adams and Cory in the peer group, determine whether there is any congress on oncogenes anywhere in the world that is deemed to be complete without them, and ask about their comparative status with the five groups that published at about the same time. I think you would find the answers very revealing indeed! Lots of kudos attach to those who strive honestly and ardently, but come in second, third, fourth or fifth. They are warmly embraced by the first discoverers and the peer group alike. You would be doing a grave disservice if you did not reveal the incredible collegiality and friendship that exists amongst fierce competitors in science. There is indeed some secrecy about highly exciting research work that is not yet published. But, once the research work is published, the whole system strives to give it maximum publicity. In fact, virtually all of the ego-satisfaction that scientists get is through the open communication of their results and through the open, public (within the peer group) acceptance of the findings and their eventual confirmation by outside observers. You claim to understand what is the norm. Well, please go to any scientific meeting devoted to an in-depth analysis of some specialised field. (I have just come back from a major conference on B lymphocytes in USA.) What you will find is about 5 individuals, all prominent but some quite young, getting up one after another talking about a recent area of discovery. None will have an obsession about who really was the first to find this or that. All will be extra keen to tell you their own tiny little contribution to making the subject brighter and clearer. With rare exceptions, each will be generous in praise of others in the same area, and this generosity is not feigned, it is real, because the fun, as you say yourself, is in seeing the clear picture gradually emerging from the fog, with the knowledge that you have yourself made some tiny contribution to this. I believe you are getting confused by the few very Olympian figures where competitiveness may or may not be more sharply etched, but then there is the risk of forgetting the literally thousands of people who are engaged not in myth-making but in real science, and I would have hoped that the description of that is really what your book is about.

Mitchell also comments very sharply on my charge that the malaria vaccine project is a competitive race. This, he says, makes 'good news' and is far more dramatic and eye-catching than reports about team co-operation. Some scientists in the malaria field are, no doubt, hung up about 'winning the race' but he himself has spent a great deal of time and energy promoting collaboration between the various groups. 'It's a pity', he says to me, 'that you didn't attend a Great Neglected Diseases annual meeting or a TDR Malaria meeting to see genuine collaboration and sharing at work'. Of course competitiveness exists and of course 'winning' is high on some people's agenda, but that is more than outweighed by co-operation.

The malaria vaccine: collaboration or competition?

What of the attempt to make a malaria vaccine? Does it live up to its original, intention to bring together scientists from different nations to work with the best available methods and knowledge in bio-medicine in order to meet a major problem of the Third World? Curing indigenous populations of malaria is not identical with developing a malaria vaccine, nor is it the only thing at stake in PNG. Some of the important stakes in the quest for a vaccine can be brought into focus by considering the race to make a malaria vaccine as it impinges on Papua New Guinea.

The main research efforts relevant to PNG form three constellations, each combining funding agencies, research institutes, and commercial connections. The Nussenzweig group in New York, which initially led the field with a synthetic peptide vaccine aimed at the sporozoite stage of the parasite, is funded largely by USAID; it is based at New York University Centre for Vaccine Research, and has as commercial partner, Hoffman-La Roche. The US army group, working on a recombinant DNA sporozoite vaccine, is funded by NIH; the research is mainly done at the Walter Reed Army Center for Medical Research with some input from the US navy, and the commercial partners are Smith, Kline and Beckman.

The Melbourne Institute malaria research has involved a PNG connection from the start. The Institute and PNGIMR started a joint project looking for a recombinant DNA merozoite vaccine funded by the TDR and GND programs and by the Australian National Health and Medical Research Council. This has, as noted before, spawned the Australian Joint Malaria Venture Group in which the research is done by the Hall Institute and the Queensland Institute of Medical Research in collaboration with PNGIMR. The commercial partners are Commonwealth Serum Laboratories (CSL) and Biotechnology Australia Pty Ltd, and the federally funded Australian Industry Development Corporation (AIDC) supports aspects of both research and development of the vaccine with, by Australian standards, very large grants.

This division into three competing enterprises reflects the way in which several researchers at the Institute see the field of play, but wider contexts need to be taken into account. At one level there are the interests of the national governments of the USA, Australia, PNG and other countries with endemic malaria or malaria vaccine research efforts. These partly overlap with the interests of the funding bodies and international medical organizations like USAID, Rockefeller, and WHO. At another level are those who are pushing rival approaches to malaria research and control (chemotherapy, larviciding, biological controls, or some mix of these elements) in biomedical and governmental organizations. Finally, at the level which usually has least access to power, there are the most interested groups of all—the malaria sufferers.

Winning the race to produce a malaria vaccine is seen to have immense scientific payoff. It may, against the odds, be as successful medically as, say, the Salk or Sabin vaccines. For the researchers, getting a vaccine and winning the race has prestige of the same order as winning the Nobel Prize. Some reflect on how seriously competition interferes with genuinely collaborative research and wonder wistfully whether there isn't some way to abolish 'the prize'. Allen, however, thinks that the competitive 'winner-take-all' idea can be over-emphasized. He says:

Of course, it's nice to be first in print but everyone acknowledges that it takes months or years to get a result, and a number of publications over several months or more really do get equal credit. Then, of course, since they are never quite the same, they tend to mutually support each other. For certain special breakthroughs (for example, Watson and Crick) priority is important. However in general it is not.

For national governments the payoff may be tangible in their ability to utilize the vaccine, or more intangible in their never-ceasing propaganda battles. The USA's major interest in PNG is to some extent coloured by their rivalry with the Russians in the Asia-Pacific region. The control of the passages between the Indian and Pacific Oceans is of great strategic importance. More generally, the Americans and Russians are vying for influence in the Third World now that it has a significant voice in the UN. The USSR has signed fishing agreements with various Pacific island states and has made approaches to PNG. Indonesia looks less attractive as an ally in the light of events in the Philippines. Thus, if the US can ultimately provide PNG with a malaria vaccine and, in the meantime, with some share of the action, the US may gain some ground in their continuing rivalry with the USSR all round the world. No doubt this is not the main motivating interest of the US, but it is a factor all the same. Back in Melbourne one of the local scientists speaks quite frankly about the vaccine as an instrument of foreign policy. The US, he says,

is going through a few problems at the moment and it wouldn't hurt them to come up with a vaccine for the Third World. It would be a public relations coup if they produced a vaccine for Equatorial Africa and South America and even for Papua New Guinea. It's naïve to believe that when you are distributing largesse you're not using it as an instrument of your own foreign policy. There are no disinterested donors in the Third World, and especially among First World countries. The aid packages from the USSR come with strings and I'm sure the USAID packages come with strings as well. From that point of view the malaria vaccine is of course an instrument of First World foreign policy *vis-à-vis* Third World countries.

The successful development of a sporozoite vaccine, I was told, is likely to provide its best protection for non-immune visitors who will be in an endemic region only for a brief period. The main groups in this category are business and government people, troops, and tourists (though it should be noted that the same argument can be used for visitors from non-endemic to endemic areas within the one country). For the US possibly the most concrete payoff of all is military. Malaria has always been a major cause of loss of combat strength in endemic regions. A lesser but nonetheless significant problem is the growing incidence of malaria among travellers and the resulting recurrence of malaria back in the United States.

The Australian Government has an interest in maintaining good relations with Papua New Guinea and is currently committed to a technology-led industrial development plan that lays special emphasis on biotechnology. The fact that it has injected $A9.3m into the Australian Malaria Vaccine Joint Venture shows that it is prepared to invest in such development. For its part, the PNG Government views malaria as a serious bar to economic development, given that it is an endemic disease throughout much of the country.

As I have already remarked, there is no general agreement about whether malaria vaccines will be commercially successful. They are high value-added, low-export cost items with a potentially vast market. It is claimed that there are 400 million cases of malaria per year world-wide, but the military and tourist market alone should be sufficient to make a vaccine a commercially attractive proposition. As one of the parties to the joint malaria venture commented, rather cynically, 'Biotech isn't interested in curing malaria [in PNG], it just wants the troops and tourists'. On the other hand if the vaccine is particularly successful, it may soon eliminate its own market. And again, if it is particularly complicated to manufacture or keep, it may lose out to rival vaccines or treatments.

Thus in the international race to develop a malaria vaccine, the political and economic payoffs seem just as significant as medical and scientific kudos. This means that decisions regarding the vaccine development and trial are made for a variety of reasons. For example, I had been told that the US Government decided to select PNG as a trial site prior to the visit of the site selection committee, and this despite the fact that PNG may not be an ideal site for such a trial. Another example is provided by the Australian Government invoking (for the first time) 'national interest' provisions of the AIDC, which require the approval of both houses of Federal Parliament, to ensure the injection of the $A9.3 million into the Australian Joint Malaria Venture. This was done despite it being a commercially high risk (an effective vaccine is still only a possibility) and despite the fact that there are other very serious contenders in the race and that, at best, Australia will only provide a component of a vaccine. Apparently the AIDC was reluctant, on purely commercial grounds, to support the venture but the Minister for Science, with his vision of a high-technology led recovery for Australia, was persuaded to give the malaria venture his blessing. Besides humanitarian reasons the Minister obviously saw the malaria project as a catalyst for other biotechnology ventures.

The Papua New Guinea Institute of Medical Research

What then is the role of the PNG Institute of Medical Research in the quest for a malaria vaccine? The strategy adopted by the Institute's Director, Michael Alpers, is very strongly tied to the concept of a malaria vaccine. When he was considering taking up the post of Director in 1976, the advent of immunoparasitology, monoclonal antibodies, and molecular biology made a vaccine a genetic engineering possibility. He took up the post with that possibility in mind following a discussion with his friend, Graham Mitchell. In their view, even if the vaccine did not come off, a good deal would still be learnt about the uncharted territory of immune response. A medical research institute's basic strategy depends very strongly on this balancing of pure and applied research.

The PNGIMR had already made a name for itself in developing a pig-bel vaccine (pig-bel is a severe disease brought on by eating too much pork). Alpers advanced that reputation further, shortly after his arrival, with a vaccine against pneumonia. Though one-third of the PNG Institute's work is research on nutrition under its Deputy Director, the rest of it is firmly committed to malaria. The research strategy for pneumonia has even been carried over into malaria. Rather than going it alone and trying to develop their own high-technology base, as other Third World institutes have tried to do unsuccessfully, they have established a collaborative connection with an already-functioning high-technology research facility, attracted funding from WHO, and worked on a fundamental health problem in co-operation with the community health services.

This requires a continuous juggling act, which is constitutive of the Institute's reality, between the national government, the Department of Health, WHO and the Melbourne Institute, all the time trying to maintain its own autonomy and authority. This has particular difficulties in an independent Third World country with a policy of nationalization. The research must be wanted and needed by the government that pays the bills, in this case 2.6 million Kina (the Kina is roughly equivalent to the US dollar) a year. The research must be sufficiently high powered to achieve credibility and recognition in the international, i.e. First World, research community: consequently at the moment few nationals have the skills and training to perform such research. This generates a tension that is reflected in the fact that though the PNG Institute's charter requires that they train national personnel, there is at present only one Papua New Guinean above the level of technician on its staff. This is a doctor undertaking a Master's degree in community medicine. The tension with the Department of Health is illustrated by the fact that though the malaria program is supposedly a co-ordinated and a collaborative effort, the PNG Institute is seen by the Department as remiss about keeping them informed on its research.

PNGIMR and the Hall Institute

The greatest tension of all for the PNGIMR arises from their collaboration with the Hall Institute. One of the PNG researchers I spoke to coined the phrase 'serum colonialists' for the people from Melbourne; in other words he was implying that the Melbourne scientists have used the PNG Institute to get ready access to blood sera. Two recent incidents haven't helped. A *Newsweek* article reporting the early success of the Melbourne team in working towards a vaccine completely failed to mention the PNGIMR. Though this oversight was due to the reporter, considerable diplomacy was subsequently required to smooth the ruffled feathers in PNG. Again when the USAID team visited the Hall Institute prior to going to PNG, they gave the impression that one of the Melbourne scientists should be in charge of the vaccine trial. Since this scientist, responsible for liaison between the Hall Institute and the PNGIMR, was in PNG when the USAID team reported this, he was acutely embarrassed and had to make it quite clear to one and all that the PNGIMR Director, Michael Alpers, was the only possible trial supervisor.

The proposed vaccine trial generated even more tension, since it was to trial the Nussenzweig vaccine, the strongest rival to the joint venture vaccine in which the Melbourne Institute and the PNGIMR are both involved.

That a vaccine should be trialled in PNG, no matter whose it might be, has always been part of the PNGIMR's game plan. This has led to an ironic over-anticipation. One of the necessary preconditions for a vaccine trial has been the establishment of an adequate data base from a full epidemiological assessment of the trial area. So much work has been done in the Yagaum region in expectation of the trial that, so I was told, the local population has become markedly less co-operative, thereby making the region unsuitable. The site, I was told, will now have to be in the East Sepik and the data base established all over again.

Malaria vaccine: costs and benefits

There are still major problems to be overcome in the quest for a malaria vaccine. A sporozoite vaccine, for example, is for only one stage of the parasite cycle. Further, it is a stage that is vulnerable to antibodies only for a few brief minutes, one circulation of the blood, before it enters the liver cells and becomes inaccessible to the immune system. In those few minutes all the sporozoites have to be destroyed. Just one entering the liver is thought to be sufficient to cause malaria, since once there it multiplies many thousand fold. Antigenic diversity means that such a vaccine will have a finite efficacy, though how long it might last is a matter of speculation.

Amongst the immune population a sporozoite vaccine may even have a negative effect. The inhabitants where malaria is endemic tend to have a high degree of immunity acquired as the result of a lifetime's exposure. However, curing them of malaria may also render them non-immune and hence highly vulnerable to a full-scale malaria attack once the effect of the vaccine wears off. A further complication is that the vaccine is specific to one of the forms of the parasite, *P. falciparum*, and not to *P. vivax* which is also common in Papua New Guinea. Papua New Guineans will not be impressed if they are cured of *falciparum* malaria but continue to get *vivax*! From the patient's point of view, the symptoms of the two malarias are indistinguishable. Similarly, in an endemic region, children may have five or six fevers a year which are indistinguishable from malaria fevers. At the very least this will lead to a decline in compliance and co-operation with the trial, and may also militate against the efficacy of a vaccine.

Nevertheless, all the parties involved, despite their varying and sometimes conflicting interests, and their awareness of these problems, are very keen to go ahead with a trial of a sporozoite vaccine in PNG. This is, in part, due to the fact that the Melbourne and PNGIMR scientists believe that it is quite likely that, to be as effective as possible, the sporozoite vaccine material will have to be mixed in a 'cocktail' with at least some of their merozoite vaccine.

The advent of recombinant DNA and other new biotechnologies have set the conditions for the possibility of a malaria vaccine; and the struggle to bring it into existence and gain the consequent prestige and other rewards is in part being played out in the field in PNG. Political and economic factors as well as scientific and medical considerations seem to have ensured that there will be a vaccine trial. That trial is seen as desirable by all parties, despite their differing interests, because it is a precondition for the possibility of human parasitic vaccines generally as well as malaria vaccines in particular. The PNGIMR and the Melbourne Institute know that the trial is a major logistical exercise requiring considerable funding and data collection to be successful. By the time it is in place their own vaccine will also probably be ready to trial, enabling a considerable cost benefit and important comparative data on efficacy. It is also likely, according to some, that, as I said before, the most effective vaccine will be a cocktail requiring both sporozoite and merozoite antigens.

In PNG the struggle is not just over who gets the credit for the discovery of a vaccine and who controls what kind it is, it is also over how and in what circumstances a vaccine is used in treating malaria. The criteria for the USAID's site selection were set at a meeting of the leading workers in the field, hosted by Sadiqqui at Hawaii in 1985. One of the PNGIMR scientists presented a paper at that meeting setting out the constraints on a vaccine trial in PNG. The paper argues strongly that there are still epidemiological and immunological problems to be resolved and that vaccination can only succeed as part of a balanced approach in which all existing and potential methods are integrated in a program which allows some degree of local responsibility.

It is feared by many at the PNGIMR, particularly those who are health professionals as opposed to those who have non-medical research interests, that unless the malaria vaccine project is integrated with the health services the vaccine will fail to help malaria sufferers in endemic areas. As one scientist put it: 'Malaria has done more for immunoparasitology than immunoparasitology has done for malaria'.

The ideal circumstances for a field trial are ones in which the subjects are relatively naïve and do not, for example, treat themselves with anti-malarials nor have access to varieties of health services. Furthermore, to reduce the number of variables the subjects should not be given any additional treatment during the trial. Fear of a disregard for the health of the subjects is expressed in the uncertainty felt by some about whether USAID would not effectively follow up on the subjects after the trial, and is reflected in the fact that they did not initially acknowledge the necessity for repeating Phase 1 and 2 trials in PNG.

This question of the importance of the subject is particularly acute in the area of 'informed consent'. Many people in PNG are concerned with the question of how to provide accurate information and reasonable estimates of the likely efficacy of the vaccine. In order to ensure full compliance, the leader of the USAID team recommended at the Madang meeting that there be an education program to inform the population of the potential benefits of vaccination; however most of the PNGIMR staff argue for a more informative approach so that the patient is not given a falsely optimistic view. (When I asked one of the field assistants responsible for 'doing the talking' exactly how he put this into practice, he acknowledged that he opted for telling the patients that the government thought it was a good idea.)

Let me now go back to some of the original questions. Why is there such a concerted effort to develop a vaccine? What are the alternatives? Will it actually help malaria sufferers in the endemic regions? The global economy has undergone a major reorientation with respect to the Third World, especially in relation to malaria. Previously the Third World was mainly a source of raw materials and labour for the First World and malaria was a problem insofar as it interfered with that. Now ironically the Third World has been turned more into a market for First World goods and services, one of which is a malaria vaccine.

The situation is one in which the technical conditions for the possibility of a vaccine exist, and the interests of national governments, research scientists, and pharmaceutical companies are all affected by the new economic order. Though we are told in the newspaper headlines, 'As malaria rampages out of control, Australian scientists race to stop it', curing malaria in the endemic regions is only one among many reasons why a vaccine is being developed. At the individual level many of the scientists are altruistic and believe that the commercial realities can be turned to advantage. As one of the Melbourne team put it to me:

I'm not philosophically against commercial connections. It is fun to be involved because we are genuinely interested in getting a vaccine into PNG and if we go along we can get rid of the financial burden of field testing and so ensure that mere tourists and army personnel are not the only ones to benefit.

Even though some of the biomedical scientists involved in the project have become disillusioned by the extent to which a conjunction of economic, political, military and self-interested factors determine important decisions, these forces do not always pull in the same direction. Nor will any one set of interests necessarily determine the outcome. The alternatives to a vaccine may be kept viable and any vaccine may actually be of long-term benefit in the endemic regions. But unless the vaccine is integrated into the local health services, political and economic forces will probably override the medical. Unless there is a dialectical interaction between the needs of particular people in particular places and the technical requirements of the vaccine, the medical program could fail just as dramatically as the eradication program based on DDT. That is, it could fail to cure the millions who get malaria each year, even though it may well succeed in promoting the interests of First World researchers, entrepreneurs, and politicians.

12

Conclusion

The 'facts' of anthropology, the material which the anthropologist has gone to the field to find, are themselves interpretations. The baseline data is already mediated by the people whose culture we, as anthropologists, have come to explore. Facts are made—the word comes from the Latin factum *'made'—and the facts we interpret are made and remade. Therefore they cannot be collected as if they were rocks, picked up and put into cartons and shipped home to be analysed in the laboratory ... The fact that all cultural facts are interpretations and multivocal ones at that, is true both for the anthropologist and for his informant, the Other with whom he works. His informant—and the word is accurate—must interpret his own culture and that of the anthropologist. The same holds for the anthropologist ... This is the ground of anthropology: there is no privileged position, no absolute perspective, and no valid way to eliminate consciousness from our activities or those of others. This central fact can be avoided by pretending it does not exist. Both sides can be frozen. We can pretend that we are neutral scientists collecting unambiguous data and that the people we are studying are living amid various unconscious systems of determining forces of which they have no clue and to which only we have the key. But it is only pretense.*

Paul Rabinow, *Reflections on Fieldwork in Morocco*[1]

Anthropologists returning from the field inevitably feel that they have merely scratched the surface of the culture they have been participantly observing. A culture or life-world is a little like the immune system—seemingly simple and graspable but in reality bewilderingly complex and will-of-the-wisp like. As we come to understand one 'black box', another black box at an even deeper level of intricacy discloses itself.

Again, one has the sense that one has discovered just what one has been allowed to discover. In Australian Aboriginal cultures there are distinct layers of meaning which are revealed only to those who are in the appropriate position or situation to receive the revelation. The outsider is given one story, which is 'true' so far as it goes, but is certainly not the full story. Within the group non-initiates are given access to another layer of meaning; initiates are provided with a deeper knowledge, and 'lawmen' and elders with deeper and richer knowledge still. I feel a little like this with respect to the scientists at the Hall Institute (although of course I am not a complete outsider since I am also a member of the same wider culture—Western European, capitalist, scientific, technological—that they belong to). While I think my account is true, I am conscious that it is true only so far as it goes. I have really only taken a limited number of soundings or, to vary the metaphor, merely drawn a sketch-map of the territory.

There is the further point—one that has been in the back of my mind during the whole of this project—that an enquiry which involves human beings trying to understand other human beings (whether individually or in social groups) is a mutually interactive process involving interpretation and translation and negotiation at all points. My 'findings' are what has come out of the interaction between me—with my own curious assortment of intellectual and cultural baggage as a philosopher/anthropologist of science—and the group of medical scientists I have been 'observing' over the last five years. Sometimes anthropologists use this situation for their own purposes; but sometimes also the anthropologists are used by their groups for the latter's purposes. When I was in Papua New Guinea I felt very strongly that I was being used by various groups involved in the malaria vaccine quest to carry messages, as it were, to other groups.

This difficulty of interpretation has been compounded in the present project because the 'I' who tells the story is a fiction. 'I' represents a kind of consensus between the views of the four people who worked on the project. Those four contributors often had conflicting opinions on crucial issues, as well as deep philosophical and methodological differences. They also had differing views about the appropriate style for writing up this account. Scholarly collaboration in projects of this kind is a beautiful ideal, but it is extraordinarily difficult to make it work in practice. At times it seemed as though the project would founder and an enormous amount of negotiation among the four was necessary to reach a consensus with regard to both content and style. It would, no doubt, have been very interesting if this 'inter-authorial' conflict and negotiation could have been incorporated into the final account, but that would have required a further higher level or 'meta' consensus, that is we would have had to agree on why we disagreed in the first place!

My story is then an account of what happens when a person with a particular set of interests and attitudes ('me') comes into contact with, and tries to understand, a group of scientists at an Institute devoted to research in immunology. Nevertheless, despite all the caveats I have referred to, I believe that my account does provide valid insights into how some scientists typically do science, and so dispels a number of what I have called mythical ideas about scientists and the scientific process.

I began my enquiry with a provisional hypothesis to guide me, namely that scientific knowledge is socially 'constructed'. Science does not take place in a social vacuum but is shaped and formed by a complex set of factors operating at the laboratory level, the Institute level, the level of the wider scientific culture of molecular biology, and also of course at the level of the general extra-scientific culture. These factors range from the conceptual and ideological (for example, the scientific paradigms or models that are dominant at any one time), to the 'political' (for example, the ways in which a new scientific field is demarcated and legitimized), to what Marx calls the 'mode of production' (the raw materials, techniques, instrumentation, organizational networks etc. that are available to the scientist) or what I call 'data generation'. Personal, or 'subjective', factors also play a large part in the way in which scientific knowledge is shaped, not just with regard to the way in which that knowledge is obtained but even with regard to the 'content' of that knowledge itself. Finally, political (in the usual sense of the word) factors, both national and international, must also be taken into account.

The notion of the 'construction' of scientific knowledge is of course a figure of speech and one must be careful not to become a prisoner of the constructivist metaphor any more than of any other epistemological metaphor. The 'construction' involved in the production of scientific knowledge is not like the building of a house from the raw materials of bricks and wood and cement, but more like the elaboration of a language. A language, such as English or French or Finnish or Australian Warlpiri, does not exist already made in nature (though the material sounds and marks that a language uses do exist in nature): it is 'made up' slowly and laboriously over many generations. It is then 'arbitrary' or 'conventional' in that, as we all know, the phonemic stock (the set of voice sounds used by a language) and grammatical and syntactical rules of a particular language could quite well have been other than they are.

Nevertheless, a language also has a certain kind of inner logic in that once certain phonemic and grammatical assumptions are made, other things follow quasi-necessarily. One cannot do just as one likes within a given language. As Lévi-Strauss has put it:

In any language, the presence of certain phonemes involves or excludes other phonemes; no language has nasal vowels if it does not also have oral ones; the presence of two opposing nasal vowels in a language implies that two oral vowels can be defined by the same opposition ... A language having one word for *red* is bound to have a pair of words for *white* and *black*, or light and dark; if there is a word for *yellow*, there will be one for *red*; and so on.[2]

It is roughly in this sense that, in my view, scientific knowledge is produced or constructed. It is as 'arbitrary' or 'constructed', and as 'given' or 'necessary', as a language. I believe that this way of putting things enables us to avoid the dichotomy I mentioned before—*either* scientific knowledge directly mirrors reality, *or* it is produced by imposing quasi-Kantian or quasi-Durkheimian schemas on the raw data of sense observation.

Adopting this perspective also enables us to outflank a related dichotomy, namely whether the social and other factors mentioned before strictly 'determine' scientific knowledge to have the form it does have, or whether those factors merely condition that knowledge. Sociologists of science refer to the first as the 'strong program' of social constructivism and the second as the 'weak program'.

Once again, if we understand the constructivist metaphor in terms of language we can evade being impaled on the horns of this either/or. Thus, although we operate within the constraints of the grammatical and syntactical rules of a language, we are also able to generate new sentences within the language. (That capacity to innovate linguistically is in fact the crucial test of whether a person is an authentic user of a language and not just a parrot repeating sentences by rote.) Although, then, we must operate in accordance with the rules of a language if we are to say anything at all, those rules do not determine or necessitate what we say. Similarly, in scientific knowledge, although we operate under certain conditions and within certain constraints, those latter do not strictly determine that knowledge: we are still able to generate new knowledge and there are always alternatives open to us. Science therefore is not 'autonomous'; it is not the inevitable outcome of the rigorous application of logic and experiment to reality. Rather, science is the product of human choices and actions. Like the rest of us, modern scientists have been raised in the belief that science is and should be autonomous. But if we and they are enabled to recognize science's intimate connections with social factors and power at all levels, we can then see that science and values are not ultimately separable. Instead of believing that a concern with the moral and political consequences of science is not the scientist's business, a constructivist approach, such as that I am arguing for here, will help all of us to see that creating knowledge carries with it the task of assuming responsibility for that knowledge.

If the construction of scientific knowledge thesis is understood in this way, I believe that my account of the production of scientific knowledge at the Institute completely vindicates it. My scientists produce data and knowledge within the constraints of a complete set of conceptual, ideological, 'political' and material factors, and personal or 'subjective' interests and attitudes. When we fill in the rich multiplicity of all these factors that constitute the total context within which the scientists at the Institute work, and without which their scientific work would have no meaning, we realize how impoverished and abstract are the various mythical views of science that many scientists and observers of science espouse. (I might also mention that one of the major features of my account is that, unlike many of the current essays in 'laboratory studies', it insists that what goes on in the laboratory must be seen in a wider setting. Thus, for example, to understand the malaria vaccine project in the Immunoparasitology Unit we have to understand the politics of international science.)

Viewed from this perspective, the sociology or anthropology of science is at the furthest remove from any kind of reductionism which would explain away the autonomy of science by purporting to show it as simply the mechanical resultant of socio-cultural forces. Rather, this approach attempts to present the scientific process in all its rich and complex, creative and human, detail.

My account of the scientific life-world of the Institute has to be left to speak for itself. I would, however, like to flag a number of issues which I think have emerged. First, what comes out of my account is the remarkably unremarkable fact that scientists are human! As I was reminded several times, for many scientists what they do is a 'job of work': something of course that they are intensely interested in, but also a way of supporting a family, paying off a mortgage and meeting the monthly gas and electricity bills. More particularly, they are very much like other professional groups—lawyers, medicos, psychiatrists, artists, academics—

although there is a good deal more mystique about scientists than about most other professionals. If I had my time again, I would do a comparative study of the scientists at the Institute and some other professional groups. The dynamics and social functions of such groups, or brotherhoods and sisterhoods, would make a fascinating historical and sociological/anthropological study, and a good deal of light could be thrown on the scientific profession and how scientists become professionalized. The professional mystique of the scientists—that they are disinterested seekers after the truth and pledged to openness and co-operation—is so powerful that the outsider tends to take it at its face value and judge deviations from the ideals (as in what I have called the ethos of competitive indivi-dualism) with excessive harshness. One has to make an effort to recognize that, like the rest of us mere mortals, they are entitled to have mixed motives.

Second, what comes through much of my discussion is how large a part 'power' plays in the scientific process, for example in staking out and legitimizing a scientific field such as molecular biology, setting a scientific research agenda (as in immunoparasitology) within a given field, securing government and private patronage, ensuring funding, promoting personal and institutional glory, and winning scientific 'races'. Foucault's insight is profoundly true, that the establishment of specific 'discourses'—ways of speaking and thinking about, for instance, illness and insanity—also provides access to power and control over the objects of those discourses. This factor is almost completely ignored by both scientists and observers of science. Kuhn, for example, dwells upon the import-ance of the models or paradigms that dictate what is acceptable (and fundable) science at any one time. But he says nothing about the 'political' work that is necessary for setting up and acceptance of those paradigms. As we have seen, the new model that came to dominate biology from the discovery of DNA only became estab-lished after a good deal of politicking and propaganda. (The Director of the Hall Institute, however, has a lively sense of the importance of scientific politics and plays the political game very adroitly, al-though of course the received rhetoric will not allow him to say so openly.) In general, as a recent commentator has put it, 'the affinities between modern science and the state, and the robber barons, entre-preneurs, statespersons and lobbyists of the "scientific community", are rarely mentioned in analyses of science and values'.[3] More generally again, it could be said that the kind of science done at the Institute supports and legitimizes the medical model of health and illness. As my colleague Dan Donald says: 'The Institute scientists are—in addition to the roles you allocate to them—the engine for the medicalization of health and illness, the validation of the medical model. I don't need to elaborate on the power ramifications, but I do think this study [he is referring to a draft of this book] is one written by a healthy person.'

Third, even in the very restricted field of immunology there is no one 'method' of scientific investigation. Science is much more anarchic and Heath Robinsonish than anyone allows. Theories are important, but the neat classical picture of deductions being made from theories and then tested by observation and experiment (the so-called hypothetico-deductive method) scarcely ever corresponds to the reality of the scientific process. Much of scientific investigation relies on a pragmatic 'let's try it and see what happens' approach, and the getting of data is all important. One might almost say that any procedure which produces reliable data is 'scientific' by definition.

Instead of concentrating on 'the method' of science as philosophers of science from Bacon to Popper have done, then, we should fix our attention on what I have called 'data generation systems', involving techniques, instrumentation, experimental materials (mice, sheep) co-ordinated organizational networks and so on. Irrational and uncontrollable factors—lucky breaks, playing one's hunches, being in the right place at the right time—also play a disconcertingly large part in scientific discovery, though no doubt the usual caveat is apposite, namely that it takes a perceptive and experienced scientist to capitalize on happy accidents and luck and intuitive hunches. The Assistant Director's entry into cancer research is a quintessential example of that.

Finally, a general point related to the more particular points I have just been making. What strikes one forcibly as one looks at the way scientists carry on in reality, is the enormous disparity between that reality and the idealized or mythical accounts of it that are given by both observers of science and scientists themselves. The rich and complex set of very diverse activities that are described as 'science' is as undefinable as the set of activities described as 'art' and one might just as well try to define 'the method' of science as one might attempt to define 'the method' of art. We can draw a rough and ready boundary around those sets of activities and demarcate them, but that is about the best we can do.

Any authentic attempt to understand a culture *ipso facto* involves critical judgements on its various aspects, and envisaging how it might be changed or transformed. One does not have to be a Marxist to recognize that to understand something is also to see how it might be changed, nor to recognize that sociological or anthropological understandings of a positivistic kind, which pretend to be purely descriptive and claim that they are simply telling it 'like it is' and eschewing critical judgement and evaluation, are in fact often surreptitiously making value judgements of their own (usually endorsing the status quo). The critical judgements I have to make are, I hope, apparent in my account. I would, however, like to single out two or three issues of importance.

First, one cannot but be struck by the contradiction between the ideal norms of science, that scientific knowledge should be disinterested and that it should be public property available to everyone, and the spirit of competitive individualism, as I have called it, that plays so large a part in the scientific enterprise. It may be that this competitiveness can be reconciled, as the Director believes, with scientific co-operation and ecumenism, or even that, like capitalist economic competition, it plays a necessary part in promoting scientific progress. However, the fact remains that there is a *prima facie* contradiction between the ideals of science and the competitive spirit. The 'winner takes all' ethos of the new biology, which began definitively with Crick and Watson's discovery of DNA, and which older biologists like Chargaff deplored, has been exacerbated by the commercialization of recombinant DNA and other forms of biotechnology. As Susan Wright has put it with regard to the development of recombinant DNA in the 1970s: 'Commercial norms with respect to scientific practice replaced academic norms, and commercial goals penetrated deep into the design of research'.[4] Marxist philosophers of science claim that this contradiction is due to the capitalist exploitation of science and technology and that in a post-capitalist society the ethos of competitive individualism would wither away. Whatever might be said about that, we can at least note the contradiction between the ideal norms of science (disinterestedness and public access) and the reality of science dominated by a competitive and individualistic ethos. And, on the basis of that we can at least envisage the possibility of a form of science where there would no longer be that kind of contradiction—where in other words, the scientific enterprise would no longer be animated to the same extent by individualistic competition.

I must admit that I was rather startled by the sharp reaction of both the Director and Mitchell to my remarks about the individualistic ethos prevailing in the malaria vaccine quest. No doubt there is and must be a kind of dialectical tension between co-operation and individualism and it would be best to say that scientific research is characterized by co-operative competition or, if you like, competitive collaboration. The major aim of all scientists is to get useable results and, given the inherent complexity and fallibility of the enterprise, every individual scientist is dependent on the work of others. Not only is the input from other scientists' work essential because of the complexity of understanding any given bit of reality, but that input has to be reliable. In the end then it cannot be a game in which the winner takes all. Though there are big prizes and big stakes, in which whole disciplines, institutes, laboratories, individual careers and reputations can be won and lost, the system has to be such that some of the spoils are distributed and there are consolation prizes for coming second. At the same time the game is essentially a struggle for authority. If you can so define the field that your own skills, techniques, instrumentation and theory are the ones that produce the results that others want, then you can ensure greater and more reliable access to funding, research students and publication. As I have said, the game then is of necessity one of competitive collaboration. I have perhaps overemphasized the competitive aspect, but in my view the Director and Mitchell exaggerate the co-operative aspect.

The second issue worthy of remark is the position of women in science. I do not believe, as some have argued, that the present style of scientific enquiry is essentially 'patriarchalist' and anti-woman, despite the aggressive and 'macho' spirit that prevails in some areas, and I do not believe that we need to envisage a distinctively feminist style of scientific enquiry or even, as Fox Keller puts it, a 'gender free' approach.[5] Some have wanted to contrast the aggressive 'male' scientific style of Crick and Watson and their successors with the comtemplative 'female' style of Barbara McClintock and other biologists of her ilk, but I do not think that one can make much out of such oppositions.[6] Certainly I found nothing in my enquiry at the Institute to support them.

Nevertheless, given the way in which science is organized, and given prevailing social structures, women do at present miss out. The whole present process of professionalization (making one's run between the ages of twenty-five and thirty five) is biased against them. As we have seen, only an exceptional few women have top jobs at the Institute. Once again, we can at least envisage an alternative form of the organization of science (entry and re-entry into science, training and professionalization) which would permit women to participate more fully at the higher levels of scientific research. One does not, however, see much at present being done about this either at the Institute or in science generally. Richmond once said facetiously to me that the reason why women do not succeed in top science must be 'in the genes'. One would almost think that most scientists really believe that men are genetically programmed to be better than women in science!

Finally, one must remark on the relative lack of interest shown by the immunologists at the Institute in the ethical and social implications of what they are doing. The spirit of ethical concern about recombinant DNA that flared up at the Asilomar Conference in 1975 is now as dead as a dodo. Asilomar has in fact assumed a legendary status: it was then that the biologists dramatically demonstrated their moral and social sensitivities about recombinant DNA and the new biotechnology, and one gets the impression that, having once shown their bona fides, they no longer need to keep doing so! Despite a few demurrers about the commercialization of biotechnology, there is not at present any real debate about the very important issues this raises. Certainly at the Institute very little time and energy is spent on these issues. Allen tells me that some scientists at the Institute are deeply concerned about the ethical and social aspects of their work; however, I cannot recall any public discussion of them at the Wednesday seminars, or in the *Annual Reviews*.

No doubt scientists are no better and no worse in this respect than any other professional groups in our community, but given the immense human importance of the biological sciences, one might expect bio-scientists to be more sensitive to the wider ethical and social implications of their work. (After reading a draft of this book Rolland makes the following rather barbed but pertinent remark: 'I notice that there is very little discussion in your opus on the ethics of *your* study and the possible effects it could have had, or might have had, on research policy, funding or the concerns of the scientists under study.')

Is it feasible to have an ethically and socially aware style of science where successful enquiry and moral sensitivity to the implications of such enquiry would go hand in hand? Once again, one can at least envisage the possibility of such a style or form of science, though it is difficult at present to give any concrete shape to that possibility.

One question which has been in my mind continually during this project is why the scientists do what they do. To put it colloquially, what's in it for them? The scientific life, at least at the top international level, is so personally arduous and demanding and so dependent on single-minded, almost obsessive, conviction and devotion, that one wonders why the Institute scientists keep at it. Again, there are very real risks in working for a long time on a project which might finally come to nothing, or one might, like Adams and Cory, find oneself pipped at the post by another competitor. There are of course some rewards in terms of prestige and recognition and prizes and money, but these are not really proportionate to the time and energy and commitment and risk that scientific research at the highest level demands.

No doubt the scientific career is like any other career, a way of paying the rent and keeping the bank manager at bay, but a basic reason why scientists keep at it must presumably be that they find scientific enquiry so intrinsically fascinating that it makes up for all the burdens and costs. Macfarlane Burnet claimed that a good scientist needs to have a strong sense of play—a willingness to follow out one's curiosity just for the sheer gratuitous pleasure of it. There are of course other more self-interested motives operating among the scientists at the Institute, but the desire to piece together at least a part of 'the lovely mosaic', as the Director once put it, of the immune system is, it seems, the thing that keeps them going. Or, as Richmond once said to me: 'When you have patiently chipped away at the marble and the statue stands revealed at last, then it is all worthwhile.'

Some people I interviewed at the Institute claimed that the pursuit of that gratuitous curiosity induces tunnel vision and often results in personal impoverishment. 'Most of the scientists I knew at the Hall were not very interesting human beings', Phyllis Bean once said to me. But of course that disjunction between professional genius and personal maturity is also to be found in other professions—art, literature, philosophy and so on. There is no necessary connection between being a good scientist (or artist, or novelist, or philosopher) and being what Aristotle would call a eudaemonic person. In any case, from what I have seen of people at the Institute, I cannot say that the scientists are less interesting or less mature as human beings than my own professional kind. Indeed, I am not at all sure if my own kind would come out nearly as well as the Institute immunologists if I were to turn my anthropological torch on them!

Right through this enquiry I have been conscious of the need to reflect on what I was doing, to observe myself observing, to anthropologize myself anthropologizing. I now see that almost all the points I have made about the scientists at the Institute could, *mutatis mutandis*, be made about what I am doing as an anthropologist of science. When I reflect upon it I think I have learned as much about my own scientific life-world as about theirs.

NOTES

Introduction

1 Bruno Latour and Steve Woolgar, *Laboratory Life: The Social Construction of Scientific Facts*, Sage, Beverly Hills, 1979, p. 11.

2 Laura Nader, 'Up the Anthropologist: Perspectives Gained from Studying Up', in D. Hymes (ed.), *Reinventing Anthropology*, Random House, New York, 1974, pp. 284–311.

3 See the stimulating essay by Clifford Geertz, 'The Way We Think Now', in *Local Knowledge: Further Essays in Interpretive Anthropology*, Basic Books, New York, 1983.

4 See ,Clifford Geertz, *Local Knowledge: Further Essays in Interpretive Anthropology*, and for a perceptive overview, Malcolm Crick, 'Anthropological Field Research, Meaning Creation and Knowledge Construction', in D. Parkin (ed.), *Semantic Anthropology*, London, Academic Press, 1982.

5 *Local Knowledge*, p. 70.

6 Cited in Jack D. Douglas, *Creative Interviewing*, Sage, Beverly Hills, 1985.

7 Robert A. Georges and Michael O. Jones, *People Studying People: The HumanElement in Fieldwork*, University of California Press, Berkeley, 1980, p. 111.

8 ibid., p. 20. For further reflections on 'observer' and 'observed' negotiation in the social sciences see Paul Rabinow, *Reflections on Fieldwork in Morocco*, University of California Press, Berkeley, 1979. See also the same author's 'Humanism as Nihilism: The Bracketing of Truth and Seriousness in American Cultural Anthropology', in N. Haan *et al.* (eds), *Social Science as Moral Inquiry*, Columbia University Press, New York, 1983. See R. F. Ellen (ed.), *Ethnographic Research: A Guide to General Conduct*, Academic Press, London, 1984, p. 11. See also Jacqui Sarsby, 'The Fieldwork Experience', in the same collection; George W. Stocking Jr. (ed.), *Observers Observed: Essays on Ethnographic Fieldwork* (History of Anthropology, vol. 1), The University of Wisconsin Press, Madison, 1983; James Clifford, 'Power and Dialogue in Ethnography : Marcel Griaule's Initiation', in George W. Stocking (ed.), *Observers Observed*, pp. 121–56; James Clifford, *Person and Myth: Maurice Leenhardt in the Melanesian World*, University of California Press, Berkeley, 1982; James Clifford, 'On Ethnographic Surrealism', in *Comparative Studies in Society and History*, vol. 23, 1981, pp. 539–64. Some anthropologists have argued that the recognition that anthropological accounts are 'constructs' puts anthropology itself into question. See, for example, K. Dwyer, *Moroccan Dialogues: Anthropology in Question*, Johns Hopkins University Press, Baltimore, 1982, and P. Rabinow, 'Representations are social facts: modernity and post-modernity in anthropology', in J. Clifford and G. E. Marcus (eds), *Writing Culture: Poetics and Politics in Ethnography*, University of California Press, Berkeley, 1986. For a 'meta-study' of anthropologists' writing of ethnographic texts see George E. Marcus and Dick Cushman, 'Ethnographies as Texts', *Annual Review of Anthropology*, vol. 11, 1980, pp. 25–69, and the

brilliant work by James Clifford, *The Predicament of Culture: Twentieth Century Ethnography, Literature and Art*, Harvard University Press, Cambridge, Mass., 1988. This latter collects some of the essays by Clifford mentioned above.

9   Thomas S. Kuhn, *The Structure of Scientific Revolutions*, University of Chicago Press, Chicago, 2nd edn, 1970. See also the same author's *The Essential Tension*, University of Chicago Press, Chicago, 1977. There is a very large body of critical studies of Kuhn's view of science. See, for example, John Krige, *Science, Revolution and Discontinuity*, The Harvester Press, Brighton, 1980, ch. 1.

10 In 'Philosophies and Human Understanding', in A. F. Heath (ed.), *Scientific Explanation*, Clarendon Press, Oxford, 1981, p. 101, Hilary Putnam argues, after Wittgenstein, that without public norms shared by a group and constituting a 'form of life', language and even thought itself would be impossible. Similarly within science 'the judgement that special relativity and quantum electrodynamics are the most successful physical theories we have is one which is made by authorities whom the society has appointed and whose authority is recognised by a host of practices and ceremonies, and in that sense institutionalised'.

11 On neo-Marxist studies of the culture of science see J. D. Bernal, *The Social Function of Science*, Routledge, London, 1936. See also the *Radical Science Journal*, London. On Marx's views of science see M. J. Mulkay, *Science and the Sociology of Knowledge*, Allen and Unwin, London, 1979. See also E. Yoxen, 'Life as a productive force: capitalising the science and technology of molecular biology', in L. Levidow and R. M. Young (eds), *Science, Technology and the Labour Process*, CSE Books, London, 1981, pp, 66–122.

12 Edward Yoxen, 'Giving Life a New Meaning: The Rise of the Molecular Biology Establishment', in N. Elias, H. Martins, R. Whitley (eds), *Scientific Establishments and Hierarchies*, Sociology of the Sciences Yearbook 1982, D. Reidel, Dordrecht, 1982, p. 125. On the influence of the Rockefeller Foundation see Pnina Abir-Am, 'The Discourse of Physical Power and Biological Knowledge in the 1930s: A Reappraisal of the Rockefeller Foundation's "Policy in Molecular Biology"', *Social Studies of Science*, vol. 12, 1982, pp. 341–82. See also A. R. Pickering, *Constructing Quarks: A Sociological History of Particle Physics*, University of Chicago Press, Chicago, 1984.

13 H. F. Judson, *The Eighth Day of Creation: The Makers of the Revolution in Biology*, Simon and Schuster, New York, 1979. See also Evelyn Fox Keller, *A Feeling for the Organism: the Life and Work of Barbara McClintock,* W. H. Freeman, New York, 1983, and the brilliant essay, 'Emigré Physicists and the Biological Revolution' by the historian Donald Fleming (in the series *Perspectives in American History*, vol. 11, 1965, Charles Warren Center for Studies in American History, Harvard University Press). See also Pnina Abir-Am, 'From Biochemistry to Molecular Biology', in *History and Philosophy of the Life Sciences*, vol. 2, no. 1, 1980, pp. 3–60.

14 For an overview of the various laboratory studies see Karen Knorr, 'The Ethnographic Study of Scientific Work: Toward a Constructivist Interpretation of Science', in K. Knorr and M. Mulkay (eds), *Science Observed: Perspectives on the Social Study of Science*, Sage, London, 1983. See also Knorr's *The Manufacture of Knowledge*, Pergamon, Oxford, 1981. Recent studies in this area include P. Abir-Am, 'How Scientists View Their Heroes: Some Remarks

on the Mechanism of Myth Construction' in *Journal of the History of Biology*, vol. 5, no. 2, 1982, pp. 281–315; Nigel Gilbert and Michael Mulkay, *Opening Pandora's Box: A Sociological Analysis of Scientists' Discourse*, Cambridge University Press, Cambridge, 1984; Marc Grenier, 'Cognition and Social Construction in Laboratory Science', in *4S Review*, vol. 1, no. 3, 1983; H. M. Collins, 'The Sociology of Scientific Knowledge: Studies of Contemporary Science', in *The Annual Review of Sociology*, vol. 9, 1983, pp. 265–85.

15   See Malcolm Crick, 'Anthropological Field Research, Meaning Creation and Knowledge Construction', p. 23. 'Recent studies going under the general label of "social studies of science" ... are exposing a great deal of philosophy of science as ideological and mystificatory, as disguising the actual operations of scientific research. They are concerned with empirical studies of how science actually gets done, how facts are constructed, negotiated and established, how various social processes play a part in producing that collective achievement called scientific knowledge. Critics of the social studies of sciences movement were quick to invoke a "muckraking" image for the enterprise. Sociologists of science were thought to be obsessed with where science had been done badly. On the contrary, however, its fundamental concern is not with what goes on when science falls short of its standards, but what exactly are the rules by which scientific knowledge is generated.'

16   See Clifford Geertz, 'Anti-Relativism', in *American Anthropologist*, vol. 86, 1984, p. 263.

17   See Robert A. Georges and Michael O Jones, *People Studying People: The Human Element in Fieldwork*, p. 22. 'Fieldwork is also a one-sided and a selfish act. Every fieldwork project has its inception in the mind of some individual who decided unilaterally that some other human being(s) will serve as the source or resource for information. Rarely are those who are considered and selected as subjects for fieldwork asked in advance if they are willing to be so identified; seldom are they requested to participate in the design of the fieldwork project or to judge and approve the plans that call for someone to observe and document their behaviour.' The authors describe the tactics used by an American anthropoligist to gain access to a potlach ceremony (giving away of goods) of the Northwest Pacific Coast Indians. In the words of this fieldworker, 'The potential prize was a firsthand look at a potlach and the attendant academic success. The potential cost was academic and personal failure, expulsion from the village, and return to Chicago as an ethnographic washout.'

18   P. Medawar, 'Lucky Jim', in *Pluto's Republic*, Oxford University Press, London, 1982, p. 273.

19   F. Jameson, *The Political Unconscious: Narrative as a Socially Symbolic Act*, Cornell University Press, Cornell, 1981, p. 106.

20   On realism and other genres of anthropological writing, see George E. Marcus and Dick Cushman, 'Ethnographies as texts', *Annual Review of Anthropology*, vol. 11, 1980, pp. 25–69.

Chapter 1

1   Howard Morphy, 'Forms of Religious Experience', in M. Charlesworth, H. Morphy, D. Bell, K. Maddock (eds), *Religion in Aboriginal Australia*, University of Queensland Press, St Lucia, 1986, p. 215.

2   G. M. Edelman, 'The Internationalism of Medical Research', *The Walter and*

Eliza Hall Institute of Medical Research: Annual Review 1985–6, p. 8.

3   See Max Delbrück, *Mind from Matter? An Essay on Evolutionary Epistem-ology*, Blackwell Scientific Publications, Palo Alto, 1986. See also Edelman's recent book, *Neural Darwinism : The Theory of Neuronal Group Selections*, Basic Books, New York, 1987.

4   'The Internationalism of Medical Research', p. 8.

5   Harrien Zuckerman, *Scientific Elite*, The Free Press, New York, 1979, p. 177.

6   Jonathan Cole, *Fair Science: Women in the Scientific Community*, The Free Press, New York, 1977.

7   Michelle Z. Rosaldo, *Knowledge and Passion: Ilongot Notions of Self and Social Life*, Cambridge University Press, Cambridge, 1980. For a study of the anthropological literature on gossip see Sally E. Merry, 'Toward a General Theory of Gossip and Scandal', in Donald Black (ed.), *Toward a General Theory of Social Control*, Academic Press, New York, 1982. For an analysis of scientists' informal talk see G. Nigel Gilbert and Michael Mulkay, *Opening Pandora's Box: A Sociological Analysis of Scientists' Discourse*, Cambridge University Press, Cambridge, 1984.

8   Melbourne University Press, Melbourne, 1971.

9   For a descriptive historical account of the Institute see V. de Vahl Davis, A History of the Walter and Eliza Hall Institute of Medical Research: An Examination of the Personalities, Politics, Finances, Social Relations and Scientific Organisation of the Hall Institute, University of NSW Thesis, 1979.

10   See Ian J. Wood, 'Burnet and Autoimmunity—A Postscript', in *The Walter and Eliza Hall Institute of Medical Research, Annual Review 1978–9: Special Volume, A Tribute to Sir Macfarlane Burnet*. 'In 1957, with singularity of purpose, he [Burnet] made a dramatic and absolute change in the researches of the Institute. Virus research would cease immediately. All would change to the study of immunology—the defence mechanisms of the body in health and disease. This courageous decision, made by Burnet alone, was criticised by some of his co-workers.' Burnet, however, in his book *Walter and Eliza Hall Institute 1915–1965*, p. 71, gives a much less dramatic account of the Institute's 'swing from virology to immunology'. According to him the Institute's viral research was becoming unproductive while at the same time the interests of several members of the Institute, including Burnet himself, were turning to autoimmune diseases: 'So the swing to immunology started almost sponta-neously and by the time I decided that we should move out of virology, there was no possibility of any other decision'.

11   I. R. Mackay, and F. M. Burnet, *Autoimmune diseases: pathogenesis, chemistry and therapy*, Charles C. Thomas, Springfield, Ill., 1963; Burnet, *Walter and Eliza Hall Institute 1915–1965*, p. 68, says that it was in 1937 that 'I first used the concept that once the simplest animals evolved, the related requirements for nutrition (by the digestion of other organisms) and for protection from bacterial infection, required a capacity to distinguish between the chemical structure of "self" and any sufficiently different chemical structure which is recognised as "not self". "Self" must remain undamaged by the enzymes and other mech-anisms that can digest and destroy "not self". That is a concept basic to modern immunology but no one applied it seriously until 1949.'

12   F. M. Burnet, 'A modification of Jerne's theory of anti-body production using the concept of clonal selection', *Australian Journal of Science*, vol. 20, 1957, p. 67.

13   Gordon L. Ada and Gustav Nossal, 'The Clonal-Selection Theory', *Scientific*

American, August, 1987, p. 53.

14   For a summary account see Niels K. Jerne, 'Burnet and the clonal selection theory', in *A Tribute to Sir Macfarlane Burnet'*, pp. 34–8.

15   G. J. V. Nossal, *Nature's Defences: New Frontiers in Vaccine Research*, Australian Broadcasting Commission, Sydney, 1978, p. 25.

16   *Walter and Eliza Hall Institute*, p. 69.

17   For an extended account of later developments in the clonal-selection theory see Gordon L. Ada and Gustav Nossal, 'The Clonal-Section Theory'.

18   *Walter and Eliza Hall Institute*, p. 155

19   See P. Medawar, 'Burnet and Immunological Tolerance', in *A Tribute to Sir Macfarlane Burnet*, pp. 31–3: 'There is a convenient theory about the contribution of Mac Burnet and myself to the discovery of immunological tolerance and it runs something like this: Burnet predicted on theoretical grounds that immunological tolerance must exist as an empirical phenomenon, whereupon Medawar and his friends showed that it did. This is a good story, very suitable for science journalists and historians of science, and it is true without qualification that Burnet predicted tolerance; but in real life nothing is ever quite so cut and dried. The full story ... is—as real life always is—somewhat messier'.

20   Pnina Abir-Am, 'How Scientists View Their Heroes: Some Remarks on the Mechanism of Myth Deconstruction', *Journal of the History of Biology,* vol. 15, 1, 1982, p. 281.

21   Thomas S. Kuhn, *The Structure of Scientific Revolutions*, University of Chicago Press, Chicago, 2nd edn, 1970.

22   Symposium on the History of Immunology, 5–6 July 1986, Victoria College, University of Toronto.

23   Symposium Abstracts.

24   Symposium Abstracts.

25   Symposium Abstracts.

26   Judith Farquhar and D. Carleton Gajdusek (eds), *Kuru: Early Letters and Field Notes from the Collection of D. Carleton Gajdusek*, Raven Press, New York, 1981, p. 298.

27   ibid., p. xv.

Chapter 2

1   James Clifford, *The Predicament of Culture: Twentieth-Century Ethnography, Literature and Art*, Harvard University Press, Cambridge, Mass., 1988, pp. 29–30.

2   See H. Judson, *The Eighth Day of Creation: The Makers of the Revolution in Biology*, Simon and Schuster, New York, 1979, p. 142, reporting Chargaff: 'I take a minority view of science of course. It's a view shared by more philosophers and humanists. The public acclaim given to scientists is exaggerated: scientists are as bright as they happen to be individually. In my opinion, present day science, especially biological science, is a direct symptom of the decline of the West: all this shameless talk about creating and multiplying will be put down as the barbarism of the twentieth century'. See also Chargaff's book, *Heracleitean Fire: Sketches of a Life before Nature*, Rockefeller University Press, New York, 1978, and Pnina Abir-Am's perceptive view of Chargaff's position, 'From biochemistry to molecular biology: DNA and the

acculturated journey of the critic of science Erwin Chargaff', *History and Philosophy of the Life Sciences*, vol. 2, 1980, pp. 3–60.

3   R. Olby, *The Path to the Double Helix*, Macmillan, London, 1974.

4   J. D. Watson, *The Double Helix: a personal account of the discovery of the structure of DNA*, Penguin, Harmondsworth, 1970.

5   'A Physicist Looks at Biology', in John Cairns, Gunther Stent, James Watson (eds), *Phage and the Origins of Molecular Biology*, Cold Spring Harbor Laboratory, Cold Spring Harbor, New York, 1966, p. 22.

6   Renato Delbucco, 'The Plaque Technique and the Development of Quantitative Animal Virology', in Cairns et. al., *Phage and the Origins of Molecular Biology*, p. 288.

7   Interview with Szilard in *International Science and Technology*, vol. 5, 1962, p. 36.

8   Donald Fleming, 'Emigré Physicists and the Biological Revolution', in *Perspectives in American History*, vol. 11, 1968, p. 161. This remarkable article, though written in 1968, is still the best account of the origins of the new biology. It is full of brilliant historical and sociological perceptions.

9   Interview with Szilard in *International Science and Technology*. For an ironic version of the same view see Delbrück in Judson, p. 52. Delbrück imagines a theoretical physicist 'who knew little about biology in general, and nothing about bacterial viruses in particular, and who accidentally was brought into contact with this field'. 'Suppose now', Delbrück goes on, 'that our imaginary physicist, the student of Niels Bohr, is shown an experiment in which a virus particle enters a bacterial cell and 20 minutes later the bacterial cell is lysed and 100 virus particles are liberated. He will say: "How come, one particle has become 100 particles of the same kind in 20 minutes? That is very interesting. Let us find out how it happens ... This is so simple a phenomenon that the answers cannot be hard to find. In a few months we will know. The experiments only take a few hours each, so the whole problem cannot take long to solve" Perhaps you would like to see this childish young man after eight years and ask him, just off hand, whether he has solved the riddle of life yet? This will embarrass him, as he has not got anywhere in solving the problem he set out to solve. But being quick to rationalise his failure, this is what he may answer: "Well, I made a slight mistake. I could not do it in a few months. Perhaps it will take a few decades, and perhaps it will take the help of a few dozen other people. But listen to what I have found, perhaps you will be interested to join me".'

10   Donald Fleming, 'Emigré Physicists and The Biological Revolution', p. 36.

11   Watson in Judson, *The Eighth Day of Creation*, p. 22.

12   Pnina Abir-Am, 'Themes, Genres and Orders of Legitimation in the Consolidation of New Scientific Disciplines: Deconstructing the Historiography of Molecular Biology', *History of Science*, vol. 23, 1985, p. 73. For a 'classical' statement on molecular biology see Jacques Monod's inaugural address in the newly established Chair in Molecular Biology at the Collège de France, 1967: 'From molecular biology to the ethics of knowledge', in *The Human Context*, vol. 1, 1969, pp. 325–60. See also A. Lwoff and A. Ullmann (eds), *Origins of Molecular Biology: A Tribute to Jacques Monod*, Academic Press, New York, 1979.

13   F. Crick, *Of Molecules and Men*, University of Washington Press, Seattle, 1966, p. 10.

14   ibid. p. 87.

15   ibid. p. 98.

16   Jacques Monod, *Chance and Necessity: An Essay on the Natural Philosophy of Modern Biology*, Alfred A. Knopf, New York, 1971, pp. 112–14.

17   For a critical discussion of the philosophical implications of molecular biology, see the remarkable book by Howard L. Kaye, *The Social Meaning of Modern Biology: From Social Darwinism to Sociobiology*, Yale University Press, New Haven, 1986. See especially ch. 2, 'From Metaphysics to Molecular Biology', and ch. 3, 'From Molecular Biology to Social Theory'.

18   See Fleming, 'Emigré Physicists and the Biological Revolution', p. 155. 'In contrast to the enormous circumspection of Avery and his colleagues in 1944, Watson and Crick in 1953 drew supremely confident inferences about the bearing of their own work on genetics. They did not argue the point, they simply took it for granted ... They were absolutely certain that the structure of DNA was the structure of genes and the secret of heredity—in fact, the secret of life. What is more, they thought that they and a handful of rivals were in striking distance of the golden fleece. How had they come to form these superbly arrogant ambitions, unbuttressed by any compelling evidence and offering total defiance to contemporary standards of good taste in biological discourse? Watson and Crick were undoubtedly slashing and imperious, conquistadores of science by native temperament. But what is equally important, they had come under the influence of a number of men who had begun to entertain in the 1940s some of the same extravagant hopes and vaulting ambitions as Jacques Loeb a generation before. They too were candidly drawing a bead on the secret of life.' These men were Schrödinger, Szilard, Delbrück and Luria. See also the interesting book by Jan Sap, *Beyond the Gene: Cytoplasmic Inheritance and the Struggle for Authority in Genetics*, Oxford University Press, Oxford, 1987, p. 223: 'Scientists are engaged in a struggle for scientific authority. What is at stake in this struggle is the power to impose a definition of the field'.

19   See the immense amount of material referred to in Pnina Abir-Am, 'Deconstructing the Historiography of Molecular Biology'.

20   Niels Bohr, 'Light and Life', in *Atomic Physics and Human Knowledge*, John Wiley and Sons, New York, 1958, p. 9; 'In every experiment on living organisms there must remain some uncertainty as regards the physical conditions to which they are subjected and the idea suggests itself that the minimal freedom we must allow the organism will be just enough to permit it, so to say, to hide its ultimate secrets from us. On this view, the very existence of life must in biology be considered as an elementary fact, just as in atomic physics the existence of the quantum of action has to be taken as a basic fact that cannot be derived from ordinary mechanical physics. Indeed, the essential non-analysability of atomic stability in mechanical terms presents a close analogy to the impossibility of a physical or chemical explanation of the peculiar functions characteristic of life'. See Henry J. Folse, *The Philosophy of Niels Bohr: The Framework of Complementarity*, North Holland, New York, 1985, pp. 183 et seq., 'Complementarity in Biology'.

21   Cited in R. C. Olby, *The Path to the Double Helix*, p. 231.

22   Erwin Schrödinger, *What is Life?* Cambridge University Press, Cambridge, 1944. Gunther Stent, 'That was the molecular biology that was', *Science*, vol. 160, 1968, p. 392.

23   E. J. Yoxen, 'Where does Schrödinger's *What is Life?* belong in the history of molecular biology?', in *History of Science*, vol. 17, 1979, pp. 17–82. See also Fleming, 'Emigré Physicists and the Biological Revolution', p. 177, on the basic

ambivalence of Schrödinger's position in the book; 'He obviously remained fearful of the conventional reductionist arguments as impoverishing the complexity of living things as he understood them. But he did believe, with however many elaborate qualifications, that biology was a branch of physics'.

24   'Deconstructing the Historiography of Molecular Biology', p. 10.
25   Cited in Olby, *The Path to the Double Helix*, p. 943.
26   'Deconstructing the Historiography of Molecular Biology', p. 105.
27   See note 2.
28   See note 3.
29   On Olby, Judson and other historians of the new biology, see Pnina Abir-Am, 'Deconstructing the Historiography of Molecular Biology'.
30   E. L. French, 'Burnet and the biology of animal viruses', *The Walter and Eliza Hall Institute of Medical Research, Annual Review 1978–79, Special Volume, A Tribute to Sir Macfarlane Burnet*, pp. 17–18.
31   G. L. Ada, 'Burnet and the biochemistry of viruses', *A Tribute to Sir Macfarlane Burnet*, p. 23.
32   Burnet, *Changing Patterns: An Atypical Autobiography*, Heinmann, Melbourne, 1968, p. 175.
33   ibid., p. 176.
34   ibid., p. 187. See also F. M. Burnet, 'Men or Molecules? A Tilt at Molecular Biology', *Lancet*, vol. 1, 1966, p. 37.
35   Edward Yoxen, 'Life as a Productive Force: Capitalising the Science and Technologies of Molecular Biology', in L. Levidow and R. M. Young (eds), *Science, Technology and the Labour Process*, pp. 66–122.
36   ibid., p. 69.
37   ibid., p. 104.
38   ibid., p. 102.
39   ibid., p. 57.

Chapter 3

1   Clifford Geertz, *Local Knowledge: Further Essays in Interpretive Anthropology*, Basic Books, New York, 1983, pp. 65, 66, 67.
2   Bertolt Brecht, *Plays, Poetry and Prose: Poems 1913–1956*, John Willett and Ralph Mannheim (eds), Methuen, London, 1976, p. 252.
3   *Annual Report 1985–86*, p. 19.
4   See G. Canguilhem, 'Techniques et problèmes de la physiologie au XIX siècle', in R. Taton (ed.), *La Science contemporaine*, Presses universitaires de France, Paris, 1961, vol. 1, p. 480.
5   Robert K. Merton, *The Sociology of Science: Theoretical and Empirical Investigations*, University of Chicago Press, Chicago, 1973, pp. 442-3.
6   Robert K. Merton, 'The Matthew Effect in Science', *Science*, 199, 5 Jan. 1968, pp. 55–63. See also Jonathan R. Cole, *Fair Science: Women in the Scientific Community*, The Free Press, New York, 1979, ch. 4, 'The Reputations of Men and Women Scientists'.
7   Otto N. Larsen, 'Social Science out of the Closet', *Society*, vol. 22, 1985, p. 12. See also, for an interesting overview of the relations between the sciences and the social sciences, Harriet Zuckerman, 'Uses and Control of Knowledge: Implications for the Social Fabric', in James F. Short (ed.), *The Social Fabric*, Sage, Beverly Hills, 1986.

8   A. Westmore, 'The steps forward are not fast enough', *Age*, 9 March 1987, p. 14.

9   Susan Wright, 'Recombinant DNA Technology and Its Social Transformation, 1972–1982', *Osiris*, vol. 2, 1986, pp. 336–7. Wright's article is one of the best surveys of this area.

10   ibid. p. 357.

Chapter 4

1   Ian Langham, *The Building of British Social Anthropology*, Reidel, Dordrecht, 1981, p. xiv.

2   *Walter and Eliza Hall Institute of Medical Research: Quinquennial Review*, 1984, vol. 1, p. 10.

3   M. Mulkay, *The Word and the World; Explorations in the Form of Sociological Analysis*, Allen and Unwin, London, 1985.

4   Quoted in James Clifford, *The Predicament of Culture*, Harvard University Press, Cambridge, Mass., 1988, p. 75.

Chapter 5

1   *Dialectical Anthropology*, vol. 10, 1985, p. 4.

2   P. Medawar, 'Is the scientific paper a fraud?', *Listener*, vol. LXX, no. 1798 12 Sept. 1963, pp. 377–8.

3   E. Mach, *The Analysis of Sensations*, trans. C. M. Williams and S. Waterlow, Dover Publications, New York, 1959, p. 24.

4   Hans Reichenbach, *The Rise of Scientific Philosophy*, University of California Press, Berkeley, 1966, p. 231.

5   Macfarlane Burnet, *Walter & Eliza Hall Institute, 1915–1965*, Melbourne University Press, Melbourne, 1971.

6   Mary Douglas, 'Institutionalised Public Memory', in James F. Short (ed.), *The Social Fabric: Dimensions and Issues*, Sage, Beverly Hills, 1986.

7   On Ostwald, see L. Feuer, *Einstein and the Generations of Science*, Basic Books, New York, 1974, pp. 346–7.

8   Abraham Maslow, *The Psychology of Science*, Harper & Row, New York, 1966.

9   ibid. pp. 92–3.

10   Ann Roe, *The Making of a Scientist*, Dodds Mead, New York, 1953.

11   D. McClelland, 'On the Dynamics of Creative Physical Scientists', in *The Ecology of Human Intelligence*, L. Hudson (ed.), Penguin Books, Harmondsworth, 1962.

12   L. Feuer, *Einstein and the Generations of Science*, Basic Books, New York, 1974.

13   ibid, p.v.

14   Ian Mitroff, *The Subjective Side of Science, A Philosophical Inquiry into the Psychology of the Apollo Moon Scientists*, Elsevier Publishing, New York, 1974.

15   ibid., pp. 8–10.

16   H. F. Judson, *The Eighth Day of Creation: The Makers of the Revolution in Biology*, Simon and Schuster, New York, 1979; Daniel Kevles, *The Physicists: The History of a Scientific Community in Modern America*, Knopf, New York,

1978; Harriet Zuckerman, *Scientific Elite*, Free Press, New York, 1977; Russell McCormach, *Night Thoughts of a Classical Physicist*, Harvard University Press, Cambridge, Mass., 1982; June Goodfield, *An Imagined World: A Story of Scientific Discovery*, Harper and Row, New York, 1981; Philip J. Hilts, *Scientific Temperaments: Three Lives in Contemporary Science*, Simon and Schuster, New York, 1982.

17   Evelyn Fox Keller, *A Feeling for the Organism: The Life and Work of Barbara McClintock*, Freeman, New York, 1983.

18   Brian Easlea, *Witch Hunting, Magic and the New Philosophy*, Harvester Press, Brighton, 1980, p. 32.

19   Evelyn Fox Keller, *Reflections on Gender and Science*, Yale University Press, New Haven, 1985. See also Vivian Gornick, *Women in Science: Portraits from a World in Transition*, Simon and Schuster, New York, 1984.

20   Jonathan R. Cole & Harriet Zuckerman, 'Marriage, Family and Scientific Publication: Truth and Illusion in Science', Macy Foundation Research Symposium, New York, 1983. This paper is reported by John T. Bruer in 'Women in Science: Toward Equitable Participation', *Science, Technology and Human Values*, vol. 9, 1984, pp. 3–7. See also Cole and Zuckerman, 'The Productivity Puzzle: Persistence and Change in Patterns of Publication of Men and Women Scientists', in Marjorie W. Steinkamp and Martin L. Maehr (eds), *Advance in Motivation and Achievement*, vol II, *Women in Science*, JAI Press, Greenwich, 1985. Cole's older study, *Fair Science: Women in the Scientific Community*, The Free Press, New York, 1979, is the standard work on the position of women scientists in the American scientific community.

21   'Marriage, Family and Scientific Publication', reported in Bruer, 'Women in Science', pp. 5–6.

22   Sharon Traweek 'High Energy Physics: A Male Preserve', *Technology Review*, Massachusetts Institute of Technology, November/December 1984, pp. 42–3.

23   ibid., p. 43.

24   Donald Light, *Becoming Psychiatrists: The Professional Transformation of Self*, W. W. Norton, New York, 1982.

25   ibid, pp. x–xi.

26   Melvin Konner, *Becoming a Doctor: A Journey of Initiation in Medical School*, Viking/Elisabeth Sefton Books, New York, 1987.

27   Mitroff, *The Subjective Side of Science*, p. 65.

28   ibid., p. 70.

29   M. Cohn, 'Burnet, Lysogeny and Creativity', *A Tribute to Sir Macfarlane Burnet*, 1979, pp. 12–13.

30   ibid., p. 13.

31   Evelyn Fox Keller, *A Feeling for the Organism*, p. 117.

32   Peter Medawar, *Pluto's Republic*, Oxford University Press, London, 1982, pp. 273–4.

33   Cited in Gerald Holton, 'Do scientists need a philosophy?', *Times Literary Supplement*, 2 Nov. 1984, p. 1231.

34   ibid., p. 1234.

35   ibid.

Chapter 6

1   Quoted in Diane E. Barwick (ed.), *Metaphors of Interpretation: Essays in*

Honour of W. E. H. Stanner, Australian National University Press, Canberra, 1985, p. 30.

2 Andre Lwoff and Agnes Ullman (eds), *Origins of Molecular Biology: A Tribute to Jacques Monod*, New York Press, New York, 1979.

3 *Journal of The History of Biology*, vol 15, no. 2, 1982, p. 281.

4 ibid., p. 184

5 ibid., p. 285.

6 ibid., p. 286.

7 G. J. V. Nossal, Australian Academy of Science, Burnet Lecture 1979.

8 *Annual Review 1978–9: Special Volume, A Tribute to Sir Macfarlane Burnet.*

9 For example, G. L. Ada, 'Burnet and the Biochemistry of Viruses', in *A Tribute to Sir Macfarlane Burnet*, p. 23.

10 G. J. V. Nossal, *Reshaping Life: Key Issues In Genetic Engineering*, Melbourne University Press, Melbourne, 1984.

11 *Women in Science: Portraits from a World in Transition*, Simon and Schuster, New York, 1984.

12 ibid., pp. 47, 61.

13 *Walter and Eliza Hall Institute, 1915-1965*, p. 83.

14 *The Impact of Genetic Engineering on Modern Medicine*, The First Ian McLennan Oration of the Melbourne University Engineering School Centenary Foundation, Melbourne, 4 October 1983, p. 13.

15 Evelyn Fox Keller, *Reflections on Gender and Science*, Yale University Press, New Haven, 1985, pp. 177–8.

16 J. Bronowski, *Science and Human Values*, revised edition, Harper and Row, New York, 1965, p. 73.

17 Charles Weiner, 'Relations of Science, Government and Industry: The Case of Recombinant DNA', in Albert H. Teich and Ray Thornton (eds), *Science, Technology and the Issues of the Eighties : Policy Outlook*, Westview Press, Boulder, Colorado, 1982, p. 74. Archival source materials on the recombinant DNA debate are contained in the Recombinant DNA Collection at the Institute Archives, Massachusetts Institute of Technology. This material contains rich and detailed accounts of the main protagonists' views on the moral and social issues involved in genetic engineering. For a description of the collection see Charles Weiner, 'The Recombinant DNA Controversy: Archival and Oral History Resources', *Science Technology and Human Values*, vol. 4, Winter 1979, pp. 17–19. See also the work by Sheldon Krimsky, *Genetic Alchemy: The Social History of the Recombinant DNA Controversy*, MIT Press, Cambridge, Mass., 1983. Krimsky's book is based upon the archival material in the Recombinant DNA Collection.

18 G. J. V. Nossal, *Reshaping Life*, p. 117.

19 ibid., p. 126.

20 G. J. V. Nossal, 'The New Biology and Human Disease', *Interdisciplinary Science Review*, vol. 8, 1983, p. 332.

21 See T. E. Mandel, 'Guidelines for the use of foetal tissues', in J. N. Santamaria (ed.), *Life in Our Power*, St Vincent's Bioethics Centre, Melbourne, 1983, p. 93.

22 William Broad and Nicholas Wade, *Betrayers of the Truth*, Simon and Schuster, New York, 1982.

23 ibid., p. 7.

24 ibid., p. 7.

25 Bruno Latour, 'Visualisation and Cognition: Thinking with Eyes and Hands,' *Knowledge and Society*, vol. 5, 1986, pp. 1–40.

26   ibid., p. 15.

Chapter 7

1   Louis Dumont, *Essays on Individualism: Modern Ideology in Anthropological Perspective*, University of Chicago Press, Chicago, 1986, pp. 2–3.
2   There are similarities between my concept of a data-generation system and Hughes's 'technical system'. See T. P. Hughes, 'Edison and the Electric Light', in D. McKenzie and J. Wacjman (eds), *The Social Shaping of Technology*, Open University, Milton Keynes, 1985, pp. 39–57. See also Robert J. Ackerman, *Rats, instruments and theory: a dialectical approach to the understanding of science*, Princeton University Press, Princeton, 1985, p. 33, and the earlier essay by Karen Knorr-Cetina, 'Tinkering towards success: prelude to a theory of scientific practice', *Theory and Society*, vol. 8, no. 197, pp. 347–75.
3   See R. M. Young, 'Science is a labour process', *Science for People*, vol. 43/4, no. 197, pp. 31–7, and 'Is Nature a Labour Process?', in L. Levidow and R. M. Young (eds), *Science, Technology and the Labour Process*, 1985. See also D. McKenzie, 'Some Notes on the Science and Social Relations Debate', *Capital and Class*, vol. 14, 1981, pp. 47–60.
4   See Bruno Latour, 'Visualisation and Cognition: Thinking With Eyes and Hands', *Knowledge and Society*, vol. 5, 1986, pp. 1–40.
5   ibid.
6   On 'technique-laden' observation see Jan Sapp, *Beyond the Gene: Cytoplasmic Inheritance and the Struggle for Authority in Genetics*, Oxford University Press, New York, 1987, p. xvi. 'By "technique-ladenness" of observations' I refer to the means by which scientific concepts become bound to phenomena studied by certain techniques. It is meant to embrace the scientific equipment, procedures, materials, tools and skills that are involved in the production of scientific results.'
7   W. T. Trager, and J. I. Jensen, 'Human malaria parasites on continuous culture', *Science*, vol. 168, 1976, pp. 673–5.

Chapter 8

1   *Local Knowledge: Further Essays in Interpretive Anthropology*, Basic Books, New York, 1983, p. 98.
2   For further details see I. Rosenfield, E. Ziff and B. Van Loon, *DNA For Beginners*, Writers and Readers, New York, 1983.
3   On the development of recombinant DNA technology see G. J. V. Nossal, *Reshaping Life*, Melbourne University Press, Melbourne 1984; J. Cherfas, *Man Made Life*, Basil Blackwell, Oxford, 1982; J. D. Watson and J. Tooze, *The DNA Story: A Documentary History of Gene Cloning*, W. H. Freeman & Co., New York, 1981.
4   See J. D. Watson and J. Tooze, *The DNA Story: A Documentary History of Gene Cloning*.
5   *Scientific American*, vol. 252, March, 1985, p. 50.
6   Recommendations of the Gene Technology Sub-Committee to the Director, 7 October 1984,
7   The Director's Report to the Board, October 1984.

Chapter 9

1 Claude Lévi-Strauss, *The Raw and The Cooked*, Harper and Row, New York, 1975, p. 7.
2 This account is based upon the article by G. Nigel Godson, 'Molecular Approaches to Malaria Vaccines', *Scientific American*, vol. 252, May 1985, no. 5, pp. 32–9.
3 D. J. Kemp, L. M. Corcoran, R. L. Coppel, H. D. Stahl, A. F. Bianco, G. V. Brown and R. F. Anders, 'Size variation in chromosomes from independent cultured isolates of *Plasmodium falciparum*', *Nature*, 315, 1985, pp. 347–50.
4 G. Nigel Godson, 'Molecular Approaches to Malaria Vaccines', p. 38.

Chapter 10

1 Nigel Barley, *The Innocent Anthropologist*, Penguin, Harmondsworth, 1986, p. 83.
2 Richard Whitley, *The Intellectual and Social Organisation of the Sciences*, Clarendon Press, Oxford, 1984.
3 ibid., p. 52.
4 See, for example, Russell C. Maulitz, '"Physician versus Bacteriologist": The Ideology of Science in Clinical Medicine', in Morris J. Vogel & Charles E. Rosenberg (eds), *The Therapeutic Revolution: Essays in the Social History of American Medicine*, University of Pennsylvania Press, Philadelphia, 1979, pp. 91–107.
5 See Kenneth E. Studer & Daryl E. Chubin, *The Cancer Mission: Social Contexts of Biomedical Research*, Sage, Beverly Hills, 1980.
6 ibid., p. 14.
7 See Mel Horwitch, 'Designing and Managing Large-Scale, Public-Private Technological Enterprises: A State of the Art Review', *Technology in Society*, vol. 1, 1979, p. 179.
8 Shrum has analysed such 'technical systems' and highlighted within them the greater range of co-workers and audiences to which scientists must relate. Wesley Shrum, 'Scientific Specialties and Technical Systems', *Social Studies of Science*, vol. 14, 1984, pp. 63–90.
9 See Michael Worboys, 'The Emergence of Tropical Medicine: A Study in the Establishment of Scientific Specialty', Gerard Lemaine *et al.* (eds), *Perspectives on the Emergence of Scientific Disciplines*, Mouton and Aldine, The Hague and Chicago, 1976, pp. 75–98.
10 Kenneth S. Warren, 'Introductory Remarks', *The American Journal of Tropical Medicine and Hygiene*, vol. 26, 1977, p. 6.
11 ibid., p. 7.
12 See W. R. Albury, 'Politics and Rhetoric in the Sociobiology Debate', *Social Studies of Science*, vol. 10, 1980, pp. 519–36.
13 'Introductory Remarks', p. 6.
14 See David S. Rowe, 'The Forgotten People', *World Health*, June 1976, pp. 18–23.
15 T. A. Lambo, 'The Evolution of WHO's Special Programmes for Research and Training', in C. Wood and Y. Rue (eds), *Health Policies in Developing Countries*, Academic Press, London, 1980, p. 44.
16 G. J. V. Nossal, 'The New Biology and Human Disease', *Interdisciplinary*

Science Reviews, vol. 8, 1983, p. 332; Charles Weiss, 'The World Bank's Support for Science and Technology', *Science*, 18 January 1985, pp. 261–5.

17 H. C. Goodman and T. A. Lambo, 'The World Health Organisation: Its Influence on Worldwide Research Policies', in H. Gudenberg (ed.), *Biomedical Institutions, Biomedical Funding and Public Policy*, Plenum, London, 1983, pp. 151–75.

18 Other American funding authorities, both government and private, have also increased their support for tropical disease research in the wake of the WHO decision to set up TDR. A number of these, including the US Agency for International Development (AID), the National Institute of Allergy and Infectious Diseases (NIAID), the Centre for Disease Control (CDC), and the Edna McConnell Clark Foundation, had already been providing funds for tropical disease research. But there was a significant increase in the total amount of US funding. See H. C. Goodman & T. A. Lambo, 'The World Health Organisation' and G. Kilata, 'The Search for A Malaria Vaccine', *Science*, vol. 176, 1984, pp. 679–82. Despite these increases, funding for tropical disease and parasitic research was still less than 2 per cent of the total US health research budget in 1979 (about $54 million out of a total of approximately $3 billion). Goodman & Lambo, pp. 154–5.

19 Kenneth S. Warren, 'Malaria: A Great Relatively Neglected Disease', *The Western Journal of Medicine*, vol. 135, 1981, p. 321.

20 *Walter and Eliza Hall Institute of Medical Research, Annual Review*, 1972–3, p. 7.

21 ibid., pp. 7–8.

22 ibid., p. 8.

23 *Walter and Eliza Hall Institute of Medical Research, Annual Review*, 1974–5, p. 185.

24 *Walter and Eliza Hall Institute of Medical Research, Annual Review*, 1978–9, p. 185.

25 All figures from *Annual Reviews*.

26 *Annual Review*, 1984–5, p. 37.

27 See, for example, Michael Alpers, 'Tropical Immunology', *Papua New Guinea Medical Journal*, vol. 21, 1978, pp. 1–10; T. A. Lambo, 'The Evolution of the World Health Organization's Special Programmes for Research and Training' in C. Wood & Y. Rue (eds), *Health Policies in Developing Countries*, Academic Press, London, 1980, pp. 63–70.

28 See W. Trager & J. B. Jensen, 'Human Malaria Parasites in Continuous Culture', *Science*, 193, 1976, pp. 673–5.

Chapter 11

1 Christine Larmer, *Witchcraft and Religion*, Basil Blackwell, Oxford, 1984, p. 142.

2 Robert K. Merton, 'Priorities in Scientific Discovery: A Chapter in the Sociology of Science', *American Sociological Review*, vol. 22, 1957, pp. 635–59; 'Singletons and Multiples in Scientific Discovery: A Chapter in the Sociology of Science', *Proceedings of the American Philosophical Society*, vol. 105, 1962, pp. 471–87; 'Resistance to Multiple Discoveries in Science', *European Journal of Sociology* (Archives) vol. 4, 1963, pp. 237–82; *On the Shoulders of Giants: A Shandean Postscript*, Harcourt Brace, New York, 1965.

3   Harriet Zuckerman, *Scientific Elite: Nobel Laureates in the United States*, The Free Press, New York, 1977, pp. 247–8.
4   Elisabeth Crawford, *The Beginnings of the Nobel Institutions: The Science Prizes, 1901–1915*, Cambridge University Press, Cambridge, 1984, p. 204.
5   Cited in *Time*, 3 July, 1985, p. 53.

Conclusion

1   Paul Rabinow, *Reflections on Fieldwork in Morocco*, University of California Press, Berkeley, 1979, pp. 150, 151, 152.
2   Claude Lévi-Strauss, *The View From Afar*, Penguin Books, London, 1987, p. 35.
3   Sal Restivo, 'Science Studies: What is to be Done?', *Science, Technology and Human Values*, vol. 12, issue 2, 1987, p. 14. See also Sal Restivo and Randall Collins, 'Robber Barons and Politicians in Mathematics: A Conflict Theory of Science', *Canadian Journal of Sociology*, vol. 6, no. 2, 1983, pp. 199–227.
4   Susan Wright, 'Recombinant DNA Technology and Its Social Transformations, 1972–1982', *Osiris*, vol. 2, 1986, pp. 360–9.
5   Evelyn Fox Keller, *Reflections on Gender and Science*, Yale University Press, New Haven, 1985.
6   Evelyn Fox Keller, *A Feeling for the Organism: The Life and Work of Barbara McClintock*, Freeman, New York, 1983; Sharon Traweek, 'High Energy Physics: A Male Preserve', *Technology Review*, November/December 1984, pp. 42–3.

BIBLIOGRAPHY

Abir-Am, Pnina, 'From biochemistry to molecular biology: DNA and the acculturated journey of the critic of science Erwin Chargaff', *History and Philosophy of the Life Sciences*, vol. 2, 1980, pp. 3–60.

Abir-Am, Pnina, 'The Discourse of Physical Power and Biological Knowledge in the 1930s: A Reappraisal of the Rockefeller Foundation's "Policy in Molecular Biology"', *Social Studies of Science*, vol. 12, 1982, pp. 341–82.

Abir-Am, Pnina, 'How Scientists View Their Heroes: Some Remarks on the Mechanism of Myth Construction', *Journal of the History of Biology*, vol. 5, no. 2, 1982, pp. 281–315.

Abir-Am, Pnina, 'Themes, Genres and Orders of Legitimation in the Consolidation of New Scientific Disciplines: Deconstructing the Historiography of Molecular Biology', *History of Science*, vol. 23, 1985, pp. 73–117.

Ackerman, Robert J., *Rats, instruments and theory: a dialectical approach to the understanding of science*, Princeton University Press, Princeton, 1985.

Ada, Gordon L., and Nossal, Gustav, 'The Clonal Selection Theory', *Scientific American*, vol. 256, August 1987, pp. 50–7.

Albury, W. R., 'Politics and Rhetoric in the Sociobiology Debate', *Social Studies of Science*, vol. 10, 1980, pp. 319–36.

Alpers, Michael, 'Tropical Immunology', *Papua New Guinea Medical Journal*, vol. 21, 1978, pp. 1–10.

Barley, Nigel, *The Innocent Anthropologist*, Penguin, Harmondsworth, 1986.

Bernal, J. D., *The Social Function of Science*, Routledge, London, 1936.

Bohr, Niels, 'Light and Life', in *Atomic Physics and Human Knowledge*, John Wiley and Sons, New York, 1958, pp. 3–12.

Broad, William, and Wade, Nicholas, *Betrayers of the Truth*, Simon and Schuster, New York, 1982.

Bronowski, J., *Science and Human Values*, revised edition, Harper and Row, New York, 1965.

Bruer, John T., 'Women in Science: Toward Equitable Participation', *Science, Technology and Human Values*, vol. 9, 1984, pp. 3–7.

Burnet, F. M., 'A modification of Jerne's theory of anti-body production using the concept of clonal selection', *Australian Journal of Science*, vol. 20, 1957, p. 67.

Burnet, F. M., 'Men or Molecules? A Tilt at Molecular Biology', *Lancet*, vol. 1, 1966, p. 37.

Burnet, F. M., *Changing Patterns: An Atypical Autobiography*, Heinemann, Melbourne, 1968.

Burnet, F. M., *Walter and Eliza Hall Institute 1915–1965*, Melbourne University Press, Carlton, 1971.

Canguilhem, H. G., 'Techniques et problèmes de la physiologie au xix siècle', in R. Taton (ed.), *La science contemporaine*, Presses Universitaires de France, Paris, 1961.

292

Chargaff, Erwin, *Heracleitean Fire: Sketches of a Life before Nature*, Rockefeller University Press, New York, 1978.

Cherfas, J., *Man Made Life*, Basil Blackwell, Oxford, 1982.

Clifford, James, *The Predicament of Culture: Twentieth Century Ethnography, Literature and Art*, Harvard University Press, Cambridge, Mass., 1988.

Clifford, James, and Marcus, G. E., (eds.), *Writing Culture: Poetics and Politics in Ethnography*, University of California Press, Berkeley, 1986.

Cohn, Melvin, 'Burnet, Lysogeny and Creativity', in *The Walter and Eliza Hall Institute of Medical Research, Annual Review 1978–9: Special Volume, A Tribute to Sir Macfarlane Burnet*, pp. 9–13.

Cole, Jonathan, *Fair Science: Women in the Scientific Community*, The Free Press, New York, 1977.

Cole, Jonathan, and Zuckerman, Harriet, 'Marriage, Family and Scientific Publication: Truth and Illusion in Science', Macy Foundation Research Symposium on Women in Science, New York, 1983.

Cole, Jonathan, and Zuckerman, Harriet, 'Marriage, Motherhood and Research Performance in Science', *Scientific American*, vol. 256, 1987, pp. 83–9.

Cole, Jonathan, and Zuckerman, Harriet, 'The Productivity Puzzle: Persistence and Change in Patterns of Publication of Men and Women Scientists,' in Marjorie W. Steinkamp and Martin L. Maehr (eds.), *Advance in Motivation and Achievement*, vol. 11, *Women in Science*, JA1 Press, Greenwich, 1985.

Collins, H. M., 'The Sociology of Scientific Knowledge: Studies of Contemporary Science', *The Annual Review of Sociology*, vol. 9, 1983, pp. 265–85.

Crawford, Elisabeth, *The Beginnings of the Nobel Institutions: The Science Prizes 1901–1915*, Cambridge University Press, Cambridge, 1984.

Crick, F., *Of Molecules and Men*, University of Washington Press, Seattle, 1966.

Davis, V. de Vahl, A History of the Walter and Eliza Hall Institute of Medical Research: An Examination of the Personalities, Politics, Finances, Social Relations and Scientific Organisation of the Hall Institute, thesis, University of NSW, 1979.

Delbrück, Max, 'A Physicist Looks at Biology', in John Cairns, Gunther Stent, James Watson (eds.), *Phage and the Origins of Molecular Biology*, Cold Spring Harbor Laboratory, Cold Spring Harbor, New York, 1966, pp. 9–22.

Delbrück, Max, *Mind from Matter? An Essay on Evolutionary Epistemology*, Blackwell Scientific Publications, Palo Alto, 1986.

Douglas, Mary, 'Institutionalised Public Memory', in James F. Short (ed.), *The Social Fabric: Dimensions and Issues*, Sage, Beverly Hills, 1986, pp. 63–75.

Dumont, Louis, *Essays on Individualism: Modern Ideology in Anthropological Perspective*, University of Chicago Press, Chicago, 1986.

Easlea, Brian, *Witch Hunting, Magic and the New Philosophy*, Harvester Press, Brighton, 1980.

Edelman, G. M., 'The Internationalism of Medical Research', *The Walter and Eliza Hall Institute of Medical Research, Annual Review 1985–6*, pp. 8–10.

Edelman, G. M., *Neural Darwinism: The Theory of Neuronal Group Selections*, Basic Books, New York, 1987.

Farquhar, Judith, and Gajdusek, Carleton D, (eds), *Kuru: Early Letters and Field Notes from the Collection of D. Carleton Gajdusek*, Raven Press, New York, 1981.

Fleming, Donald, 'Emigré Physicists and the Biological Revolution', in *Perspectives in American History*, vol. 11, 1965, Charles Warren Center for Studies in American History, Harvard University Press, Cambridge, Mass., pp. 152–90.

Folse, Henry J., *The Philosophy of Niels Bohr: The Framework of Complementarity*, North Holland, New York. 1985.

French, E. L., 'Burnet and the Biology of Animal Viruses', *A Tribute to Sir Macfarlane Burnet*, pp. 14–19.

Geertz, Clifford, *Local Knowledge: Further Essays in Interpretive Anthropology*, Basic Books, New York, 1983.

Georges, Robert A., and Jones, Michael O., *People Studying People: The Human Element in Fieldwork*, University of California Press, Berkeley, 1980.

Gilbert, Nigel, and Mulkay, Michael, *Opening Pandora's Box: A Sociological Analysis of Scientists' Discourse*, Cambridge University Press, Cambridge, 1984.

Godson, Nigel G., 'Molecular Approaches to Malaria Vaccines', *Scientific American*, vol. 252, May 1985, pp. 32–9.

Goodfield, June, *An Imagined World: A Story of Scientific Discovery*, Harper and Row, New York, 1981.

Goodman, H. C., and Lambo, T. A., 'The World Health Organisation: its Influence on Worldwide Research Policies', in H. Gudenberg (ed.) *Biomedical Institutions, Biomedical Funding and Public Policy*, Plenum, London, 1983, pp. 151–75.

Gornick, Vivian, *Women in Science: Portraits from a World in Transition*, Simon and Schuster, New York, 1984.

Haan, N., *et al.* (eds), *Social Science as Moral Inquiry*, Columbia University Press, New York, 1983.

Heath, A. F., (ed.), *Scientific Explanation*, Clarendon Press, Oxford, 1981.

Hilts, Philip J., *Scientific Temperaments: Three Lives in Contemporary Science*, Simon and Schuster, New York, 1982.

Hughes, T. P., 'Edison and the electric light', in D. McKenzie and J. Wacjman (eds.) *The Social Shaping of Technology*, Open University, Milton Keynes, 1985, pp. 39–57.

Jerne, Niels K., 'Burnet and the clonal selection theory', in *A Tribute to Sir Macfarlane Burnet*, pp. 34–8.

Judson, H. F., *The Eighth Day of Creation: The Makers of the Revolution in Biology*, Simon and Schuster, New York, 1979.

Kaye, Howard L., *The Social Meaning of Modern Biology: From Social Darwinism to Sociobiology*, Yale University Press, New Haven, 1986.

Keller, Evelyn Fox, *A Feeling for the Organism: The Life and Work of Barbara McClintock*, W. H. Freeman, New York, 1983.

Keller, Evelyn Fox, *Reflections on Gender and Science*, Yale University Press, New Haven, 1985.

Kevles, Daniel, *The Physicists: The History of a Scientific Community in Modern America*, Alfred Knopf, New York, 1978.

Kilata, G., 'The Search for a Malaria Vaccine', *Science*, vol. 226, 1984, pp. 679–82.

Knorr-Cetina, Karen, 'Tinkering towards success: prelude to a theory of scientific practice', *Theory and Society*, vol. 8, no. 197, pp. 347–75.

Knorr-Cetina, Karen, *The Manufacture of Knowledge*, Pergamon, Oxford, 1981.

Knorr-Cetina, Karen, and Mulkay, Michael, (eds.), *Science Observed: Perspectives on the Social Study of Science*, Sage, London, 1983.

Konner, Melvin, *Becoming a Doctor: A Journey of Initiation in Medical School*, Viking/Elisabeth Sefton Books, New York, 1987.

Krige, John, *Science, Revolution and Discontinuity*, The Harvester Press, Brighton, 1980.

Krimsky, K. Sheldon, *Genetic Alchemy: The Social History of the Recombinant DNA Controversy*, MIT Press, Cambridge, Mass., 1983.

Kuhn, Thomas S., *The Structure of Scientific Revolutions*, University of Chicago Press, Chicago, 2nd ed., 1970.

Kuhn, Thomas S., *The Essential Tension*, University of Chicago Press, Chicago, 1977.

Lambo, T. A., 'The Evolution of WHO's Special Programmes for Research and Training', in C. Wood and Y. Rue (eds.), *Health Policies in Developing Countries*, Academic Press, London, 1980, pp. 63–70.

Langham, Ian, *The Building of British Social Anthropology*, Reidel, Dordrecht, 1981.

Larsen, Otto N., 'Social Science out of the Closet', *Society*, vol. 22, 1985, pp. 11–15, Sage, Beverly Hills, 1979.

Latour, Bruno, and Woolgar, Steve, *Laboratory Life: The Social Construction of Scientific Facts*, Sage, Beverly Hills, 1979.

Latour, Bruno, 'Visualisation and Cognition: Thinking with Eyes and Hands', *Knowledge and Society*, vol. 5, 1986, pp. 1–40.

Lévi-Strauss, Claude, *The Raw and the Cooked*, Harper and Row, New York, 1975.

Lévi-Strauss, Claude, *The View From Afar*, Penguin, London, 1987.

Light, Donald, *Becoming Psychiatrists: The Professional Transformation of Self*, W. W. Norton, New York, 1982.

Lwoff, A., and Ullmann, A., (eds.), *Origins of Molecular Biology: A Tribute to Jacques Monod*, Academic Press, New York, 1979.

Mach, E., *The Analysis of Sensations*, trans., C. M. Williams and S. Waterlow, Dover Publications, New York, 1959.

Mandel, T. E., 'Guidelines for the use of foetal tissues,' in J. N. Santamaria (ed.), *Life in Our Power*, St. Vincent's Bioethics Centre, Melbourne, 1983, pp. 87–94.

Maslow, Abraham, *The Psychology of Science*, Harper and Row, New York, 1966.

Maulitz, Russell C., 'Physician versus Bacteriologist: the Ideology of Science in Clinical Medicine', in Morris J. Vogel and Charles E. Rosenberg (eds.), *The Therapeutic Revolution: Essays in the Social History of American Medicine*, University of Pennsylvania Press, Philadelphia, 1979, pp. 91–107.

McClelland, D., 'On the Dynamics of Creative Physical Scientists', in L. Hudson (ed.), *The Ecology of Human Intelligence*, Penguin, Harmondsworth, 1962, pp. 309–41.

McCormach, Russell, *Night Thoughts of a Classical Physicist*, Harvard University Press, Cambridge, Mass., 1982.

McKenzie, D., 'Some Notes on the Science and Social Relations Debate', *Capital and Class*, vol. 14, 1981, pp. 47–60.

Medawar, P., 'Is the scientific paper a fraud?', *The Listener*, vol. LXX, no. 1798, 1963, pp. 377–8.

Medawar, P., 'Burnet and Immunological Tolerance', in *A Tribute to Sir Macfarlane Burnet*, pp. 31–3.

Medawar, P., *Pluto's Republic*, Oxford University Press, London, 1982.

Merry, Sally E., 'Toward a General Theory of Gossip and Scandal', in Donald Black (ed.), *Toward a General Theory of Social Control*, Academic Press, New York, 1982.

Merton, Robert K., 'Priorities in Scientific Discovery: A Chapter in the Sociology of Science', *American Sociological Review*, vol. 22, 1957, pp. 635–59.

Merton, Robert K., 'Resistance to Multiple Discoveries in Science', *European Journal of Sociology*, vol. 4, 1963, pp. 237–82.

Merton, Robert K., *On the Shoulders of Grants: A Shandean Postscript*, Harcourt Brace, New York, 1965.

Merton, Robert K., *The Sociology of Science: Theoretical and Empirical Investigations*, University of Chicago Press, Chicago, 1973.

Merton, Robert K., 'The Matthew Effect in Science', *Science*, vol. 159, 1968, pp. 56–63.

Mitroff, Ian, *The Subjective Side of Science: A Philosophical Inquiry into the Psychology of the Apollo Moon Scientists*, Elsevier Publishing, New York, 1974.

Monod, Jacques, 'From Molecular Biology to the Ethics of Knowledge', in *The Human Context*, vol. 1, 1969, pp. 325–60.

Monod, Jacques, *Chance and Necessity: An Essay on the Natural Philosophy of Modern Biology*, Alfred A. Knopf, New York, 1971.

Mulkay, Michael, *Science and the Sociology of Knowledge*, Allen and Unwin, London, 1979.

Mulkay, Michael, *The Word and the World: Explorations in the Form of Sociological Analysis*, Allen and Unwin, London, 1985.

Nader, Laura, 'Up the Anthropologist: Perspectives Gained from Studying Up', in D. Hymes (ed.), *Reinventing Anthropology*, Random House, New York, 1974, pp. 284–311.

Nossal, G. J. V., *Nature's Defences: New Frontiers in Vaccine Research*, Australian Broadcasting Commission, Sydney, 1978.

Nossal, G. J. V., *The Impact of Genetic Engineering on Modern Medicine*, Ian McLennan Oration, University of Melbourne, Parkville, 1983.

Nossal, G. J. V., 'The New Biology and Human Disease', *Interdisciplinary Science Reviews*, vol. 8, 1983, pp. 34–8.

Nossal, G. J. V., *Reshaping Life: Key Issues in Genetic Engineering*, Melbourne University Press, Melbourne, 1984.

Olby, R., *The Path to the Double Helix*, Macmillan, London, 1974.

Pickering, A. R., *Constructing Quarks: A Sociological History of Particle Physics*, University of Chicago Press, Chicago, 1984.

Rabinow, Paul, *Reflections on Fieldwork in Morocco*, University of California Press, Berkeley, 1979.

Reichenbach, Hans, *The Rise of Scientific Philosophy*, University of California Press, Berkeley, 1966.

Restivo, Sal, and Collins, Randall, 'Robber Barons and Politicians in Mathematics: A Conflict Theory of Science', *Canadian Journal of Sociology*, vol. 6, no. 2, 1983, pp. 199–227.

Roe, Ann, *The Making of a Scientist*, Dodds Mead, New York, 1953.

Rosaldo, Michelle Z., *Knowledge and Passion: Ilongot Notions of Self and Social Life*, Cambridge University Press, Cambridge, 1980.

Rosenfield, I., Ziff, E., and Van Loon, B., *DNA For Beginners*, Writers and Readers, New York, 1983.

Sap, Jan, *Beyond the Gene: Cytoplasmic Inheritance and the Struggle for Authority in Genetics*, Oxford University Press, Oxford, 1987.

Schrödinger, Erwin, *What is Life?*, Cambridge University Press, Cambridge, 1944.

Shrum, Wesley, 'Scientific Specialties and Technical Systems', *Social Studies of Science*, vol. 14, 1984, pp. 63–90.

Stent, Gunter, 'That was the molecular biology that was', *Science*, vol. 160, 1968, pp. 390–5.

Stocking, George W., Jr. (ed.), *Observers Observed: Essays on Ethnographic Fieldwork*, The Wisconsin Press, Madison, 1983.

Studer, Kenneth E., and Chubin, Daryl E., *The Cancer Mission: Social Contexts of Biomedical Research*, Sage, Beverly Hills, 1980.

Trager, W. T., and J. I. Jensen, 'Human malaria parasites on continuous culture', *Science*, vol. 168, 1976, pp. 673–5.

Traweek, Sharon, 'High Energy Physics: A Male Preserve', *Technology Review*, Massachusetts Institute of Technology, November/December 1984, pp. 42–3.

Walter and Eliza Hall Institute of Medical Research: *Annual Review*, 1920– .

Warren, Kenneth S., 'Introductory Remarks', *The American Journal of Tropical Medicine and Hygiene*, vol. 26, 1977, pp. 35–7.

Warren, Kenneth S., 'Malaria: A Great Relatively Neglected Disease', *The Western Journal of Medicine*, vol. 135, 1981, pp. 320–1.

Watson, James D., *The Double Helix: a Personal Account of the Discovery of the Structure of DNA*, Penguin, Harmondsworth, 1970.

Watson, J. D., and Tooze, J., *The DNA Story: A Documentary History of Gene Cloning*, W. H. Freeman and Co., New York, 1981.

Weiner, Charles, 'The Recombinant DNA Controversy: Archival and Oral History Resources, *Science, Technology and Human Values*, vol. 4, 1979, pp. 17–19.

Weiner, Charles, 'Relations of Science, Government and Industry: The Case of Recombinant DNA', in Albert H. Teich and Ray Thornton (eds.), *Science, Technology and the Issues of the Eighties: Policy Outlook*, Westview Press, Boulder, Colorado, 1982.

Weiss, Charles, 'The World Bank's Support for Science and Technology', *Science*, vol. 227, 1985, pp. 261–5.

Whitley, Richard, *The Intellectual and Social Organisation of the Sciences*, Clarendon Press, Oxford, 1984.

Wood, Ian J., 'Burnet and Autoimmunity—A Postscript', in *A Tribute to Sir Macfarlane Burnet*, pp. 46–9.

Worboys, Michael, 'The Emergence of Tropical Medicine: A Study in the Establishment of a Scientific Speciality', in Gerard Lemaine *et al.* (eds.), *Perspectives on the Emergence of Scientific Disciplines*, Mouton, The Hague, 1976, pp. 75–98.

Wright, Susan, 'Recombinant DNA Technology and its Social Transformation, 1972–1982', *Osiris*, vol. 2, 1986, pp. 360–9.

Young, R. M., 'Science is a labour process', *Science for People*, vol. 43/4, no. 197, pp. 31–7.

Yoxen, Edward, 'Where does Schrödinger's *What is Life*? belong in the history of molecular biology?' *History of Science*, vol. 17, 1979, pp. 17–52.

Yoxen, Edward, 'Life as a productive force: capitalising the science and technology of molecular biology', in L. Levidow and R. M. Young (eds.), *Science, Technology and the Labour Process*, CSE Books, London, 1981, pp. 66–122.

Yoxen, Edward, 'Giving Life a New Meaning: The Rise of the Molecular Biology Establishment', in N. Elias *et. al.* (eds.), *Scientific Establishments and Hierarchies*, Sociology of the Sciences Yearbook 1982, D. Reidel, Dordrecht, 1982, pp. 123–43.

Zuckerman, Harriet, *Scientific Elite*, The Free Press, New York, 1979.

Zuckerman, Harriet, 'Uses and Control of Knowledge: Implications for the Social Fabric', in James F. Short (ed.), *The Social Fabric: Dimensions and Issues*, Sage, Beverly Hills, 1986, pp. 334–48.

INDEX

Abir-Am, Pnina, 11, 44, 45, 105, 124, 142

Academic science, 223, 225, 238

Ada, G. L., 46, 174

Adams, Jerry, 165, 173, 177–92, 254, 275

Africa, 212

AIDS (Acquired Immune Deficiency Syndrome), 2, 55, 77, 253

Albury, Randall, 229

Allergens, 88

Alpers, Michael, 259, 260

Alvarez, Luis, 143

Ancestor Spirits, 5, 20

Anders, Robin, 188, 199, 236, 240

Anthropology, 4, 7, 13, 82, 98, 122, 148, 219, 220, 221, 265

Anthropology of science, 13, 14, 48, 142, 144, 146, 275

Antibodies, 27–31, 69, 153, 183, 207, 210

Antigenic variation, 209, 261

Antigens, 28, 29, 69, 88, 239

Apollo moon rock project, 104, 111, 112

Aristotle, 275

Artefacts, cultural, 16, 213; scientific, 157, 160–5

Asilomar Conference, 134, 136, 184, 274

Australian Aborigines, 14, 20, 265–6

Australian Industry Development Corporation (AIDC), 224, 238, 256

Australian Malaria Vaccine Joint Venture, 258

Authorship, scientific, 87, 91, 110, 169, 170

Autoimmune diseases, 27, 55, 202

Autoradiographs, 161–3

Azande, African, 6, 13

Babesia bovis, 188, 211, 237

Bachelard, Gaston, 144

Barley, Nigel, 222

Barthes, Roland, 41

Basel Institute for Immunology, 68, 71, 72, 74, 76, 89, 154, 155, 158, 206

Berg, Paul, 70, 134

'Berkeleitis', 143

Bernard, Ora, 183

'Big' science, 35, 36, 143, 239

Biology, new, 38, 39, 41, 45, 202

Biomedical research, 225–6; funding of, 230–2; politics of, 229–30

Biotechnology, 68, 69; *see also* Recombinant DNA

Biotechnology Australia, 224, 239, 256, 258

Bohr, Niels, 43, 44, 120

Borges, Jorges Luis, 213

Boyle, Robert, 53, 54

Brecht, Bertolt, 53

Broad, William, and Wade, Nicholas, 121, 140–1

Brown, Graham, 224, 236, 240

BT14, biological control, 248–9

Burkitt's lymphoma, 166, 186–8

Burnet, F. Macfarlane, 21, 25, 26–34, 38, 39, 55, 61, 74, 101, 116, 127; as 'culture hero', 32–3, 36–7, 79, 124, 125; as Director, 26–7; and Gajdusek, 35–6; and Nossal, 34–5; and molecular biology, 46–7, 174, 184; opposition to 'big' science, 34, 36, 239; *see also* Clonal Selection Theory